THE LYRIC POEM

As a study of lyric poetry, in English, from the early modern period to the present, this book explores one of the most ancient and significant art forms in western culture as it emerges in its various modern incarnations. Combining a much-needed historicisation of the concept of lyric with an aesthetic and formal focus, this collaboration of period-specialists offers a new cross-historical approach. Through eleven chapters, spanning more than four centuries, the book provides readers with both a genealogical framework for the understanding of lyric poetry within any particular period, and a necessary context for more general discussion of the nature of genre.

MARION THAIN is Reader in English Literature and Culture at Sheffield University. She has published primarily on late-nineteenth-century poetry and poetics, and is author of *'Michael Field': Poetry, Aestheticism and the Fin de Siècle* (Cambridge, 2007).

THE LYRIC POEM

Formations and Transformations

EDITED BY

MARION THAIN

Sheffield University

CAMBRIDGE
UNIVERSITY PRESS

University Printing House, Cambridge CB2 8BS, United Kingdom

Published in the United States of America by Cambridge University Press, New York

Cambridge University Press is part of the University of Cambridge.

It furthers the University's mission by disseminating knowledge in the pursuit of education, learning and research at the highest international levels of excellence.

www.cambridge.org
Information on this title: www.cambridge.org/9781107010840

First published 2013

Printed in the United Kingdom by CPI Group Ltd, Croydon CR0 4YY

A catalogue record for this publication is available from the British Library

Library of Congress Cataloguing in Publication data
The lyric poem : formations and transformations / edited by Marion Thain.
pages   cm
Includes bibliographical references and index.
ISBN 978-1-107-01084-0 (hardback)
1. Lyric poetry–History and criticism.   2. Lyric poetry–Themes, motives.
I. Thain, Marion, editor of compilation.
PN1356.L94 2013
809.1′4–dc23
2013015853

ISBN 978-1-107-01084-0 hardback

Contents

v

Contributors

JONATHAN CULLER, Class of 1916 Professor of English and Comparative Literature at Cornell University, has published widely on contemporary literary theory. A chapter of his *Structuralist Poetics* on 'Poetics of the Lyric' and a widely cited article, 'Apostrophe', form the point of departure for the book he is completing, entitled *Theory of the Lyric*.

HEATHER DUBROW, John D. Boyd, SJ, Chair in the Poetic Imagination at Fordham University, has published six scholarly books, most recently *The Challenges of Orpheus: Lyric Poetry and Early Modern England*, a co-edited collection of essays, and an edition of *As You Like It*. A collection of her poetry, *Forms and Hollows*, was published by Cherry Grove Collections.

DAVID DUFF is Professor of English at the University of Aberdeen. His books include *Romance and Revolution: Shelley and the Politics of a Genre* (1994), *Scotland, Ireland, and the Romantic Aesthetic* (co-edited, 2007), and *Romanticism and the Uses of Genre* (2009). He is editor of the forthcoming *Oxford Handbook of British Romanticism*.

DAVID FAIRER is Professor of Eighteenth-Century English Literature at the University of Leeds. His most recent book, *Organising Poetry: The Coleridge Circle, 1790–1798* (2009) traces the development of English poetry during the 1790s, building on the concerns of his previous comprehensive study, *English Poetry of the Eighteenth Century, 1700–1789* (2003). With Christine Gerrard he has edited *Eighteenth-Century Poetry: An Annotated Anthology* (second edition, 2003).

THOMAS HEALY is Professor of Renaissance Studies and Head of the School of English at the University of Sussex. He has published widely on sixteenth- and seventeenth-century English literature, including studies of Richard Crashaw, Christopher Marlowe, and theory and Renaissance literature.

DAVID LINDLEY, Professor of Renaissance Literature at the University of Leeds, has published monographs on Lyric (1983), *Thomas Campion* (1985), and *Shakespeare and Music* (2006). He has edited Jonson masques for the *Cambridge Ben Jonson* (2012), and *The Tempest* for *New Cambridge Shakespeare* (second edition, 2013).

PETER NICHOLLS is Professor of English at New York University. His publications include *Ezra Pound: Politics, Economics and Writing*, *Modernisms: A Literary Guide, George Oppen and the Fate of Modernism*, and many articles and essays on literature and theory. He is currently US associate editor of *Textual Practice*.

IAN PATTERSON teaches English at Queens' College, Cambridge, and is the author of *Guernica and Total War* (2007), and the translator of Proust's *Finding Time Again* (2003). He has written on a variety of topics in the literature of the last 100 years.

NEIL ROBERTS is Emeritus Professor of English Literature at the University of Sheffield. He is the editor of the Blackwell *Companion to Twentieth Century Poetry* and author of ten books, including *Narrative and Voice in Postwar Poetry, Ted Hughes: A Literary Life*, and, most recently, *A Lucid Dreamer: The Life of Peter Redgrove*.

NIGEL SMITH is William and Annie S. Paton Foundation Professor of Ancient and Modern Literature at Princeton University. His major works are *Andrew Marvell: The Chameleon* (2010), *Is Milton Better than Shakespeare?* (2008), the Longman Annotated English Poets edition of *Andrew Marvell's Poems* (2003), *Literature and Revolution in England, 1640–1660* (1994), and *Perfection Proclaimed: Language and Literature in English Radical Religion, 1640–1660* (1989).

MARION THAIN is Reader in Literature and Culture at Sheffield University. Her research interests are primarily in nineteenth-century and early- twentieth-century poetry and poetics; recent publications include *'Michael Field': Poetry, Aestheticism and the Fin de Siècle* (2007; issued in paperback in 2010), and *Michael Field, the Poet: Published and Manuscript Materials* (2009).

MARCUS WALSH is Kenneth Allott Professor of English Literature at the University of Liverpool. His research interests focus on eighteenth-century poetry, and the theory, practice, and history of editing. His publications include *Shakespeare, Milton, and Eighteenth-Century Literary Editing* (1997), and editions of Swift's *A Tale of a Tub* (2010) and Smart's *Song to David* and *Hymns and Spiritual Songs* (1983).

Acknowledgments

We thank everyone who has advised and commented on draft versions of these chapters; Marion Thain offers thanks to the Victorian Seminar group at CUNY. Particular thanks are due also to Stephen Gill for being so supportive of this project at its inception. 'Glamour of Gold' by Olive Custance is reproduced here with kind permission of John Rubinstein and John Stratford – literary executors of the Estate of Lord Alfred Douglas – all rights reserved.

Introduction

Marion Thain

This book is a study of the concept of 'lyric' poetry, in English, from the early modern period to the present. It is a study of one of the most ancient and significant art forms in western culture, as it emerges in its various modern incarnations. As David Lindley notes in our opening chapter, '*The Oxford English Dictionary*'s first recorded uses of "lyric" as an adjective or noun come from the 1580s' (p. 10).

In recent years, literary study has seen something of a return to questions about the aesthetic, in which genre has begun to emerge as one important focus. Indeed, as the most historically and culturally reflexive incarnation of text's rhetorical operation, genre is well placed to reflect the continuing importance of historical methodologies to literary study while at the same time enabling an insistence on the importance of aesthetic and formal considerations of text. Within the recent renewed interest in literary genre more generally there has been a particular focus on the lyric poem. Some explore key features of lyric by anchoring themselves primarily in a particular historical milieu or author, and others take a more aesthetic orientation in relation to a contemporary understanding of lyric. Those studies that are anchored in a particular historical milieu include Heather Dubrow's *The Challenges of Orpheus: Lyric Poetry and Early Modern England* (2008), G. Gabrielle Starr's *Lyric Generations: Poetry and the Novel in the Long Eighteenth Century* (2004), and Virginia Jackson's *Dickinson's Misery: A Theory of Lyric Reading* (2005). Of the primarily aesthetically situated type there are two books that stand out over the last five years or so: Susan Stewart's *Poetry and the Fate of the Senses* (2002); and Mutlu Konuk Blasing's study, *Lyric Poetry: The Pain and Pleasure of Words* (2007). Recent work by Simon Jarvis marks another important recent critical dimension. The issues he poses about the rhetorical operations of poetry are primarily philosophical, and although he doesn't use the term, his work on verse asks questions about the relationship between, for example, music and language, that are entirely relevant to thinking about the nature of lyric.[1] Offering a complementary focus within this burgeoning field of studies of lyric and the lyrical (and the above are just a few examples of a rapidly growing field), we explore the development of the concept of lyric over a long historical trajectory through eleven separate case studies. Through this approach we aim to take on a broad temporal remit while avoiding the imposition of a generalised grand-narrative of lyric constructed through a particular historical perspective, or any fixed definition of the genre.

As a work of historical poetics, this book is a long way from the 'genre theory' of the 1970s. Drawing on a tradition of genre theory from E. D. Hirsch and Croce, William Elford Rogers' *The Three Genres and the Interpretation of Lyric* states its aim as a delineation of 'lyric' as an interpretive category: one that aids current classification.[2] Yet lyric is as much a historical category of production as of interpretation, and one whose changing conceptualisation has affected the work of poets as well as the way we read their texts. Moreover, in these days of frequent polarisation between 'historical' and 'theoretical' literary methodologies, genre might have a particularly interesting role to play in determining a reconsideration of this binary. As Friedrich Schlegel put it, the study of genre can be nothing short of 'a classification which at the same time would be a history and theory of literature'.[3] It is this simultaneous history and theory of literature that we aim to reflect in our engagement with the concept of lyric.

As Derek Attridge, amongst others, notes, 'the history of English poetry could be written as a history of the gradually increasing importance of its visual dimension – but always as this interacts with its aural dimension'.[4] The term 'lyric poem' has come today to denote a genre of poetry perhaps most commonly circulated primarily in print, and read, whether silently or aloud, from the page. It is the conceptualisation of lyric poetry that has, in addition to an investment in oral forms, a significant and independent life on the page that we trace in this study. While the genre has its origins in a sung form of Classical antiquity, the term had certainly come to acquire, in addition, a textual meaning by the time it was used in Sidney's *An Apology for Poetry* in 1595. So, this is a study whose remit is not defined by 'song' as such, but by the shifting conceptualisation of the lyric poem, which in the period we study must be linked particularly to the development of textual and print cultures. The historical boundaries of the lyric we study coincide with modern printing methods that mark a specifically modern phase in textual history. It is this printed incarnation that over time was to bring a characteristic embodiment of, and particular possibilities for, the lyric poem in the contemporary world. While seeing this as a central thread to our study, however, we also reflect the importance of manuscript culture and the continuing potential of lyric in its textual embodiment to contain as a palimpsest an aural echo: sometimes actual, sometimes an imagined memory.

In 1970, René Wellek called for critics to 'abandon attempts to define the general nature of the lyric or the lyrical'.[5] To begin with a fixed definition of the lyric genre would be to beg the question. Although the significance of its origins in Classical and medieval song forms provides a necessary touchstone for this study, they do not provide a yard stick against which to measure subsequent forms. This book does not aim to present a 'definition' of the lyric poem, but something more like a loose genealogy. It is only in this way that we can begin properly to understand how this concept has shaped the production and reception of literary texts past and present. Each chapter uses sources contemporaneous to the poetry studied in order to give evidence for the meaning and significance of the term at that time, with a particular awareness of whether it refers to a form, a mode, or a genre. Where 'lyric' is a form, it has often been used to denote primarily song forms of poetry; as a 'mode', it has described a particular type (or types) of writing that could be found within a variety of forms and genres; as a genre, lyric represents one overall type of poetry in distinction to others such as 'epic' or 'dramatic'. The genealogy of the concept of 'lyric' that we trace is not a smooth or consistent movement from one type of meaning to another: indeed the term might be used, in different instances, in all three of these ways within the same historical period. Yet this messiness is a part of what makes the concept of lyric so interesting an object of study.

Current orthodoxy regards some ages as more 'lyrical' than others. High points are generally thought to include notable early modern writers, the Romantic period, modernism, and contemporary poetry (now poetry has, in the minds of many, become synonymous with definitions of the lyric). In contrast, the earlier eighteenth century is seen as an age more interested in political commentary than in the personal introspective effusion that came to be associated with lyric. The Victorians too, with the popularity of the novel and poetic forms that turned away from lyric, are more readily associated with other genres. Are these characterisations based primarily on a retro-projected definition of lyric, or are they rooted in contemporaneous experience? To what extent does the conceptualisation of lyric respond to the dominant concerns of the age, waxing and waning in connection with changing political, cultural, or philosophical contexts?

These are questions we will be investigating in order to interrogate current characterisations of the lyric tradition. This book will not only chart the shifting conceptualisation of lyric in a series of contexts, but will discover something of the interconnections between the aesthetics of lyric form and the context of its production in order to read the cultural and intellectual concerns inscribed in the contours and fortunes of the concept.

More specifically, an established critical narrative sees our current understanding of the lyric genre as originating largely in the Romantic period. Most recently, Scott Brewster begins his study of lyric with that claim that our current understanding of the lyric as a textual poetic genre was 'developed in the later eighteenth century, which defined lyric in terms of heightened emotion and authentic sentiment, and presented it as a (usually brief) moment of intensified awareness'.[6] This was the point, argues M. H. Abrams, at which 'lyric' became not just *a* poetic genre, including under its umbrella a variety of poetic forms that might previously have been considered to have separate trajectories, but *the* poetic genre: the pre-eminent form of poetry.[7] Yet was this point in lyric history a revolution or an evolution?[8] If 'lyric' was first recorded as an adjective or noun in the late sixteenth century, what did it mean before the Romantic codification of genre? And what about the investment in this Romantic understanding of lyric in the following centuries? From at least the 1960s the following formulation has been dominant: 'from the late eighteenth century the lyric impulse became diffused over an ever-widening area, till today one could almost say there is no lyric poetry since every poem has a lyrical quality'.[9] More recently, Virginia Jackson has taken up this idea to describe a process of 'the lyricization of poetry itself – the historical transformation of many varied poetic genres into the single abstraction of the post-Romantic lyric'.[10] Jackson has suggested that 'the lyric takes form through the development of reading practices in the nineteenth and twentieth centuries that become the practice of literary criticism'.[11]

Jackson's work appears with other position papers (mainly from scholars whose own specialisms lie in post-Romantic literature) in the 2008 *PMLA* issue that put the 'New Lyrical Studies' on the map. Here, in response to challenges to the notion of 'lyric' as a transhistorical category, Jonathan Culler responded with cautious optimism that an essential core of qualities might characterise the genre over time, and with a call for an investigation.[12] This call has begun to be taken up by critics in various forms, but not yet in a longitudinal study.[13] The current book aims to provide an arena for the historical investigation of the concept of lyric spanning more than four centuries, undertaken by scholars qualified to make this assessment in their particular historical area of expertise. In this way, we provide the first book-length study to respond to these questions.

In what follows we present no definitive single narrative of lyric formation. Rather, we present evidence drawn from many sources in many different ways to establish a multi-vocal, multi-perspectival history that we hope will raise more questions than it answers. This method responds to the need to avoid a retrospective mapping of a 'lyric' tradition in the image of any one moment in that history. Presenting case studies within a broadly chronological structure, we also aim to avoid a homogenising survey of literary periods. In each chapter a different author engages with what they identify as a key moment of formation or transformation in the idea of lyric poetry. While grounding the argument in a historicised understanding of 'lyric' that will orient the non-period-specialist reader, each author seeks to present an original reflection on it. In this way, a substantial historical and collective endeavour is given a tight focus within each chapter that enables its theme to be worked out in detailed and specific arguments. Each chapter takes, as its central object of study, a small number of poems – sometimes canonical and sometimes little known. Close reading is a key shared methodology and will unite the studies, grounding the analysis in a focus on the works themselves. The chapters take diverse approaches and methodologies, and we have also tried to highlight different issues within the concept of lyric within each chapter (each particularly relevant to the historical period in question) at the same time as attending to a shared remit. Overall, however, these studies collectively offer a sustained interrogation of the concept of lyric that focuses around an exploration of its historical conceptualisation and, at times, the relevance of current definitions of the genre to reading poetry from the past.

David Lindley's opening chapter explores the relationship between early modern 'lyric' poetry and the crucible of song and text in which it was formed. Analysing the experience of song in the period, he highlights distinctions, are crucial (although often overlooked) to our understanding of lyric, between metrical regularity on the page and the musicality of lyrics written to a particular tune. Heather Dubrow continues many of the same concerns while using an analysis of deictics to offer a very different kind of reflection on lyric in the sixteenth century. Interrogating generic assumptions of lyric immediacy, she questions the relevance of twentieth-century definitions of lyric to reading sixteenth-century poems, at the same time as exploring what it might mean to think about 'lyric' in the period. Moving on thematically from lyric's generative connection with song, and moving, historically, into the seventeenth century, Thomas Healy explores what it means for lyric to exist in both print and manuscript cultures. Focusing on the work of John Donne, he looks at how the instabilities of both textual media create not only fluidity of meaning and interpretation but also interesting challenges for reading poetic subjectivity that have profound consequences for our understanding of what it might mean to read 'lyric' poems in this period. Nigel Smith offers a complementary focus on seventeenth-century poetry through an exploration of lyric's fate and function in a time of intense unrest. Through an original account of the new wave of song study among the musicographers of the seventeenth century, Smith finds a discourse on the idea of lyric within a poetic landscape in which the epic and heroic formed a more recognised focus. In spite of lyric's subordinated position within poetics of the period, he finds it playing an innovative role both in political action and in the understanding of a time of 'deep perplexity'. Considering the eighteenth century, David Fairer traces the conscious translation of lyre music into 'modern' poetry, identifying an understanding of 'lyric' poetry not as a formal genre but as the playing of an instrument in a textual medium. Revealing how poets sought in the modal and expressive features of poetry an equivalent for something derived from the ancient lyrists, Fairer argues that the idea of lyre music was taken up in ways that could 'make the transition to modern lyric poetry and become a defining aspect of it' (p. 94). In the context of an eighteenth-century shift from the satiric modes associated with Pope towards a poetry of the imagination, Marcus Walsh takes as his focus the ode. Identifying this form as central to an attempt to 'reconstitute the high lyric as a leading genre for British poetry' (p. 113), Walsh explores the potential for such poems themselves to offer a commentary on the development of a poetics of affect and imagination, and, more generally, on the difficult status of the modern lyric poet in relation to an inheritance of multiple Greek, Hebraic, and English models.

David Duff takes as his focus the Romantic expansion of 'lyric' as a generic term that included a rapidly growing number of different poetic forms. Yet, far from presenting a single, unified conceptualisation of lyric, his chapter considers the relationship between different Romantic ideas of lyric, and how they overlap or, sometimes, combine. Focusing both on the idea of lyric as an introspective mode, and the reassertion of a tie between lyric poetry and music, Duff looks in detail at poems by Burns and Shelley in order to argue for the complexity and multiplicity of lyric in this period (from popular song to a return to ancient forms). In my own chapter, I turn away from the centrality of music to lyric in order to think about the importance to Victorian poetry of a constitutively printed rather than sung conceptualisation of lyric, and what this means for the identity of a genre recognised at the time to be in tension with cultural modernity. Struggling with a conceptualisation of lyric they frequently identify as inherited from the Romantics, mid-Victorian poets such as Browning pathologise the form, yet later Victorian poets, I argue, reclaim the idea of lyric through the very terms of that sickness. Exploring the work of Pound and twentieth-century modernism, Peter Nicholls interrogates the binary that sees modernist lyric as affiliated with the eye in opposition to the ear. While arguing for the continuing significance of sound (and of Swinburne) to Pound's melopoeia, Nicholls also highlights the profound scepticisms around lyric musicality present not only in high modernism but also in the work of the following generations. From Oppen's distrust, to Susan Howe's sense of the limits of lyric, Nicholls considers the ways in which lyric has come to seem to some poets a damaged or compromised form. The final two chapters both address issues of lyric subjectivity and can be seen to work as parallel reflections on two very different traditions of poetry that emerged in the second half of the twentieth century. Neil Roberts' analysis draws together Philip Larkin and Ted Hughes, arguing that 'Both poets combine a conservative-seeming attachment to the idea of lyric with a historically inevitable suspicion of its integrity' (p. 214). Moreover, however opposed the two poets may appear stylistically, he recognises in both the need to seek strategies for the escape of the ego via the construction of the lyric 'I' through language and through something similar to what Blasing describes as the rhythmic pulse that 'makes audible an intending "I"' (p. 195).[14] Finally, Ian Patterson turns to a major strand of contemporary poetry that might be called 'late modernist' (with J. H. Prynne a major focus), and that Patterson defines in opposition to the 'mainstream' of contemporary British poetry explored in the previous chapter. Ultimately, Patterson's analysis shows that however pathologised, broken, irrelevant, or, now in Patterson's terms 'fragmented', lyric has become, it persists as an uncanny echo in contemporary poetry: a force that is never completely rejected. 'Lyric' has become for Patterson too intrinsic to the process of articulating the subject in poetic language. The volume ends with a reflection on the whole, and on the utility of genre categorisations, from a scholar seminal to our critical study of lyric: Jonathan Culler.

This book aims to offer a fresh approach to the study of lyric by taking a long historical remit and employing a multi-authored approach in order to maintain the specificity and expertise throughout. Collaboration of this type amongst scholars of English literature is surprisingly rare. Such connections do not easily fall under the banner of 'interdisciplinarity',[15] but nor are they fostered by conferences and groupings within university disciplines that are predominantly historically based. Marjorie Perloff has written about the dangers of a current configuration of the discipline in which the '"merely" literary is so suspect'.[16] The casualties of this have sometimes been the formal features of the text itself as an aesthetic object and the larger *literary* trajectories or frames of reference in which those texts might be located. There is a danger of leaving scholars without enough of a sense of the larger trajectory in which they are working; this is the reason why certain questions remain unanswered, and why historical parochialism is a real risk for current scholarship.

It should by now be clear that this book is not an introductory guide or a comprehensive historical survey of lyric poetry. It achieves what can only be achieved through a collective, bringing together many scholars and giving a shape to a long period of literary history. In short, this book attempts to offer a combination of qualities usually polarised between the frequently very specialist academic monograph and the less narrow, but often simplified, overview of the historical survey or guide book. The authors involved in this project reflect a range of additional interests crucial to the topic: as well as being eminent critics, some also bring with them an editor's understanding of the importance of genre (for example David Fairer, Neil Roberts, Nigel Smith, Marcus Walsh), some are published lyric poets themselves (such as Heather Dubrow and Ian Patterson), some bring a particular understanding of the development of print culture (for example Thomas Healy) and of the relationship between literature and music (David Lindley), some bring expertise in Anglo-American literature that is crucial to understanding twentieth-century developments in English poetry (for example Peter Nicholls), and some specialise in genre theory itself (David Duff). The focus of the book on 'English' literature means, for most of its historical range, a focus on poetry within the British Isles. The sheer range and diversity of poetries in English in contemporary literature is a subject for another book, but the later chapters reflect the significance of, particularly, North American poetry to the English lyric. Although this collection cannot attempt to reflect the reach of contemporary global criticism, its historical breadth aims to appeal to any reader interested in poetry and the concept of lyric. Readers who have a particular interest in poetry of any one of the historical periods covered will gain an important context for their study, while the book also provides a necessary framework for thinking about the nature of genre.

Notes

1 Simon Jarvis, 'Musical Thinking: Hegel and the Phenomenology of Prosody', *Paragraph* 28.2 (2005), 57–71 (*passim*).
2 William Elford Rogers, *The Three Genres and the Interpretation of Lyric* (Princeton University Press, 1983), p. 56.
3 Friedrich Schlegel, *Dialogue on Poetry and Literary Aphorisms*, trans. Ernst Behler and Roman Struc (University Park: Pennsylvania State University Press, 1989), p. 76.
4 Derek Attridge, *Poetic Rhythm* (Cambridge University Press, 1995), p. 2.
5 René Wellek, 'Genre Theory, the Lyric, and Erlebnis', in *Discriminations: Further Concepts of Criticism* (New Haven: Yale University Press, 1970), pp. 225–52 (pp. 251–2).
6 Scott Brewster, *Lyric* (London and New York: Routledge, 2009), pp. 1–2.
7 M. H. Abrams, *The Mirror and the Lamp*, (Oxford University Press, 1963), pp. 84, 96.
8 See David Duff, *Romanticism and the Uses of Genre* (New York: Oxford University Press, 2009), p. 210; Brewster, *Lyric*, p. 72.
9 C. Day Lewis, *The Lyric Impulse* (London: Chatto and Windus, 1965), p. 13.
10 Virginia Jackson, 'Who Reads Poetry?', *PMLA* 123.1 (2008), 181–7 (p. 183).
11 Virginia Jackson, *Dickinson's Misery* (Princeton University Press, 2005), p. 8.
12 Jonathan Culler, 'Why Lyric?', *PMLA* 123.1 (2008), 201–6 (p. 202).
13 See, for example, Rachel Cole's essay, 'Rethinking the Value of Lyric Closure: Giorgio Agamben, Wallace Stevens, and the Ethics of Satisfaction', *PMLA* 126.2 (2011), 383–97, in which she posits lyric's formal closure as part of its 'transhistorical' nature and asks how we might think about that feature ethically.
14 Mutlu Konuk Blasing, *Lyric Poetry: The Pain and Pleasure of Words* (2007), p. 55.
15 For example, the UK Arts and Humanities Research Council classes the study of English literature across all historical periods as one subject area.
16 Marjorie Perloff, 'Presidential Address 2006: It Must Change', *PMLA* 122.3 (2007), 652–62 (p. 655).

CHAPTER ONE

'Words for music, perhaps'
Early modern songs and lyric

David Lindley

In the sixteenth century most people made their primary contact with
poetry or verse when it was accompanied by music. Whether in the ballads sold by itinerant sellers such as Shakespeare's Autolycus in *The Winter's
Tale*, or in the metrical Psalms that were the only music permitted in the
average parish church, or in the songs heard in the theatre, or in music
sung for domestic entertainment, verses came most frequently attached
to tunes.

The *Oxford English Dictionary's* first recorded uses of 'lyric' as an adjective or noun come from the 1580s.[1] It is very evident that the label had
very little direct connection with modern, or post-Romantic, definitions
of lyric by its individual and personal utterance. Instead, virtually all the
uses of the term until well into the seventeenth century made their primary connection to Classical tenets, and especially to metrical distinctions
of one literary kind from another. The early modern generic definition
was, therefore, much less by subject matter or by forms of address than we
expect. Above all, 'lyric' was a category prescribed by metrical form. At the
same time, most definitions in the period, either explicitly or implicitly,
also gesture towards the etymological connection of 'lyric' to the lyre, and
therefore to music. Puttenham's generic categorisation is entirely typical of
the period, and therefore instructive:

> As the matter of poesy is diverse, so was the form of their poems and man-
> ner of writing, for all of them wrote not in one sort, even as all of them
> wrote not upon one matter. Neither was every poet alike cunning in all as
> in some one kinde of poesy, nor uttered with like felicity. But wherein any
> one most excelled, thereof he tooke a surname, as to be called a Poet *Heroic*,
> *Lyric, Elegiac, Epigrammatist* or otherwise. Such therefore as gave them-
> selves to write long histories of the noble gests of kings and great Princes
> … they called poets *Heroic*, whereof *Homer* was chief and most ancient
> among the Greeks, *Virgil* among the Latins. Others who more delighted
> to write songs or ballads of pleasure, to be sung with the voice, and to

the harpe, lute, or citheron and such other musical instruments, they were called melodious poets [*melici*] or by a more common name *Lyric* Poets, of which sort was *Pindarus*, *Anacreon* and *Callimachus* with others among the Greeks: *Horace* and *Catullus* among the Latins. There were another sort, who sought the favour of fair ladies, and coveted to bemoan their estates at large, and the perplexities of love in a certain pitious verse called *Elegie*, and thence were called *Eligiack*: such among the Latines were *Ouid*, *Tibullus*, and *Propertius*.[2]

There is a very general sense here of particular subjects attached to genre or mode, but Classical love poems, which we would certainly label 'lyrics', are called 'elegies' entirely on metrical grounds, while the highly formal odes of Pindar, precisely because of their musical connection, earn the generic title of lyrics.

Metrical discrimination is also the marker for Thomas Campion in his treatise on Classical, quantitative metres in English verse, where he writes: 'To descend orderly from the more simple numbers to them that are more compounded, it is now time to handle such verses as are fit for *Ditties* or *Odes*, which we may call *Lyricall*, because they are apt to be soong to an instrument, if they were adorn'd with convenient notes.'[3] He continues with examples of the Sapphic, a dimeter, and a five-line stanza; his basic point is that it is complex, or compound metres, that are 'lyrical', and they are so *because of* their suitability for musical setting.

It is on the same metrical basis that the Psalms of David were categorised as lyrics. Thomas Churchyard, in a marginal note to his *A musicall consort of heauenly harmonie*, writes that: 'David sung the Liricke verses to his harp and those ebrue songs consisted of divers feet and unequall numbers'.[4] Philip Sidney commented in similar terms:

> And may I not … say that the holy David's Psalms are a divine Poem? If I do, I shall not do it without the testimony of great learned men, both ancient and modern. But even the name psalms will speak for me, which, being interpreted, is nothing but songs; then, that it is fully written in metre, as all learned hebricians agree, although the rules be not yet fully found.[5]

The versions of the Psalms by Sidney and his sister, Mary, are themselves notable for their metrical virtuosity, no doubt intended at some level to represent the rhythmic qualities ascribed to the original language. Sidney's best-known and most often-quoted formulation on lyric poetry, however, defines the poet himself as one who 'cometh to you with words set in delightful proportion, either accompanied with, or prepared for, the well enchanting skill of Music'.[6]

His assertion of the close link between music and poetry is a persistent one in definitions of lyric both as a mode and as a genre. Heather Dubrow quotes the twentieth-century poet C. Day Lewis: 'A lyric is a poem written for music – for an existing tune, or in collaboration with a composer, or in an idiom demanded by contemporary songwriters, or simply with music at the back of the poet's mind.' But, as she observes, 'the interdisciplinary linkage Day Lewis posits is … fraught and sometimes debatable'.[7] Nonetheless, this is the definition of lyric that early modern writers would most readily have acknowledged, and it is important to tease out the potential implications of that understanding of lyric, both for writers at the time, and for modern critics.

Some of the problematic nature of the critical observations that can – or cannot – be drawn from the frequently asserted connection of words and music can be illustrated by considering briefly the case of Thomas Wyatt. Poets, from the Classical writers onwards, may often gesture towards the notion that they are writing 'songs', and Wyatt is no exception, appearing explicitly to acknowledge his accompanying lute in a number of poems. Exactly what this might mean, however, is not transparent. John Stevens sets out the problem:

> A theory that words were written to be set to music in this period will probably rest on one of the following beliefs: the poet wrote words in a special way – either, because he was himself a creative musician and able to set them; or because he worked in close collaboration with a composer and could be told what was needed; or because the active music-making of his environment forced him to think imaginatively in terms of music.[8]

According to this definition, Wyatt, he concludes, 'blames his lute, or not, as the fancy takes him, but never talks about it in the way of a man who really understands and cares for it'.[9] It is, for Stevens, merely a conventional gesture towards lyric's musical origin.

Winifred Maynard attempted to revise this opinion by considering a rather different possibility: that Wyatt wrote words with actual tunes of a more popular cast in his mind, though she notes the problem that 'since many of the metres are common ones, it is easy to find possible partners for many lyrics, but hard, theoretically at least, to tell whether a poem was really made for a specific tune, or simply happens to go to it'.[10] This does not dissuade her from pursuing the possibility that Wyatt did have particular tunes in his head as he composed some of his lyrics.

Elizabeth Heale is more cautious, noting that 'the question of how much English courtly verse was, or was intended to be, sung, and in what manner, is a vexed and to some extent an unanswerable one'.[11] While she does cite evidence that poems might have been fitted to known tunes, she concentrates her discussion of music's influence on verse forms that originally were explicitly associated with musical settings, and that then could be imitated, whether or not a writer knew anything of individual musical examples, and whether or not a poet had an ounce of actual knowledge of or interest in music. Here she is connecting Wyatt with the medieval fashion of writing poems in stanzas, such as the *virelai*, *ballade*, and *rondeau*, whose patterns of formal repetition originate in their preparedness for musical setting.[12] Her argument is that new models were imported, especially from Italy, and focuses on the musically derived form of the *frottola* as inspiration for some of Wyatt's lyrics. But this is a term that encompasses both a stanzaic song with refrain and a number of other lyric forms, and is therefore perhaps too general a label for any great claims to be made for specifically musical influence in particular individual cases. Nonetheless, Wyatt's work manifests some of the ways in which newer verse forms found their way into early Tudor poetry, and were almost certainly assisted in their assimilation by the international circulation of music and musicians.

The problem with using Wyatt as an example, however, is that it is virtually impossible to demonstrate that he possessed any actual musical knowledge, or to identify any specific piece of music that might have influenced him. There is surer ground to be discovered in various different kinds of verse writing spanning all social classes across the sixteenth and early seventeenth centuries, where words are explicitly linked to named tunes, or clearly destined for musical performance. For the populace at large this meant both the ballad, where a repertoire of familiar tunes was invoked at the top of a printed broadside, and also the Psalms in their metrical form, which were accommodated to a limited range of well-known tunes.[13] In both genres some tunes came to have specific association with particular subjects or words. The popular tune 'Fortune my foe', for example – a gravely melancholy air – was regularly invoked for ballads dealing either with the execution of criminals or else with religious meditation.[14] The 'Old Hundredth', a hymn tune associated with the hundredth Psalm in the Sternhold and Hopkins Psalter, is still sung to the words 'All people that on earth do dwell' today. But there are significant differences between the poetry in the two genres of ballad and Psalm.

The first four lines of Psalm 1 in the Sternhold and Hopkins Psalter edition of 1564 read:

> The man is blest that hath not bent,
> To wicked rede his ear,   *rede*: counsel
> Nor led his life as sinners do
> Nor sat in scorner's chair.

This is in the metre that is the most frequently employed throughout the book, with lines of alternating eight and six syllables. In its time it was known as 'Sternhold's metre', and has persisted as 'common metre' in hymn books down to the present. It is relentlessly iambic and insistently regular.

Compare that with the opening of 'The Famous Battle between Robin Hood and the Curtal Friar: To a New Northern Tune':

> In summer time when leaves grow green
>   And flowers are fresh and gay
> Robin Hood and his merry men,
>   Were disposed to play.
> Then some would leap and some would run,
>   And some would use Artillery,
> Which of you can a good Bow draw,
>   A good Archer for to be.[15]

If these lines are to be interpreted as forming two four-line stanzas, they have roughly the same shape as the Psalm, but each stanza is realised slightly differently, with more or fewer syllables than the norm and with frequent departures from a regular stress-pattern. These are words written with a tune in mind, but a tune that the singer can modify by introducing extra notes, omitting upbeats and the like. This illustrates very clearly the significant difference between verse timed by beats with an indeterminate number of intervening syllables on the one hand, and accentual-syllabic metres, describable in the language of Classical prosody, on the other. For Northrop Frye, indeed, this was a key differentiator for poetry that could be considered 'musical', as he suggested: 'When in poetry we have a predominating stress accent and a variable number of syllables between two stresses … we have musical poetry, that is, poetry which resembles in its structure the music contemporary with it.'[16]

This formulation has an obvious appeal – and Derek Attridge's excellent study, *The Rhythms of English Poetry*, might seem to afford it some support as he begins his analysis with nursery rhymes and other stress-timed verse.[17] It is, however, an oversimplification, since it takes no account of

the crucial difference between, on the one hand, writing *for* a musical setting and, on the other, writing *to* an existing tune. Both activities might
be expected to show the potential influence of music on poetry, and both
offer challenges and opportunities to poets, but they do so in quite distinct
ways. In the former case a poet might choose to employ existing metrical
and stanzaic forms that had already been set to music. As we have seen in
the discussion of Wyatt, poets need have no musical knowledge in order
to produce such verbal structures, since they can model their poems on
other texts whose rhythms and shapes are discernible without recourse to
any supporting music. There will be technical demands if the poet actually imagines a musical destiny for the poem, in particular in confronting
the problem of making the rhythms and patterns of second and subsequent stanzas analogous to the first.

Where the music exists before the words, however, poets face a very different challenge, and one that writers of more sophisticated poems than
the average ballad were ready to take on. Such a poet must consider the
music carefully, and match both overall form and local stress-patterns to
its dictates. One form of such an exercise is the provision of English words
to the Continental music that was increasingly being collected by musicians, amateur and professional, during the sixteenth century.

Nicholas Yonge, a chorister at St Paul's, produced in 1588 an anthology
of translated madrigals, and his collection was rapidly followed by others,
including the poet Thomas Watson's *Italian Madrigals Englished* (1590),
which on its title-page informed the user that the madrigals were Englished
'not to the sense of the dittie, but to the affection of the note'. Here the
poet departed on occasion entirely from the sense and subject of his original, providing, for example, an elegy on Philip Sidney in place of a 'love
message a young goatherd sends with a nosegay to his beloved'.[18] At one
level this illustrates very obviously the ways in which quite different words
may be perfectly satisfactorily accommodated to the same music. This possibility is exploited, for example, in the composition of *contrafacta* supplying religious words to secular tunes, a practice that stretches from 'Sumer is
icumen in', to which the words 'Perspice Christicolas' were supplied in the
thirteenth century; through the Lutheran appropriation of 'the devil's best
tunes' in the sixteenth century; to modern hymnody, where, for example,
folk tunes are invested with new religious lyrics. The capability of music to
sustain such adaptation, even where the words have quite different subjects,
is explained by William Mahrt: 'Even in the most explicit word-painting, it
is the link between the musical gesture and the connotation given it by the
text which accounts for its concreteness. It should not be surprising, then,

that the same musical figure can bear texts of diverse meaning and still be received as word-painting.'[19] This is, of course, even more true when a tune is relatively characterless or implies only the most general of moods. The sense that it is words that nail down the generalised emotion that music generates is an axiom frequently invoked in the musical treatises of the period. Words, as it were, make music 'safe'.

Such exercises in translation may have encouraged experimentation with line and phrase length, but they scarcely produced poems that might stand on their own. The opening six lines of the fourth madrigal from Yonge's collection make this evident:

> False Love, now shoot and spare not,
> Now do thy worst, I care not; and to dispatch me
> Use all thine art and all thy craft to catch me.
> For youth amiss bestowed
> I now repent me, and for my faults I languish
> That brought me nothing else but grief and anguish …[20]

Apart from its struggle with Italian feminine endings, the lyric, after a promising enough opening, limps in the third and sixth lines with the effort of producing a single unit of continuous sense that could fit the melodic contours of Palestrina's madrigal.

The most studied of such words-to-existing tunes are the poems of the Sidneys, Philip and Robert. Frank Fabry's identification of some of the airs to which Sidney, in *Certain Sonnets*, wrote new words is complemented by Gavin Alexander's work on a poem of Robert Sidney.[21] The latter's assertion that 'each time an English song was made out of imported material, the relations between music and poetry, and the styles and structures of English song, were extended and altered' (p. 381) is in many ways convincing – it is generally claimed, for example, that Philip Sidney's words-to-music introduced trochaic metres into English verse. But it is not as straightforward a matter as he suggests.

Anthony Munday, in the 'Address to the Gentle Reader' of his *Banquet of Daintie Conceits* (1588) wrote:

> Fyrst, thou art to consider, that the Ditties heerein contained, are made to seuerall set Notes, wherein no measure of verse can be obserued, because the Notes will affoorde no such libertie: for looke how they rise and fall, in iust time and order of Musique, euen so haue I kept course therewith in making the Ditties, which will seeme very bad stuffe in reading, but (I perswade me) wyll delight thee, when thou singest any of them to thine Instrument.[22]

Rather later, in 1629, Edward Filmer, in his preface to *French Court-Aires*, writes equally anxiously about the challenges in fitting words to notes:

> Now, because translated Ditties and Originals differ chiefly in this Preposterous Point, that, whereas the Musicall Notes are fitted to the Originals, the Translations are, contrarily, to be fitted to the Musicall Notes, I have been forced by this new Taske, for the more even Accord with the Musicke, in divers Aires, to alter the Naturally first Cast of the Verse, and to ordaine, in the proper place of an *Iambicke* Foot, a dissonant *Trochaicke*, as more sutable to the nature of the Note. For this cause, when the most busie Examiners shall, in some of the Ditties, find heere and there *Iambick* Meeters that seeme to faulter in their Pace, through the unlawfull frequencie of Troachaike motions let them forbeare Censure till they have tried them with the Streame of the Aire or Note.[23]

The important thing registered by both writers here is the way that words written to fit existing music are often rhythmically problematic to a reader who is simply contemplating them as a lyric poem on the page. In the absence of a tune one might grope with difficulty after the underlying rhythm. This is true for the modern poetry of Linton Kwesi Johnson, which is rhythmically indecipherable to anyone not familiar with dub-reggae, or with the poet's own readings, and it was true in the early modern period for many of these lyrics written as *contrafacta*. The praise that has been offered to Sidney's efforts could scarcely be given to many of the words provided for the instrumental pieces of Dowland. His most often-quoted song, 'Flow my teares', for example, is evidently a lyric provided to fit the music of the already existing *Lachrimae* pavan, and illustrates exactly Filmer's 'faltering pace' in the first and third lines of the first stanza:

> Flow my teares fall from your springs,
> Exilde for euer: Let me morne
> where nights black bird her sad infamy sings,
> there let mee liue forlorne.[24]

To anyone who knows the music the emphasis in the first line on both 'teares' and 'fall', and 'sad' and 'infamy' are unproblematic when the tune is in one's ear, whereas the unknowing reader might well hesitate over the allocation of stresses.

Even more obviously, in the thirteenth song from the *Second Book of Airs* a reader will struggle to find any metrical shape (or even coherent sense) in the following lines:

> One faith one loue,
> Makes our fraile pleasures eternall, And in sweetnesse proue.
> New Hopes new ioyes,
> Are still with sorrow declining, Vnto deepe anoies.[25]

The almain dance-form of the song suggests that the tune was written first and the words rather desperately seek to accommodate themselves to its rhythm – though even then not particularly successfully, since the articulation of the lyrics is almost as difficult in singing as it is in reading. Dowland might well himself have supplied these words, and other similar lyrics, to already-existing dance tunes, and their conventionality of sentiment, awkwardness of expression, and elusive metrics do not in any way prevent them from being perfectly successful as words for a song. Whether a poet could learn anything from them of use in writing 'literary' lyrics, however, might seem doubtful indeed. Dowland illustrates vividly the abiding paradox that lyrics having the most demonstrably close connection to music are yet frequently those whose metrical shape, or verbal 'music', is most incoherent when simply read on the page.

While the impulse to provide words for music has always been an active one, the motivation for supplying words to these existing dance tunes in this period may have been a commercial one, as the advent of printed music (of which more later) offered a market in which songs and madrigals might well have had wider appeal than instrumental ensembles. This is certainly the case in Campion's published version of *The Lord Hay's Masque* of 1607, where he supplied words to pre-existing tunes at the end of the description of the entertainment, explaining that 'though the last three Ayres were devised onely for daucing, yet they are here set forth with words that they may be sung to the Lute or Violl'.[26] This publication, then, is both a memento and a record of a fleeting court occasion (masques were generally performed only once before a select audience), and at the same time one that offers its readership the opportunity to translate courtly pastime into domestic entertainment. These, it must be said, are not amongst Campion's best lyrics, exhibiting some of the same awkwardnesses as have been noted in other *contrafacta*. The first is made of straggling long lines; the third manifests in its eighth and tenth lines a similar metrical 'faltering pace' to that exhibited in Dowland's 'Flow my teares'. But Campion, of course, made special claim for himself as both poet and musician in the address 'To the Reader' prefaced to *Two Bookes of Ayres* (?1612/13), where he wrote: 'In these *English* Ayres, I have chiefely aymed to couple my Words and Notes lovingly together, which will be much for him to do that hath not power over both.'[27] If even he could find accommodating words to existing tunes a problematic activity, it suggests that the significance of *contrafacta* in stimulating metrical innovation in the early modern lyric has been somewhat overstated.

And yet, though in general it would seem likely that Campion's lyrics were written before the music to which they were then set, and are examples, therefore, of words written *for* rather than *to* music, a lyric like

'Faire, if you expect admiring', from *A Booke of Ayres*, usefully signals what can still be claimed for music's influence. Its first stanza runs:

> Faire, if you expect admiring,
> Sweet, if you provoke desiring,
> Grace deere love with kinde requiting/
> Fond. but if thy sight be blindnes,
> False, if thou affect unkindnes,
> Flie both love and loves delighting.
> Then when hope is lost and love is scorned,
> Ile bury my desires, and quench the fires that ever yet in vaine have burned.[28]

The first six lines are straightforwardly trochaic – the metre, we have seen, whose musical origin is claimed for Sidney's *contrafacta*. But what of the last straggly line? The rhymes might tempt one to relineate it as:

> Ile bury my desires,
> And quench the fires
> That ever yet in vaine have burned.

But the analogous final line of the second stanza is rather differently shaped by rhyme:

> Ile flie to her again, and sue
> For pity to renue
> My hopes distressed.

No conventional, Classically derived prosodic description will serve. But consider the musical setting (see Fig. 1). Here the 'spondee' at the beginning of the third and sixth lines becomes much more obvious – an indication of Campion's attention to 'quantity' as well as rhythm, which found its expression in the *Observations in the Art of English Poesie* (1602)[29] – but it is the organisation of the final line, in which the rhyme words are, as it were, incidental chimes rather than structuring sounds, that most clearly indicates the way in which thinking 'musically' might affect the writing of verse. It is, of course, possible that Campion had written the tune first, but it is much more likely that word and tune evolved together, the rhythmical contrast of the rapid movement in the second section with the steady crotchet pace of the first being a fairly standard musical climactic quickening.

There are, then, at least two important ways in which this song suggests things that might be especially significant in the influence of music on poetry. The first is the way the larger structure of the poem might be suggested by, or reflect, a musical pattern. When Shakespeare wrote Ariel's song of freedom, 'Where the bee sucks', he presumably did so

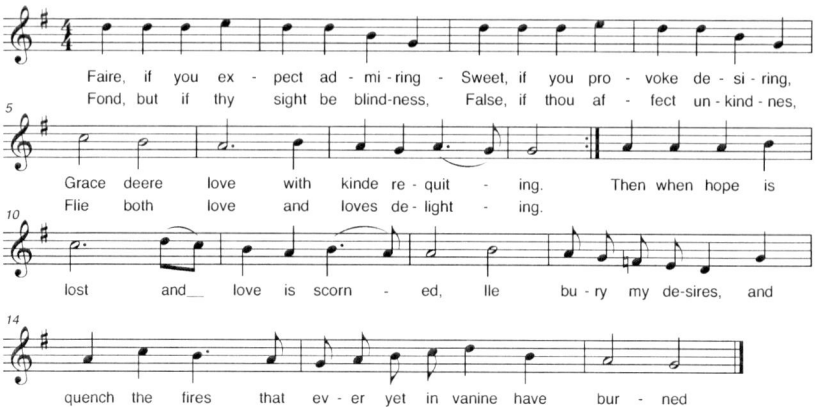

Figure 1 Thomas Campion, *A Booke of Ayres* (London: printed by Peter Short, 1601), no. 11

before it was set by a composer; but its shift into a dactylic triple rhythm at 'Merrily, merrily, shall I live now' feeds naturally into a setting such as that by Robert Johnson, which may have been used at an early performance. The second is the more interesting, and the more difficult to tie down explicitly to musical influence. In Campion's lyric, units of sense of different lengths are counterpointed against the rhyme units, with the patterning of accent and stress further enriching the mixture. And it is precisely the way in which music might suggest and prompt relationships between shorter and longer phrasal units within an overall organisation of syntactical sense and chimings of sounds in rhyme that is fundamental to the richness of, for example, Herbert's poetry. His widely varied stanza forms manifest continuously an almost unparalleled sensitivity to and control of these relationships. He was, as Izaak Walton informs us, an adept musician.

> His chiefest recreation was Musick, in which heavenly Art he was a most excellent Master, and, compos'd many divine Hymns and Anthems, which he set and sung to his Lute or Viol; and, though he was a lover of retiredness, yet his love to Musick was such, that he went usually twice every week on certain appointed dayes, to the Cathedral Church in Salisbury; and at his return would say, That his time spent in Prayer, and Cathedral Musick, elevated his Soul, and was his Heaven upon Earth: But before his return thence to Bemerton, he would usually sing and play his part, at an appointed private Musick meeting; and, to justifie this practice, he would often say, Religion does not banish mirth, but only moderates, and sets rules to it.[30]

It might, then, seem entirely probable that Herbert learnt his verbal and metrical artistry in part at least from the frequent exercise of musical performance. It is, however, impossible to demonstrate as a fact. For Ben Jonson – an author who seems to me not to have been particularly enamoured of practical music,[31] and one who, in any case, claimed in conversation with William Drummond 'that he wrote all his [verses] in prose, for so his master Camden had learned him'[32] – could yet write odes in complex quasi-Pindaric metres, and lyrics of delicate verbal music such as the poem 'Her Triumph' in the *Celebration of Charis in Ten Lyric Pieces*, with its adept deployment of triple- and duple-time beats. Drummond reported, indeed, that Jonson 'said to the King his master, Mr G. Buchanan, had corrupted his ear when young, and learned him to *sing* verses when he should have *read* them'.[33] To the dichotomy of reading–singing we will return, but for the moment Jonson is sufficient evidence that it is not necessary to be immersed in music to write 'musical' poems.

Though Frye considered it was the roughness of Donne's verse that actually could be considered 'musical', most readers have counterposed his conversational rhythms with the measured quality of Herbert's lyrics to suggest quite the opposite. And yet consider, for example, the familiar opening lines of Donne's 'Sun Rising':

> Busy old fool, unruly sun,
>   Why dost thou thus,
> Through windows, and through curtains call on us?

The extension of the third line and delightful postponement of the arrival of the rhyme word manifest precisely the kind of control that the lyric quoted above from Yonge's collection cannot quite bring off – and might signal some kind of relationship with music.[34] Many of Donne's lyrics were resistant to setting until a more flexible, declamatory musical style came into being in the mid seventeenth century, but yet, according to Walton, he commanded his 'An Hymne to God the Father'

> to be set to a most grave and solemn Tune, and to be often sung to the Organ by the Choristers of St. Pauls Church, in his own hearing, especially at the Evening Service; and at his return from his Customary Devotions in that place, did occasionally say to a friend, The words of this Hymne have restored to me the same thoughts of joy that possest my Soul in my sickness when I composed it.[35]

This implies not merely that Donne was sensitive to music but, in its suggestion that it was when the words were actually set that he was enabled to recall their original feeling, that this account stands in interesting relationship to his earlier lyric, 'Triple Fool', and leads this chapter on to consider what the musical relationship of lyric poetry might mean for the transition from manuscript to print. In 'Triple Fool', having argued that writing a love poem 'tames' grief, the second stanza continues:

> Some man, his art and voice to show,
>   Doth set and sing my pain,
> And, by delighting many, frees again
>   Grief, which verse did restrain.
> To love and grief tribute of verse belongs,
> But not of such as pleases when 'tis read,
>   Both are increased by such songs:
> For both their triumphs so are published,
> And I, which was two fools, do so grow three;
> Who are a little wise, the best fools be.
> And I, which was two fools, do so grow three;
> Who are a little wise, the best fools be.[36]

This stanza presents a layered view of the purposes and effects of poetic composition, musical setting, and publication. For the individual poet, writing is represented as a therapeutic activity, softening the pains of love and grief. But when set to music the complications are several. First, such setting subjects the poem to the self-display of the musician, thereby taking it out of the control of the writer. But then, whereas Donne's hearing of his musically clothed religious poem reawakened the original joy, it seems that here it merely releases grief again. Yet it does not do so directly – since the song's listeners take pleasure in the singing, rather than re-enacting the originary grief. Instead it 'publishes' the triumph of both love and grief, in part to the humiliation of the poet at the broadcasting of private emotion.

The tension between private and public purposes is exposed here. And the songbooks share with a good deal of published verse a problematic sense of the relationship between the two. Thomas Healy considers Donne's poem in the light of this tension in his chapter below (pp. 63–5). Campion may stand for many other writers when, in the address to the reader for *Two Bookes of Ayres* he writes: 'Out of many Songs, which, partly at the request of friends, partly for my owne recreation, were by mee long since composed, I have now enfranchised a few.'[37] Yonge, in his dedication of *Musica transalpina*, claimed that he had received the translated lyrics from a high-placed gentleman, and then recorded that when he had collected

> sufficient to furnish a great sett of Bookes, diuers of my friends afore-said, required with great instance to haue them printed, whereunto I was

as willing as the rest, but could neuer obtaine the Gentlemans consent, though I sought it by many great meanes. For his answere was euer, that those trifles beeing but an idle mans exercise, of an idle subiect, written onely for priuate recreation, would blush to be seene otherwise then by twilight, much more to bee brought into the common view of all men.[38]

These are, of course, perfectly conventional protestations, which can be met with again and again in the published works of the period. At one level they confirm simply that music and poem belong to the same cultures. But yet there are important distinctions to be made. Poems in print can be read by anyone who is literate, where songs demand a performing skill if they are to be realised in their musical form. Even in the case of *A handefull of pleasant delites* (1584), a collection made of 'pleasaunt songs to ech new tune',[39] the address of 'The Printer to the Reader' encouragingly writes:

> Here may you haue of sundrie sorts,
>   Such Songs as you require
> Wherefore my friend, if you regard
>   such Songs to reade or heare:
> Doubt not to buy this pretie Booke.

In this collection the tunes were not printed but, like the broadside ballad, were simply identified and, presumably, were well known to the majority, at least, of purchasers. Nonetheless, the compiler, Clement Robinson, offers the poems equally to the ear or the eye. At an artistically higher level, the 1590s saw the fitful beginnings of the publication of solo airs in England (well behind the European Continent), and the creation of a market for printed music. Nonetheless, Campion himself issued a very similar invitation to the dedicatee of his *Two Bookes of Ayres*, Francis, earl of Cumberland:

> These Leaves I offer you, Devotion might
> Her selfe lay open, reade them, or else heare
>   How gravely with their tunes they yeeld delight
> To any vertuous, and not curious eare.[40]

Campion's comment raises significant questions about the audience for printed songbooks, about the ways in which they might have been used, and therefore about the nature of the musical lyric itself.

The shift from manuscript to print at the very least meant that composers, like poets, could take charge of the structuring of their works. At the simplest level, these two books of Campion's compositions are divided into the 'grave and pious' and the 'amorous and light'. Long ago I argued for the thematic coherence that might be found in the organisation of most of Campion's books.[41] Those claims now seem perhaps overstated, but I would still suggest that the *Third Booke*, which is explicitly offered to his patron, Thomas Monson, on the occasion of his release from the Tower, and which claims that its songs were conceived privately under his patronage, makes in its structure a comment on the misfortunes that he and his patron had suffered in the Overbury affair. The printed collection then retains some of its private relationship with the individual patron, and, indeed, after this very high-profile misfortune, may have been an attempt to vindicate Monson in the public eye. But, inevitably, at the same time it offers itself differently to the general music-buying public.

Kirsten Gibson has explored the implications of publication for Dowland's *First Booke of Songes or Ayres*, and makes interestingly similar claims. She notes Dowland's apparent reluctance to commit songs to print, but argues: 'When the songs and their associated texts were transferred from specific socially situated instances of performance to the pages of a printed book, they became, like the book itself, material objects, whose interpretation might be refigured by their new form and context.'[42] And she observes that: 'The songs, moreover, become mutually informing of each other as they are gathered together to form a discrete collection.'[43] From this perspective a published book of songs is not unlike the contemporary sequences of sonnets, with their very varying degrees of coherent narrative or thematic organisation. The importance of such connections should not, therefore, be overstated.

In other respects, however, the print publication of songs raises significant questions about the nature of lyric itself, and about the kinds of experience song might offer to its performers and to its audience. There are questions that arise about the way in which a singer positions him or herself in relation to the 'I' of a song when performing musically, rather than reading the lyric. So, too, there are interesting problems in formulating exactly what it is that audiences are responding to when they hear a song in a performative context.

Heather Dubrow has valuably questioned many of the assumptions that have characteristically been made about the relationship of a reader to the 'I' of a lyric. She writes persuasively about 'the unstable fluidity of audiences that is so central to early modern lyric',[44] thereby unsettling the notion that a reader simply absorbs the voice of a lyric to him or herself, identifying with the first person of the lyric.

Songbooks add further dimensions. A song, or a Psalm, like a poem, might be performed privately and solitarily, and an individual certainly might take on the voice of the poem for him or herself. Margaret Hoby, for example, recorded that on 26 January 1600, 'to refresh my selfe being dull, I plaied and sunge to the Alpherion'.[45] But, as Donne's 'Triple Fool' makes evident, there is always, precisely because of the element of performance, a distance established between the spoken voice of the poem and the sung voice of its performer. Sarah Iovan follows through some of the implications of the performative nature of the experience for the lyric speaker in a suggestive discussion. She notes that 'at first glance the musical setting seems to simplify the traditional questions surrounding the lyric speaker by giving the speaker and listener physical presence. At the most basic level, the singer enacts the position of speaker, and the audience enacts the position of listener.' She argues that this simple binary is always disturbed by the dialogic relationship between the singer and the accompanying lute.[46] There are, as it were, simultaneously the voices of the poet and composer, of vocalist and accompanist, being experienced by the song's audience.

One might go further and say that even if the song is sung for solitary recreation, the very fact of taking pleasure in the act of singing means that the relationship with the lyric can never be simply one of identification; the 'I' of the lyric is always someone else, the emotion always mediated. Even more obviously is this the case if one considers the physical form that the printed books of songs frequently took. One page offered a melody and accompaniment, which could be used either by a solo singer accompanying him or herself, or else by a singer and an accompanist side by side. The facing page arranged alto, tenor and bass parts on the page so that it would be possible for a quartet standing round a table, with or without lute, to sing together.

Campion explained why he provided this arrangement:

> These Ayres were for the most part framed at first for one voyce with the Lute, or Violl, but, upon occasion, they have since beene filled with more parts, which who so please may use, who like not may leave. Yet doe wee daily observe, that when any shall sing a Treble to an Instrument, the standers by will be offring at an inward part out of ther owne nature; and, true or false, out it must, though to the perverting of the whole harmonie.[47]

The note of regret is unmissable, and Campion clearly would have preferred to keep the purity of his coupling of word and note by confining performance to one singer. But his comments demonstrate the fundamental sociability of the act of singing, and, though publication in this form might have been undertaken for the benefit of sales, it obviously responds to something very basic in our response to lyric-as-song.

How to describe the experience of song is a much contested matter. Mark W. Booth, writing of the member of an audience listening to a song recital, contends that 'because song comes to us in a voice, without dramatic context, to pass through the consciousness of the listener, it fosters some degree of identification between singer and audience', arguing that 'we are drawn into … the self offered by the song'. But he adds to this perhaps rather solipsistic account the claim that 'the individual member of the audience enters into a common pattern of thought, attitude and emotion, and achieves by it concert with his society'.[48] Jeanette Bicknell is even more categoric: 'The fact that music can have a private or individual use does not make it any less a social product … Communing with music is a form of communing with human reality, and that is social.'[49]

Following Classical theory and medieval practice, then, the lyric is defined in the early modern period principally through its relationship with music, whether actual, or only notional. The connection with its sister art contributed significantly to the development of varied metrical and stanzaic forms, assisting in opening up the ears and eyes of poets to Continental forms, and in freeing lyric verse from the tyranny of jog-trot metres. The exercise of providing words to fit existing tunes, however, exposes also the difference between verse written *for* music and that written *to* an already existing tune. In the absence of the music such verse can be problematic for a reader to negotiate. Music, like poetry, moved from manuscript to print, and the process emphasised its essentially communal nature, complicating the nature of the relationship of performers and audience to the lyric 'I'. If this offers a definition at variance with standard post-Romantic assumptions about the individual and personal nature of the lyric as a genre, it is well to remind ourselves that song is still the dominant mode in which the majority of the population experience any poetry at all.

Notes

1 Though there is at least one antedating, from Drant's translation of Horace in 1567.
2 George Puttenham, *The Arte of English Poesie* (1589), pp. 19–20.
3 Thomas Campion, *The Works of Thomas Campion*, ed. Walter R. Davis (London: Faber and Faber, 1969), p. 309.
4 Thomas Churchyard, *A musicall consort of heauenly harmonie (compounded out of manie parts of musicke) called Churchyards charitie* (London, 1595), p. 35.
5 Philip Sidney, *An Apology for Poetry*, ed. Geoffrey Shepherd (London: Nelson, 1965), p. 99.

6 *Ibid.*, p. 113.

7 Heather Dubrow, *The Challenges of Orpheus: Lyric Poetry and Early Modern England* (Baltimore: Johns Hopkins University Press, 2008), p. 5. And see her chapter below, pp. 30–50.

8 John Stevens, *Music and Poetry in the Early Tudor Court* (London: Methuen, 1961), p. 108.

9 *Ibid.*, p. 134.

10 Winifred Maynard, 'The Lyrics of Wyatt: Poems or Songs?', *Review of English Studies*, n.s. 16 (1965), 1–13 (p. 2). Stevens also notes that poems were written to fit existing tunes, but is dismissive of the significance of this (Stevens, *Music and Poetry*, p. 131). That lyrics might fit a variety of tunes is exemplified in Ross Duffin, *Shakespeare's Songbook* (New York and London: Norton, 2004), where tunes are selected for the plays' lyrics, with no claim that they were in Shakespeare's mind as he wrote them.

11 Elizabeth Heale, *Wyatt, Surrey and Early Tudor Poetry* (London and New York: Longman, 1998), p. 78.

12 For a witty exemplification of these and other stanzaic forms, see John Hollander, *Rhyme's Reason: A Guide to English Verse*, rev. edn (New Haven and London: Yale University Press, 2001).

13 On the metrical Psalms and their music see Nicholas Temperley, *The Music of the English Parish Church*, 2 vols. (Cambridge University Press, 1979).

14 The tune can be heard sung to a variety of ballads in the *English Broadside Ballad Archive* at http://ebba.english.ucsb.edu/.

15 'The Famous Battle between Robin Hood and the Curtal Friar: To a New Northern Tune', http://ebba.english.ucsb.edu/ballad/30375/xml.

16 Northrop Frye, *The Anatomy of Criticism* (Princeton University Press, 1957) p. 255.

17 Derek Attridge, *The Rhythms of English Poetry* (London: Longman, 1982); see also his *Poetic Rhythm: An Introduction* (Cambridge University Press, 1995).

18 Winifred Maynard, *Elizabethan Lyric Poetry and Its Music* (Oxford University Press, 1986), p. 45. She discusses, but is dismissive of, the poetic value of such translations, pp. 40–5. Rather more positive insights into the two translators are offered by Laura Macy, 'The Due Decorum Kept: Elizabethan Translation and the Madrigals Englished of Nicholas Yonge and Thomas Watson', *Journal of Musicological Research* 17 (1997), 1–21; and William Peter Mahrt, 'Yonge versus Watson and the Translation of Italian Madrigals', *John Donne Journal* 25 (2006), 245–66.

19 Mahrt, 'Yonge versus Watson', pp. 265–6.

20 E. H. Fellowes, *English Madrigal Verse, 1588–1632*, ed. F. W. Sternfeld and David Greer, 3rd edn (Oxford University Press, 1967) p. 320.

21 Frank J. Fabry, ' Sidney's Verse Adaptations to Two Sixteenth-Century Italian Art Songs', *Renaissance Quarterly* 23 (1970), 237–55, and 'Sidney's Poetry and Italian Song-Form', *English Literary Renaissance* 3 (1973), 232–48; Gavin Alexander, 'The Elizabethan Lyric as Contrafactum: Robert Sidney's "French Tune" Identified', *Music and Letters* 84 (2003), 378–402.

22 Anthony Munday, 'Address to the Gentle Reader', in *Banquet of Daintie Conceits* (London: printed by I. C[harlewood] for Edwarde White, 1588), sig. A3r.

23 Edward Filmer, *French Court-Aires With their Ditties Englished … Collected, Translated, Published by Ed. Filmer, Gent* (London, 1629), sig. A4r.

24 John Dowland, 'Flow my teares', in *Lyrics from English Airs 1596–1622*, ed. Edward Doughtie (Cambridge, MA: Harvard University Press, 1970), p. 101.

25 John Dowland, 'Now cease my wand'ring eyes', in *ibid.*, p. 106.

26 Campion, *Works*, p. 230.

27 *Ibid.*, p. 55.

28 *Ibid.*, p. 33.

29 For the most comprehensive treatment of Campion's ill-fated efforts to introduce Classical quantitative metres into English poetry, see Derek Attridge, *Well-Weighed Syllables: Elizabethan Verse in Classical Metres* (Cambridge University Press, 1974). See also Christopher R. Wilson, 'Number and Music in Campion's Measured Verse', *John Donne Journal* 25 (2006), 267–89.

30 Izaak Walton, *The lives of Dr. John Donne, Sir Henry Wotton, Mr. Richard Hooker, Mr. George Herbert* (London, 1670), pp. 59–60 (each of the lives is paginated separately). For a very different take on Herbert's use of musical imagery, which argues that he is not interested in the actual performance of music, see Andrew Mattison, '"Keep Your Measures": Herrick, Herbert, and the Resistance to Music', *Criticism* 48 (2006), 323–46.

31 See David Lindley, 'Music', in *Ben Jonson in Context*, ed. Julie Sanders (Cambridge University Press, 2010), pp. 162–70.

32 Ben Jonson, *The Cambridge Edition of the Works of Ben Jonson*, ed. David Bevington, Martin Butler, and Ian Donaldson, 7 vols. (Cambridge University Press, 2012), Vol. v, p. 378.

33 *Ibid.*, p. 386 (my italics). Jonson is here echoing Quintilian.

34 Helen Gardner suggested that Donne wrote some poems with tunes in mind. See her edition of John Donne, *The Elegies and the Songs and Sonnets* (Oxford: Clarendon Press, 1965), p. 238. On the settings of Donne's poetry see Bryan N. S. Gooch, 'Music for Donne', *John Donne Journal* 15 (1996), 171–88.

35 Walton, *Lives*, p. 55.

36 Donne, *Elegies and the Songs and Sonnets*, p. 81.

37 Campion, *Works*, p. 55.

38 Nicholas Yonge, *Musica transalpina* (London: printed by Thomas East, 1588), sig. A2r.

39 As John Ward authoritatively demonstrated, neither words nor tune were 'new'; see his 'Music for *A Handefull of pleasant delites*', *JAMS* 10 (1957), 151–80.

40 Campion, *Works*, p. 54.

41 David Lindley, *Thomas Campion* (Leiden: E. J. Brill, 1986), pp. 3–29.

42 Kirsten Gibson, 'The Order of the Book: Materiality, Narrative and Authorial Voice in John Dowland's *First Booke of Songs or Ayres*', *Renaissance Studies* 26 (2012), 13–33 (p. 19).

43 *Ibid.*, p. 24.

44 Dubrow, *Challenges of Orpheus*, pp. 69, 77.

45 Margaret Hoby, *The Private Life of an Elizabethan Lady: The Diary of Lady Margaret Hoby, 1599–1605*, ed. Jane Moody (Stroud: Sutton, 1998), p. 56. The 'Alpherion' is the orpherion, a wire-strung, lute-like instrument.

46 Sarah Iovan, 'Performing Voices in the English Lute Song', *SEL* 50 (2010), 63–81.

47 Campion, *Works*, p. 55.

48 Mark W. Booth, *The Experience of Songs* (New Haven and London: Yale University Press, 1981), p. 15.

49 Jeanette Bicknell, *Why Music Moves Us* (London: Palgrave, 2009), p. 93.

CHAPTER TWO

Neither here nor there
Deixis and the sixteenth-century sonnet

Heather Dubrow

Directions, definitions, delimitations

[Mad] in pursuit and in possession so,
Had, having, and in quest to have, extreme,
A bliss in proof, and prov'd, [a] very woe,
Before, a joy propos'd, behind, a dream.
    All this the world well knows, yet none knows well
    To shun the heaven that leads men to this hell.[1]

Shakespeare's Sonnet 129 evokes desire, sliding from a straightforward condemnation to a representation of its dream-like allures and a challenge to the didactic agenda of the poem. All that the critical world well knows, yet few or none knows well why the deictic 'this' appears twice in the couplet – and why we have devoted so little attention to the deictics that establish, or appear to establish, temporal and spatial positions in early modern lyric, notably *here/there*, *now/then*, and *this/that*.[2]

Despite that neglect, other critics have engaged with deictic practices in narratives and dramas of this and many other periods. Deixis, narratologists have repeatedly demonstrated, establishes positionalities constitutive of narrative, notably the relationship between story and discourse and between an external world and the mind of an observer.[3] 'Deixis is immensely important to the drama, however, being the primary means whereby language gears itself to the speaker and receiver … and to the time and place of the action … as well as to the supposed physical environment at large and the objects that fill it', Keir Elam announces, a position seconded by many other students of theatre.[4] In encouraging cognate inquiries into lyric, arguments like Elam's foreshadow potential comparisons and contrasts. Henry V's 'Then call we this the field of Agincourt' (4.7.90) at once intensifies the pretence that 'this' is already a battlefield and reminds us that he is miming the work of theatre in turning a stage into a battlefield, much as he transforms French property into English booty. Yet, as the final sonnet reminds us, all these charms are eventually o'erthrown in both the political and theatrical realms. In other words, deictics in performed drama often code representation in terms of the material stage. As we will see, lyric deixis draws attention to the material page, a practice that in more senses than one rhymes with its analogue in drama.

Comparisons like these risk evoking the expectation that contrasting dramatic and lyric deixis can conveniently crystallise representations of lyric in the sixteenth century, thus extending arguments in the chapter that opens this volume (David Lindley's powerful analysis of song) by slotting in clear-cut definitions and descriptions of lyric in its print and manuscript versions.[5] Not so. To be sure, such an argument would conveniently enable a trajectory that could aptly structure this entire volume by historicising changing conceptions of lyric. But, as Hemingway's Jake puts it in *The Sun Also Rises*, 'isn't it pretty to think so'. For in fact the category of lyric, if indeed it should be called a category in its sixteenth-century incarnations, was discussed too sporadically and inconsistently in that period to produce that sort of clear-cut trajectory. Indeed, committed to interpreting lyric as a label serving poetic and critical ends rather than an objectively discerned and stable entity, many students of later periods would distrust such a trajectory on other grounds.[6] Nonetheless, deixis can in fact illuminate the development of lyric both by directing our attention to sixteenth-century practices that characterised it in that era and by anticipating more theoretical representations of the mode in subsequent centuries.

All discussions of genre demand caveats. Genres are, as so many critics have observed, variable and volatile. Hence, the family resemblance model that Alastair Fowler's *Kinds of Literature* influentially adapts from Wittgenstein can resolve many problems through defining forms as labile as, for example, the sonnet, epigram, and lyric itself, as well as successfully bracketing additional dilemmas.[7] But it remains all too easy to present the texts on which one is focusing as normative; thus statements rendering solitary meditation as the sine qua non for the genre ignore the communal renditions of lyric in the Greek ode, and Jonathan Culler's instantiation of apostrophe as the signature trope of lyric is rooted in the Romantic poetry in which he specialises.[8] Particularly important is distinguishing twentieth- and twenty-first-century usages from those in the culture one is exploring. Witness, for example, the ways the polemical rejection of a hypostasised version of lyric by LANGUAGE poets has shaped – and misshaped – perceptions of that form by both critics and defenders.

But how about the specific subject of this chapter, lyric in the sixteenth century?[9] A useful analogue is the status of the Classical epigram, which could vary in content from a gravestone memorial to a satirical commentary and was variously inscribed, written, and spoken.[10] The extent of the analogous challenge posed by this chapter registers in the fact that some critics have even claimed that the very term 'lyric' was virtually unknown in the sixteenth and earlier seventeenth centuries; but in fact it does appear very occasionally. As the preceding chapter by Lindley has effectively indicated, however, such references are very rare, and these and the few other surviving allusions to lyric per se either use the term in relation to music, as in the passage from Puttenham that he cites, or in relation to metre, which was the determinant of generic classifications in many Classical texts; in particular, those texts often refer to 'melic', or song-like poetry. Thus, anticipating the triadic division of modes that we also find in the mid seventeenth century in Milton's *Reason of Church Government*, Roger Ascham's *Scholemaster* divides poetry into comic, tragic, epic, and melic. We might well see this adoption of the Classical category of melic poetry as signalling the emphasis on song discussed by Lindley, though presumably it would also need to encompass such unsong-like forms as that slippery epigram.

Despite their rarity elsewhere, we do also find references to lyric per se in statements by George Puttenham and Sir Philip Sidney, as well as two later writers, Michael Drayton and John Milton. The influence of Classical metrical practices is especially apparent when Sidney writes, 'Is it then the Pastoral poem which is misliked? ... Or is it the lamenting Elegaic? ... Is it the bitter but wholesome Iambic? ... Is it the Lyric that most displeaseth?'[11] As these rhetorical questions indicate, Sidney's categories are primarily based on metre, not the characteristics related to lyric in its later and expanded sense in other chapters in this volume; pastoral, the exception to that generalisation about Sidney's classifications, reminds us yet again that lyric, when discussed at all, was not discussed consistently in the sixteenth century.

Although they cannot yield a more definitive argument about how lyric was seen in the period, statements on related subjects are germane. References to the Pindaric ode, which were very common in the period, may suggest that it offered a potential prototype for lyric – that is, celebratory public poetry – much as the ode and lyric were often conflated in later eras. The association of poetry with iconic mythological figures – notably Orpheus but also Pan and Arion – variously connected that mode with, paradoxically, both rhetorical power and failure; arguably such characters were especially linked to what we today would call lyric. And the use of words like 'air' and 'turn' also brought to bear a range of associations, some relevant to cultural anxieties about the erotic temptations of love lyrics. 'Turn', for instance, could suggest both the skill with which Jacobean furniture was designed and the deceit with which seductive songs were associated; moreover, the sexual undertow of 'turn', neglected in my exposition of it in the book cited above, demonstrates ambivalences and ambiguities surrounding lyric, thus further complicating definitions.

Similarly, perceptions of lyric in its many and volatile incarnations were surely informed, in the several senses of that term, by the sonnet and pastoral. Pastoral drew attention to the dialogic characteristics denied in many commentaries on lyric, as well as that problematical connection with song. And the propensity of both the genre of shepherds and that of lovers to participate in groupings of poems – a shepherd's calendar, a series of replies like those attracted by Marlowe's 'Passionate Shepherd to His Love', and of course the many varieties of sonnet cycles and sequences – complicates the project of defining the mode in terms of length. The putative immediacy of lyric is not the only apparent signature of the form that is liable to misreadings and even forgeries.

In exploring such issues, I rely especially on the sonnet, in part because it offers a convenient microcosm of issues that arise in other versions of lyric as well – and, paradoxically, in part because it simultaneously involves intriguing potentialities for distinctive forms of deixis. As I argued in detail elsewhere, a transhistorical comparison of the sonnet and lyric yields predictable connections among their putative characteristics, notably the sonnet's propensity to represent heightened emotion and intense personal experience. (As the example from Samuel Daniel below reminds us, however, the sonnet often is not overheard but rather implicitly or explicitly addressed to human listeners, thus challenging a characteristic so often attributed to lyric.)[12] Moreover, the special status the sonnet variously enjoyed for both readers and writers in the early modern period gestures towards connections with some ways lyric was represented then and later. If, as David Lindley's chapter argues, audiences in that period often encountered lyric in the form of song, in the sixteenth century the sonnet was arguably the principal genre in which they encountered written poetry focusing on personal experience. And so many of that era's authors felt inspired or impelled to experiment with the sonnet, whether to assert nationalistic claims over a Continental form; or to demonstrate their skill with a difficult one; or to explore love, a subject central to the writings of their period.

Hence arguably they associated this literary type with the potentialities of poetry in general and with how they may have conceived lyric in particular, to the extent that they held such a conception. Several chapters in this volume, notably Marion Thain's 'Victorian Lyric Pathology and Phenomenology', scrutinise practices of representing the lyric as a synecdoche for all poetry; arguably in the sixteenth century the sonnet often occupied a similarly synecdochal role.

This does not of course guarantee that analysing the sonnet, that repository of images of storm-tossed seas, is itself smooth sailing. In approaching this form we encounter no paucity of direct references to its workings, but, like the more sporadic allusions to lyric, they too prove slippery and inconsistent in the sixteenth century. To be sure, the pervasive impact of not only Petrarch but his commentators and Continental imitators had established a conception of a fourteen-line poem following predetermined rhyme schemes. But the term 'sonnet', etymologically a 'little song', was by no means confined to the types of fourteen-line poems that our own handbooks typically specify. Witness, *inter alia*, the assignment of the title *Songs and Sonets* to Donne's posthumous publication, while Sir Philip Sidney's *Apology for Poetry* similarly refers to 'that lyrical kind of songs and sonnets'.[13] Yet as Donne's volume and collections like Mary Wroth's *Pamphilia to Amphilanthus* conclusively remind us, poems called 'sonnets' were sometimes distinguished from those labelled 'songs'. In any event, the fact that the term 'song' was itself multifarious and inconsistently used, as David Lindley's chapter has demonstrated, further complicates issues about the sonnet. Hence describing lyric in general or the sonnet in particular as 'song-like' involves blithely skiing down one of many slippery slopes in this perilous terrain.

But all these problems in addressing sixteenth-century conceptions of lyric, song, and even the sonnet do not mean that I need to take my deictics and go home again. Fortunately, useful analogues abound in the critical literature on periods other than the early modern, as a few instances winnowed from many can demonstrate, and they begin to suggest some ways deixis can be relevant to the study of lyric. Commentaries on deictics often focus on pronouns in particular, as does Jonathan Culler when arguing that these usages help establish the distinctive literariness of poems; although those pronouns are largely outside the purview of this chapter, their implications for studying the fraught issue of lyric subjectivity are evident.[14] Analysing T. S. Eliot, David Trotter argues that 'this' and 'that' serve less to locate an object precisely than to indicate its relationship to the speaker; his emphasis on a scale of proximity anticipates my point about degrees of deixis, though he does not develop that observation at any length.[15]

A handful of exceptions to the relative neglect of scholarly discussions of deixis in early modern lyrics hints at directions for future study and crystallises the need for further work. Astute and subtle, Scott Newstok's analysis of 'here' in epitaphs has many implications for the cognate but distinct arenas of lyric that are outside the scope of his own study. In particular, his suggestion that the 'here' of epitaphs resembles its cousin in theatre in its insistence on a presence that doesn't exist anticipates and buttresses my own argument that lyric deixis, paradoxically, often turns place in the sense of a determined and delimited region into space in the sense of the unbounded.[16] In one of the most important discussions of lyric deixis, Roland Greene establishes its centrality to Petrarchism; his problematical emphasis on binary patterns, however, invites the challenges below.[17]

A revisionist examination of deixis in sixteenth-century lyric can, therefore, draw attention to transhistorical issues about that mode, notably its putative immediacy and internalisation within a single consciousness. Equally important, that examination crystallises characteristics distinctive of, though not always unique to, the period in question; most relevant to this volume are the workings of metatextuality and spatiality, especially in relation to print culture, and the cultural conditions that triggered these and additional subterranean issues within deictics. Varied though these arenas in which deixis operates are, affects and effects of instability and multi-directionality unite them: *here*, *this* and similar words often both define and destabilise space through multiple referents, and they interact with a whole range of sixteenth-century cultural practices, from the habits of printers to the rituals of priests.

Samuel Daniel: a case study

A well-known sonnet by Daniel aptly introduces patterns traced throughout this chapter. On the one hand, its deictics unsettle place and time rather than fixing them – fixing in the sense of both creating stasis and repairing potential problems. In this and other ways the poem anticipates how deictics challenge assumptions about immediacy and other putative lyric characteristics not only in the sixteenth century but also in later eras. And on the other hand the same practices provide some answers by signalling the workings of print culture and the material text in the sixteenth century and by drawing attention to spatiality.

When Winter snowes upon thy golden heares,
And frost of age hath nipt thy flowers neere:
When darke shall seeme thy day that never cleares,
And all lyes withred that was held so deere.
　　Then take this picture which I heere present thee,
Limned with a Pensill not all unworthy:
Heere see the giftes that God and nature lent thee;
Heere read thy selfe, and what I suffred for thee.
　　This may remaine thy lasting monument,
Which happily posteritie may cherish:
These collours with thy fading are not spent;
These may remaine, when thou and I shall perish.
　　　　If they remaine, then thou shalt live thereby;
　　　　They will remaine, and so thou canst not dye.[18]

Less aggressive than other sonnets in its *carpe diem* tradition, this sonnet emphasises not the need to respond to the threat of aging through sexuality but rather the ways the poem itself will control that threat through the devices traced in this chapter: deictics that variously and sometimes simultaneously perform gestures and establish, or seem to establish, place and time. Line 5, 'Then take this picture which I heere present thee', initiates these patterns by setting up a contrast between the *then and there* when the aged woman will read the poem and the *here and now* in which it is presented.

But in a poem that turns on so many binaries, why does the text resist the obvious alternative of 'which I now present thee'? In so doing, it activates the many meanings of *here* traced throughout this chapter – and forcefully demonstrates why *here* and *now* need to be distinguished. In other words, 'heere' in 'which I heere present thee' may refer to an occasion – that is, the time and place when the book is being handed over; to the volume itself, and thus again to the process of representation; and arguably it also thus hints at the gestural meaning of *here*, to which I'll return shortly. Notice now, though, that a couple of these meanings introduce spatiality in a way that 'now' could not.

Here also can hint at handing the poem to the lady, as in Keats' famous conclusion to a poem to which I'll turn shortly, 'This living hand': 'here it is— / I hold it towards you'.[19] This reading reminds us that 'here' both creates and marks interactions, that it *performs* hereness through a process of leaning and reaching. That is, it establishes an emotive and spatial relationship between the voice that is speaking and the person to whom something is being handed. And as in the proffer of Keats' hand, the person to whom the poem is handed in this putative undertow of meaning is close enough to hear and receive it, and yet may need to draw near – to be gathered in by the poem and its author – in order actually to receive it. At the same time that these references to handing something and to that something as the material text build their versions of immediacy, however, 'here' again signals representation, the poem itself.

In any event, the establishment of a *here and now* when the book is being given to its recipient introduces an effect of immediacy, intensified by 'this', a classic example of deictics as pointers. But observe again how that is complicated if 'heere' refers to the material book – that is, 'I am presenting the poem within this book'. The possibility that the lady is holding it draws attention to the tactility that can contribute to immediacy; but that possibility also reminds us that the poem exists in the realms of representation. Moreover, these lines clearly refer primarily to a printed text ('Limned with a Pensill not all unworthy' (6)), but all these interpretations are further complicated in ways traced above when one considers that the poem might be sung or recited – that is, presented in a performance as well as a book. For example, whereas visceral reactions to sound can intensify effects of immediacy, the possibility that a song is performed by someone other than the original creator of the words and indeed performed by multiple people on multiple occasions vitiates those effects and their implications for subjectivity, as we will see below.

If 'heere' in line 5 thus introduces a range of spatial and other references while appearing to establish the *then/now* temporality about which Roland Greene has written, as the sonnet progresses time becomes as various and unsettled as space. Thus 'Heere see' (7) and 'Heere read' (8) primarily represent commands to examine the poem at a future date – reminding us of how often, for all the commonplaces about a lyric present, anticipation is the dominant mode of such poetry. Associated with an anticipated future, 'Heere see' and 'Heere read' conflate and confound a spatial *here* and a temporal *there*. At the same time, surely these phrases also function as imperatives in the present moment at which the lady is receiving the poem. This conflation uncovers the doubleness, in more senses than one, of the poem.

And should we read these imperatives in lines 7 and 8 as command or invitation, recognising that the latter might embed the power plays of the former? As a suggestion, however authoritarian, that will be fulfilled in the future, the lines reassure the lady that reading about her beauty will mitigate the losses of aging. But surely the invitation to read them now opens up the possibility of a different kind of invitation: the seduction of the *carpe diem* motif. Hence the apparent tentativeness of the subsequent promises, though qualified by the final assertion, may warn the woman that she cannot rely completely on being memorialised by poetry. Unsure that she can gather her poetic posies when she may in the future, she should gather her roses while she may now.

The possibility that the woman is being invited to read in the *here and now* as well as in an anticipated future also in effect asks us to consider the ghostly traces of a comma after these 'heere's' – in other words, to attribute to them the gestural force we will encounter shortly in poems by John Keats and Elisabeth Frost. This reminds us that 'heere' both creates and marks interactions, that it *performs* hereness through a process of leaning and reaching. That is, it establishes an emotive and spatial relationship between the voice that is speaking and the person to whom something is being handed. And as in the proffer of Keats' hand, the person to whom the poem is handed in this putative undertow of meaning is close enough to hear and receive it, and yet may need to draw near – to be gathered in by the poem and its author – in order actually to receive it. At the same time that these references to handing something and to that something as the material text build their versions of immediacy, however, 'heere' again signals representation, the poem itself.

And that poem also again complicates the trajectories of literary history and the simplified definitions of lyric by reminding us how often early modern lyrics address the beloved directly or, as many critics have noted, implicitly address a coterie of male friends. If, *pace* John Stuart Mill and his heirs, the lyric poetry of later eras cannot simply be classified as solitary speech, the sixteenth century offers important antecedents and analogues. Similarly, as I have demonstrated elsewhere, many early modern lyrics include characteristics that students of nineteenth-century poetry have seen as unique to the dramatic monologues of their era.[20] Marshall Brown has gone so far as to argue that all poems are in some sense dramatic monologues;[21] whereas poems by Donne support this tendentious point better than our sonnet by Daniel, in the silent but felt presence of the lady and the hints that the speaker is being held up to judgement do we not find elements of a mode whose origins are sometimes seen as distinctively Victorian?

Reconceiving lyric: transhistorical implications

The challenge deixis offers to common assumptions about lyric is among the most compelling reasons for studying it; the recurrent ways it does so in work as diverse as sonnets by Shakespeare and Wordsworth, a lyric by Keats, and a postmodern poem, encourage contextualing my focus on sixteenth-century poetry with passages like those, thus demonstrating how frequently and intensely deictics challenge long-standing assumptions clinging to the mode of lyric.

Lyric immediacy, often summarised by citing the home address of the mode as the *here and now*, remains a staple, even a shibboleth, of criticism, and one would expect words like 'here' conveniently to demonstrate that imputed characteristic. Yet, as Daniel's poem reminds us, in many lyrics *here* is a moving target, a point that can complicate attempts to define the mode in other periods as well. To be sure, this deictic often leans towards *herein*, hence suggesting enclosure in a stable place, but it also gestures outwards to encompass multiple contiguous positions. In subtly tracing the process by which lyric poets from a range of centuries address an invisible listener with what she terms a 'vertical' relationship to themselves, Helen Vendler demonstrates a range of instances of our moving target, though she does not analyse them in these terms, nor does she fully confront their challenge to the isolated, meditative speaker whose normative status she still asserts.[22] Winnowing the sixteenth century itself for poems that complicate their references to *here* yields a range of examples. In adducing the idiom 'here and there' in his opening line, 'Alas, 'tis true, I have gone here and there' (110.1), Shakespeare invokes through it not a single contrast between polar opposites but a vague geography with many possible coordinates to his 'here' and 'there'. But even passages that do not rely on the resonances of that idiom have similar effects. Complaining to the moon about Stella's disdain, Sir Philip Sidney asks that celestial expert in couples-counselling, 'Are Beauties there as proud as here they be?'.[23] Whereas the contrasting deictics indubitably invoke the commonplace contrast between the sublunary world and the sphere above it, the 'here' may also refer to the court in general; to the more specific locales in which Astrophil interacts, or attempts to interact, with Stella; and, as I will maintain shortly, to discourse and its material realisation. And although this volume focuses on English literature, Richard Helgerson's demonstration that the '*Aquí*' in Garcilaso de la Vega's 'Sonnet from Carthage' encompasses not only contemporary Carthage, but its predecessor inhabited by Dido, and Toledo as well.[24] Helgerson's argument that 'here' within this sonnet may attempt to recapture the past, the *then*, emphasises its multidirectional workings.

Cognate examples from other periods are thick on the ground (an appropriate locale for a 'here' in particular). In Wordsworth's sonnet 'The Stepping Stones', 'here' draws attention to a particular locale, the area of the River

Duddon, but, as the title of the poem indicates, it is used to evoke not a single point but movement and change. Similarly, when Robert Lowell intones 'This is the end of the whaleroad and the whale' in his 'Quaker Graveyard in Nantucket' (69), the deictic 'this' functions like a colon when alluding both to a particular epistemological recognition (we have learned the relationship among various types of violence and exploitation); but surely it also refers to neighbouring but separable geographical locales, ranging from that cemetery itself, to the New England locales to which the poem refers, to the country as a whole.[25] Such deictic usages, then, challenge the immediacy associated with lyric: often, I maintain, it involves not establishing a static and single position but moving among a series of points.

Similarly, the gestural propensities of deixis challenge other assumptions about lyric, thus again introducing issues relevant throughout this volume. *Here* differs from *now* not least in its ability to suggest handing to or handing over. Often that gesture is metatextual, as when Daniel writes, 'Heere read thy selfe, and what I suffred for thee' (8). But the putative agency of Daniel's lyric is transferred to and transformed into that icon of agency, the human hand, in a hauntingly ambiguous poem (or, some critics have claimed, fragment) by John Keats:

> This living hand, now warm and capable
> Of earnest grasping, would, if it were cold
> And in the icy silence of the tomb,
> So haunt thy days and chill thy dreaming nights
> That thou would wish thine own heart dry of blood,
> So in my veins red life might stream again,
> And thou be conscience-calm'd. See, here it is—
> I hold it towards you.

To begin with, although the 'here' in the penultimate line mainly signals a gesture, it also reinforces my earlier point that the word typically marks not a single point but a series of them: if speaker and addressee were in exactly the same place, the 'towards' would not be necessary. Thus the poem itself introduces some revisionist approaches to the isolation and immateriality often associated with lyric: it exemplifies, as does our instance from Daniel, the presence of more than one person – not just the overhearer posited in certain traditional theories of lyric – and demonstrates the relevance of embodiment and physical gesture. (All this is of course further complicated by the possibility that not the living hand but the anticipated dead one is being held out, in which case the possessor of the hand and the addressee invited to regard and possibly touch it are indeed in different places, ontologically and spatially.)

But is that proffered hand accepted? Although one critic asserts that the reader reaches towards it in sympathy, surely even the possibility of its being a dead hand is as likely to produce recoil.[26] A comparable reminder of the unstable reactions to gestural deixis occurs in a poem entitled 'Happiness' by the contemporary American poet Elisabeth Frost. Its speaker is attempting to say – and convey – the concept in the title to an unreceptive listener, though within a context that itself calls into question communication ('all talk is slippery … Who can say how a thing in words turns and flowers like that' (1, 5)).[27] The poem ends,

> We're in this room, and you're not hearing
> how I'm still trying to say this thing to you.
>
> I'll say it again. Here. *Happiness*.
>
> (13–15)

The 'Here' (15) may refer to locale, with 'this room' (13) signalling an enclosure of two people who are really far apart, but primarily, of course, it is a gestural deictic: happiness is being verbally and acoustically handed to someone who wants to refuse it. As in Keats' extraordinary lines and many other poems, a deictic gesture establishes the presence in some form of a hearer, and anchors the poem in a space where the gesture may be perceived if not necessarily accepted, an analogue to the soundscapes to which I'll turn shortly. And as in Daniel's poem, the object that the speaker attempts to pass on is discursive, involving both a philosophical concept and the word through which it is conveyed. Above all, in all these cases the deixis establishes lyric as a process involving more than one consciousness and a complex relationship to space and place. But how are that process, and that relationship, inflected by the matrices of sixteenth-century lyric poetry?

Deixis and sixteenth-century lyric

Identifying the distinctive forms these and other transhistorical deictic patterns assume in sixteenth-century poetry involves a centripetal reinterpretation of issues traced in the preceding section, especially a re-examination of metatextuality in relation to the material texts of print culture, as well as a centrifugal examination of the cultural resonances of deixis in the sixteenth century. Having successively demonised looking closely at anything but the text, and looking closely at the text in lieu of looking at history and culture, the United States academy has recently become more capacious in accepting and connecting those approaches – a shift appropriate to these fraternal twins.

Although we have seen that deictics are characteristically metatextual in many periods, in the sixteenth century that characteristic is typically shaped by early modern versions of spatiality, by their relationship to the material text, and by the relationship of that text in its printed form to other means of transmission; references to local literary conventions may also be at play. Specific to sixteenth- and early seventeenth-century culture, many resonances of the line cited earlier from Sidney's thirty-first sonnet – 'Are Beauties there as proud as here they be?' (31.11) – thus distinguish Sidney's 'here' from the usages by Keats and Frost flagged above. Not only does cosmology of the period evoke a sublunary world; Sidney's 'here' also gestures towards a series of literary conventions characteristic of its era, especially Petrarchism, and to their expression on a particular page of a particular poem printed according to particular conventions. Thus the types of Petrarchism Sidney variously explores, extends, and excoriates distinguish his 'here' from that of, say, Romantic poets like Charlotte Smith working with that tradition. But more to my purposes now, the material page to which the word can refer had distinct and intriguing characteristics in Sidney's day. As Thomas Healy's contribution to this collection, '"Trewly wrote": Manuscript, Print, and the Lyric in the Early Seventeenth Century', also reminds us, printers often inserted borders at the bottom or, in many instances, both the top and bottom of every page. An extreme and extremely interesting version is the 1595 edition of Spenser's 'Epithalamion' and *Amoretti*, where each sonnet and each stanza of the wedding poem is encased in this way. Thus the metatextual 'here' as well as 'this', both words that frequently appear in that collection, again become associated with 'herein', turning the potentially amorphous space of the book into a defined and controlled place, and thus encouraging us to adduce space/place theory more often when reading lyric. The contrast throughout the 'Epithalamion' between the putatively safe world of the wedding and the dangers lurking at its borders lend resonance to that attraction to enclosure, even though its visualisation through printing practices was probably fortuitous. In addition, in the 'Epithalamion', the tension between the borders of the stanzas and the narrativity often enacted in their content extends the interplay between lyric and narrative elements throughout the poem. More broadly, in other sixteenth-century collections using large borders, such as the anonymous and perhaps satirical collection *Zepheria*, and Thomas Watson's *Hecatompathia; or, Passionate Centurie of Love*, those borders insistently separate linked poems, in particular countering the connections established in other ways in groups of sonnets. In instances like these, defining the referent of a metatextual 'this' or 'here' as the poem at hand rather than its neighbours as well is encouraged, though the alternative is not precluded.

That signal is, however, complicated, and other issues about representations of *here* introduced, through catchwords. Early modern printers regularly relied on these devices: at the bottom of the page, positioned far right, appears the first word of the next poem, a system that helped keep the pages in order during composition and production. But this deliberate placing of a word not in the text at hand in fact operated like a different and accidental characteristic of sixteenth-century texts: the propensity of ink from the succeeding page to bleed into the preceding one, thus on occasion leaving a ghostly anticipation of what is to come. In both instances, the trace of the next page is at once *here* and a reminder of a page that in one sense is *there* but still relatively close to *here*. We also encounter yet another version of *here* as contiguous and shifting points. These catchwords, which at least lack and at times conflict with the authorial agency expressed in creating closure at the end of a given poem, are, however, intriguingly analogous to the poetic devices skilfully deployed by writers to link poems – the repeated line in *concatenatio* or, of course, the very concept of groups of poems and of a sonnet sequence or cycle.

Joshua Calhoun has recently demonstrated another way the material page could interact with pointers like *here* and *this* in sixteenth-century England. Quite literally putting the material back in materialism, he traces the processes by which paper was made, showing that it often contained discernible fragments of, for example, wood and old clothing.[28] Thus when the word 'here' refers to the book and page it gestures as well towards the past life of the incorporated objects, a *there* that draws closer and again unsettles the *here/there* binaries fallaciously seen as normative in lyric. And, returning to Spenser's 'Epithalamion', the afterlife of those fragments is serendipitously thematic there. The poem repeatedly gathers the woods closer to the world of the poem, notably through the refrain that refers to the woods answering. Calhoun's work demonstrates that the physical text, like the refrain, incorporates, gathers the woods into the song, in the first instance quite literally. In this sense print culture physically enacts properties of deictics.

But among the most important characteristics of sixteenth-century print culture is its interaction with coexisting types of transmission, notably manuscript culture and song, the latter recently coming into its own as a subject of study after its appearance in important but isolated volumes. Deixis both shapes and is shaped by that interaction, whose broader implications for lyric are cogently discussed in the opening chapter of this volume.[29] Whereas Fredric Jameson's commentary on remediation, the adaptation of a text in a different medium, attempts to position it as a characteristic of postmodernism, other analyses have noted the vitality of that practice in preceding centuries as well.[30] Indeed, whether or not one challenges John Guillory's alternative location of remediation in the early modern period (claims that a major movement started in the area in which one specialises should always be greeted with suspicion), his observation that remediation makes one more conscious of the medium is persuasive and germane.[31] That consciousness, one should add, is intensified by deictics: their meaning shifts depending on whether they appear in a scribal or print context or in a performed song.

What happens if we reinterpret the metatextual meaning of Sidney's 'as here they be' (31.11) as extending to scribal circulation as well as print? Although some might cite the sales figures on volumes like Spenser's *Shepheardes Calender* (five editions in the sixteenth century, not to mention adoption by Oprah's book club) to qualify the primacy assigned to scribal documents in Thomas Healy's '"Trewly wrote": Manuscript, Print, and the Lyric in the Early Seventeenth Century', the pervasiveness of manuscript versions of poems is unassailable. Given the frequent changes and errors associated with that mode of transmission, the deictic 'here' is further destabilised, with a reminder that the poem to which it now refers may differ significantly from a later rendition. Moreover, since manuscript culture involved passing of poems among members of coteries, the usage reminds us that besides all the other possibilities traced above – 'here' as the sublunary world but also as Petrarchan discourse, a particular page, the court, and so on – the word could refer to a small circle examining the poem. Or to the group attending to it as it is read aloud.

Deictic references are further complicated if the lyric is sung – or even perceived as a text that might be sung. First of all, Sarah Iovan has demonstrated that the musical accompaniment often functions as a different voice, not merely an echo of that of the performer.[32] Thus a metatextual 'here' and 'this' could refer to significantly different versions of the text variously performed by a human voice and an instrument, an intriguing parallel to the multiple versions and voices encouraged by manuscript culture. Moreover, expanding the concept of soundscape, developed by Bruce Smith and others, demonstrates that the process of singing works like deixis (and is sometimes actually marked by deictics) for the original singer, a potential subsequent singer, and the audience.[33] Song interpellates all three into complex relationships to spatiality – but also may bestow more agency than the concept of interpellation usually acknowledges. The original singer helps to create a soundscape, in effect reaching outwards towards others much as Keats' and Frost's poems do. At the same time the sound reverberates within the body of the singer. As Sharon Harris cogently puts it, 'A sound-producer makes a sound that both enters her ears and travels out away from her into her surrounding soundscape. She is a participant in that soundscape and shapes and alters her surroundings.'[34] The audience is drawn into the soundscape, recalling the person invited to take Keats' hand or the listener to whom Elisabeth Frost offers happiness – but if they are in earshot, this, unlike the hand or the concept of happiness, is an offer they cannot refuse. The visceral power of song contributes to the imperative force of the invitation.

Moreover, in the instance of song, unlike the analogues in Keats and Frost, subsequent singers redefine and expand the *here and now* of the original song so that it includes the potentially different place and inevitably different time when they are singing. All this implicit deixis is even knottier when actual deixis is included. Returning to a poem probably written in the sixteenth century, though by a poet who became an icon of Jacobean sensibility for an earlier generation of literary historians, John Donne's 'The Indifferent' includes the line, '*Venus* heard me sigh this song' (19).[35] Recalling my allusion to Spenser's 'Epithalamion', this deictic conflates the earlier version Venus heard, the current rendition if we assume the line in question is itself part of a song rather than a commentary on one, and a possible rendition of it by some other singer at some point in the future – perhaps even someone within the current soundscape who is hearing it and will then repeat it. In short, in this as other instances, the coexistence of print with manuscript and sung versions expands the potential references of deictics, again ensuring in particular that when 'here' or 'this' or 'now' appears in a given poem, it signals not the single, stable place or time conventionally associated with lyric but multiple and volatile possibilities. These interactions are, of course, further complicated by the fact that songs were experienced not only through performance but also through the print versions of them that circulated in the period, thus complicating yet another binary.

The felt presence of a specified emotive speaker, certainly cornerstone and arguably shibboleth of so much critical analysis of lyric, is thus challenged as well. Subjectivity also becomes an arena for those volatile possibilities. My earlier arguments about spatiality do imply a realised voice, indeed an embodied person. Yet the pervasiveness of song, its status as a synecdoche for lyric, suggests that even poems that were neither sung nor written in ways that facilitate musical settings were associated with a first-person pronoun that could wander among successive voices.

The second principal reason deictics operate distinctively in sixteenth-century poetry is their interaction with cultural practices and problems ranging from the astrological to the theological to the architectural. Paradigms contrasting the sublunary world and heavenly worlds, explicit in Sidney's Sonnet 31, arguably lie behind even contrasts that do not refer explicitly to that model. More often, however, Christian doctrines are the whirling undertow in passages that introduce, then blur, the contrast between *here* and *there*. Above all, of course, the Eucharistic debates, a major if not the major source of controversy in the English Reformation, sometimes pivot on the 'hoc' in 'hoc est corpus meum'. Does it refer to Real Presence or to representation? And is the point that Christ is uniquely present at that holy moment or that, as the doctrine of virtualism would indicate, that he is always present in the world?[36] Intensifying as the seventeenth century progressed, millenarianism was also present in England and on the Continent in the sixteenth century, and of course earlier as well, and it too drew attention to spatial and temporal binaries, suggesting that *here* was rapidly approaching a moment spatially and temporally *there*. (Without allowing abstractly theoretical explanations to override the quotidian social conditions motivating groups like the Levellers, might one speculate that the desired redistribution of property also served to render literal other types of spatial and temporal volatilities?)[37] In short, so potent and pervasive were a range of theological debates involving versions of *here* versus *there* and *now* versus *then* that they informed and on occasion electrified secular allusions to such concepts.

Architecture and interior design, I maintain, also contributed to early modern interpretations of deixis by rejecting the simple binaries of *here* versus *there* often cited in analyses of lyric immediacy. Characteristic of, though by no means unique to, the period were architectural features such as a moat or the enclosed courtyards created by the common H or E designs, all of which blurred the distinction between inside and outside, and hence *here* and *there*.[38] And how about the bedrooms designed so that a couple could maintain erotic privacy within the curtains of a four-poster bed while others still slept within the room? Once again, if the room is *here*, it contains many different points.

Turning from the broader culture to the literary cultures of early modern England, many generic practices interacted with the forms of deixis I have outlined. As significant here as in many other issues about of the early modern period is the popularity of the sonnet and pastoral to which I referred above. I have already indicated how the propensity of the former to appear in groupings complicates *here* and *there*. Pastoral is grounded in interlocking but sometimes antagonistic binaries. Poems that contrast the *here* of pastoral tranquillity with the *there* of busy companies of men often express their uneasy awareness of another contrast: the *there* of the original lost Eden versus the *here* of its latter-day imperfect analogues. That original Eden may not be regained, but the *there* of the outer world may impinge all too effectively, as the invasions by soldiers and brigands in that protopastoral Virgil's first eclogue and that metapastoral Book VI of *The Faerie Queene* remind us.

From here to there

My initial focus on a poem about invitations, Daniel's sonnet, is fortuitously appropriate for one of the initial chapters in a volume like this one. The potentialities and problems of sixteenth-century lyric invite us to see how historical changes inflect them in the periods to which this volume now turns; for example, the distinctive workings of print when it coexists in the ways it does in the sixteenth century invite, indeed impel, further explorations of how lyric changes because of, and despite, the evolutions of print. And that pointing device deixis points us as well towards revisionist explorations of concepts fundamental to many definitions of lyric, from immediacy to interiority.

Notes

1 William Shakespeare, Sonnet 129, 9–14. I cite throughout *The Riverside Shakespeare*, ed. G. Blakemore Evans, 2nd edn (Boston, MA: Houghton Mifflin, 1997).

2 Throughout this chapter, I italicise the names of deictics when referring to the concepts and use quotation marks for a usage within a particular text.

3 David Herman, *Basic Elements of Narrative* (London: Wiley-Blackwell, 2009), pp. 115–16 (pp. 123–4).

4 Keir Elam, *The Semiotics of Theatre and Drama* (London: Routledge, 1980), pp. 26–7.

5 Because of the structure of this volume, my chapter focuses specifically on the sixteenth century; but I share the widespread perception that in many literary and cultural arenas periodisation should not posit a firm divide between the sixteenth and earlier seventeenth centuries.

6 For this position and analyses of the related issue of lyricisation, see for example Virginia Jackson, 'Lyric', in *The Princeton Encyclopedia of Poetry and Poetics*, ed. Roland Greene, Stephen Cushman, Clare Cavanagh, Jahan Ramazani, Paul F. Rouzer, Harris Feinsod, *et al.*, 4th edn (Princeton University Press, 2012); Yopie Prins, *Victorian Sappho* (Princeton University Press, 1999),

esp. pp. 3–22; and Marion Thain's chapter, 'Victorian Lyric Pathology and Phenomenology' in this volume, pp. 156–76.

7 Alastair Fowler, *Kinds of Literature: An Introduction to the Theory of Genres and Modes* (Cambridge, MA: Harvard University Press, 1982), pp. 40–4.

8 Jonathan Culler, *The Pursuit of Signs: Semiotics, Literature, Deconstruction* (Ithaca, NY: Cornell University Press, 1981), pp. 135–74. Culler himself argues for focusing on those Classical roots in his essay 'Why Lyric?', *PMLA* 123 (2008), 204–5.

9 See my book *The Challenges of Orpheus: Lyric Poetry and Early Modern England* (Baltimore: Johns Hopkins University Press, 2008), pp. 15–53 for more detailed discussions of arguments later in this paragraph and in the two sub-sequent ones; the references to mythological characters appear on pp. 18–26 and the discussion of terminology on pp. 26–39.

10 Niall Livingstone and Gideon Nisbet, *Epigram*, Greece and Rome: New Surveys in the Classics 38 (Cambridge University Press, 2010).

11 I cite throughout Sir Philip Sidney, *An Apology for Poetry; or, The Defence of Poesy*, ed. Geoffrey Shepherd (London: Nelson, 1965). This quotation appears on pp. 116–18.

12 See my chapter 'The Sonnet and the Lyric Mode', in *The Cambridge Companion to the Sonnet*, ed. A. D. Cousins and Peter Howarth (Cambridge University Press, 2001), pp. 25–45.

13 Sidney, *Apology*, p. 137.

14 Jonathan Culler, *Structuralist Poetics: Structuralism, Linguistics, and the Study of Literature* (Ithaca, NY: Cornell University Press, 1975), pp. 164–70.

15 David Trotter, *The Making of the Reader: Language and Subjectivity in Modern American, English and Irish Poetry* (New York: Macmillan, 1984), pp. 44–6. I would also take issue with some implications of his argument for subjectivity, though doing so is outside the scope of this chapter.

16 Scott L. Newstok, *Quoting Death in Early Modern England: The Poetics of Epitaphs beyond the Tomb* (Houndmills: Palgrave Macmillan, 2009), esp. pp. 33–58.

17 Roland Greene, *Post-Petrarchism: Origins and Innovations of the Western Lyric Sequence* (Princeton University Press, 1991), esp. pp. 22–62.

18 Samuel Daniel, Sonnet 34. The citation is to Samuel Daniel, *Poems and 'A Defence of Ryme'*, ed. A. C. Sprague (University of Chicago Press, 1965 [1930]). I have regularised 'v'/'u'.

19 John Keats, *The Poems of John Keats*, ed. J. Stillinger (Cambridge, MA: Harvard University Press, 1978).

20 Dubrow, *Challenges of Orpheus*, pp. 9, 236–7.

21 Marshall Brown, 'Negative Poetics: On Skepticism and the Lyric Voice', *Representations* 86 (Spring 2004), 120–40 (p. 131).

22 Helen Vendler, *Invisible Listeners: Lyric Intimacy in Herbert, Whitman, and Ashbery* (Princeton University Press, 2005).

23 Philip Sidney, *Astrophil and Stella*, 31.11. Throughout, citations from Sidney's poetry are to *The Poems of Sir Philip Sidney*, ed. William A. Ringler, Jr (Oxford: Clarendon Press, 1962).

24 Richard Helgerson, *A Sonnet from Carthage: Garcilaso de la Vega and the New Poetry of Sixteenth-Century Europe* (Philadelphia: University of Pennsylvania Press, 2007), pp. 40–7,

25 I cite Robert Lowell, *Collected Poems*, ed. Frank Bidart and David Gewanter (New York: Farrar, Straus, and Giroux, 2003).

26 Sympathy is suggested by Lawrence Lipking in *The Life of the Poet: Beginning and Ending Poetic Careers* (University of Chicago Press, 1981), p. 181.

27 Elisabeth Frost, *All of Us*, Marie Alexander Poetry Series (Buffalo: White Pines Press, 2011), lines 1, 5.

28 Joshua Calhoun, 'The Word Made Flax: Cheap Bibles, Textual Corruption, and the Poetics of Paper', *PMLA* 126 (2011), 327–44.

29 Compare Joshua Calhoun's observation that the word 'that' in Shakespeare's *Sonnets* 'identif[ies] the text without identifying a specific incarnation of it' ('Ecosystemic Shakespeare: Vegetable Memorabilia in the Sonnets', *Shakespeare Studies* 39 (2011), 64–73 (p. 70)). But whereas I maintain that such references evoke lyrics' multiple statuses as written, recited, and sung without privileging any, he argues that 'this' contrasts the flimsiness of paper with the successful memorialisation the text performs.

30 Fredric Jameson, *Postmodernism; or, The Cultural Logic of Late Capitalism* (Durham, NC: Duke University Press, 1991), pp. 161–80.

31 John Guillory, 'Genesis of the Media Concept', *Critical Inquiry* 36 (2010), esp. p. 324.

32 Sarah Iovan, 'Performing Voices in the English Lute Song', *SEL* 50 (2010), 63–81.

33 The concept of the soundscape is developed throughout Bruce R. Smith, *The Acoustic World of Early Modern England: Attending to the O-Factor* (University of Chicago Press, 1999). Also cf. Gina Bloom, *Voice in Motion: Staging Gender, Shaping Sound in Early Modern England* (Philadelphia: University of Pennsylvania Press, 2007).

34 Sharon Harris, 'The Orbit of Music and Motion in the Eighth Song of *Astrophil and Stella*', unpublished essay presented at 'Inarticulacy: A National Early Modern Conference', University of California, Berkeley, 12 November 2012.

35 John Donne, 'The Indifferent', line 19, in *The Elegies and the Songs and Sonnets*, ed. Helen Gardner (Oxford University Press, 1965).

36 The Eucharistic controversies have of course been exhaustively analysed by both theologians and literary critics. For a valuable though not uncontroversial version of those debates, see Judith H. Anderson, *Translating Investments: Metaphor and the Dynamic of Cultural Change in Tudor-Stuart England* (New York: Fordham University Press, 2005), pp. 36–60.

37 For a useful overview of the millenarian movement, see David Loewenstein, *Milton and the Drama of History: Historical Vision, Iconoclasm, and the Literary Imagination* (Cambridge University Press, 1990), pp. 8–12. Also see the lengthier analyses in David S. Katz and Richard H. Popkin, *Messianic Revolution: Radical Religious Politics to the End of the Second Millennium* (New York: Hill and Wang, 1998), esp. pp. 3–57; Norman Cohn, *The Pursuit of the Millennium:*

Revolutionary Messianism in Medieval and Reformation Europe and Its Bearing on Modern Totalitarian Movements, 2nd edn (New York: Harper and Rowe, 1961 [1957]), esp. appendix.

38 On these styles, see e.g David Watkin, *English Architecture: A Concise History*, rev. edn (London: Thames and Hudson, 1979), pp. 77–95.

CHAPTER THREE

'Trewly wrote'
Manuscript, print, and the lyric in the early seventeenth century

Thomas Healy

I

In his *Civil Wars* (1595, extended 1609), Samuel Daniel proclaimed that the devil's principal instruments are the printing press and gunpowder. A wide circulation of texts through printing enables 'the vulgar' to grow wise, 'deepest mysteries debate', and 'Controule their betters'.[1] Yet even when chastising print, Daniel's words convey sentiments that to current ears seem precisely why the medium might be fêted; its technology allows:

> that instamped Characters may send
> Abroad, to thousands, thousand mens intent;
> And in a moment may dispatch much more,
> Then could a world of Pennes performe before.[2]

Daniel's view is an extreme reflection of an anxiety around print and what may be termed its democratic tendencies.[3] Proclaiming about high truths in eloquent language needing to be veiled from those incapable of appreciating their transcendent qualities is a familiar Renaissance proposition, but it is a sentiment that other contemporary thinkers rejected. John Foxe, for example, celebrated printers along with players and preachers as bulwarks of the Reformation.[4] Daniel, too, was hardly reluctant to see his poetry in print, and in 1601 became the first English poet to gain the distinction of having his verse published in a dedicated folio volume. Richard Tottel addresses the readers of his 1557 collection *Songes and Sonettes written by the right honourable Lorde Henry Howard late Earle of Surrey, and others* (the book usually termed *Tottel's Miscellany*), acknowledging that while he may offend some sensibilities in printing these lyrics, he is enabling wide reading 'to the honor of the English tong' in contrast to those 'ungentle horders up of such treasure'.[5] Yet even when broadly content with a printed medium, writers often expressed a preference for manuscript circulation.

In a playful Latin poetic address, John Donne proposes that printed books
tend to be ignored in contrast to readers' reverence towards handwritten ones ('sed que scripta manu, sunt veneranda magis').[6] Ben Jonson is
much celebrated for his 1616 folio, *The Workes of Beniamin Ionson*, which
printed selections of his lyrics and epigrams along with his plays, but it
is less acknowledged that Jonson returned to coterie manuscript circulation for his later lyrics after this folio's publication.[7] The relation between
manuscript and print, in which the latter is assumed gradually to replace
the former because it allowed more reliable texts to circulate in greater
numbers, needs to be reassessed. In this chapter I wish to address some
implications for our interpretive practices in thinking about lyric through
manuscript.

Before exploring lyric in sixteenth- and early seventeenth-century
manuscript, however, it is useful to reflect upon this era's understanding of the category of lyric itself. As Heather Dubrow reminds us, while
perceptions and representations of 'lyric' exist in this period, they were
'many and volatile', and similarly the term 'song' was equally 'multifarious and inconsistently used'.[8] Citing *The Arte of English Poesie* (1589),
David Lindley illustrates how Puttenham classified Classical poets such
as Pindar, Horace, and Catullus as lyric, whereas Ovid and Propertius are
labelled 'Eligiack' and considered 'another sort, who sought the favour of
fair ladies and coveted to bemoan their estates at large'.[9] In contrast, our
current perceptions usually consider shorter Renaissance poetic addresses
to lovers as quintessentially exemplifying the period's lyric verse. Sir Philip
Sidney's *Defence of Poesie* (1579/1595) uses poesy broadly to mean any forms
of eloquent, decorous language and not strictly poetry. For Sidney, serious
writers are 'makers' – derived from his etymology of the Greek *poiein* – a
label that carries associations both with the divine (God is also a maker)
and with skilled artisans such as scriveners who copy out texts.[10] Samuel
Daniel similarly perceives successful poetry resting in language's careful
crafting in his essay 'A Defence of Rhyme' (1603). Daniel's remarks about
sonnets may be applied generally to contemporary perceptions of lyric
verse. It is the form's compactness that gives lyric notable intensity:

> For the body of our imagination, being as an vnformed *Chaos* … if by the
> divine power of the spirit it be wrought into an Orbe of order and forme, is
> it not more pleasing to Nature, that desires a certaintie, and comports not
> with that which is infinite, to haue these clozes rather than not to know
> where to end, or how farre to goe … Besides, is it not most delightfull to
> see much excellentlie ordred in a small roome … [that] would not appeare
> so beautifull in a larger circuite … And these limited proportions, and rests

> of stanzes, consisting of six, seven or eight lines, are of that happines, both
> for the disposition of the matter, the apt planting the sentence where it
> may best stand to hit, the certaine close of delight with the full body of a
> iust period well carried.[11]

The sonneteer is imitating God's creation of earth in fashioning his poem,
creating an effect that also resonates with musical composition. Although
many manuscripts in which verse circulated in this period also include
prose extracts, one of the things that attracted the compilers to shorter
poems was their language being 'excellentlie ordred in a small roome'.

As Nigel Smith details, the cultural environment that nurtured poetry
in the sixteenth and seventeenth centuries developed out of schoolroom
practices in which Classical forms – perhaps most critically the epigram –
provided the building blocks to develop expression that celebrated imitation.[12] Copying enabled readers to recognise both similarity and difference
(for instance, by exploiting familiar lines or tropes or generic conventions
in altered contexts), but a consequence is that while the best lyrics power-
fully persuade us of their speakers' characters, these are inevitably constructed *personae* and it would be misleading to imagine this poetry as
designed to reflect its authors' authentic experiences. Poetic accomplishment was celebrated for displaying a general capability in *eloquentia* – the
employment of language correctly, truthfully, and ethically according to
humanist norms. Christopher Marlowe won a scholarship to Cambridge
endowed by Matthew Parker, a former archbishop of Canterbury. It was
gained on merit by a student with high proficiency in grammar and 'if it
may be such as can make a verse'.[13] The premise underlying this stipulation
was that the holder's ability in composing verses elegantly in Latin (the
language of Elizabeth education) was a likely sign of his moral soundness,
as the recipient was intended to follow a career in the English Church.
Parker scholarships were not envisaged as nurturing an aesthetic sensibility that might lead to a release of personal thought and feeling into individual poetic expression.

The poetic culture that prompted Renaissance lyric was fundamentally
different from that of the Romantic poets and their successors. The lyric
later comes to be envisaged as engaging with singular experience, seeking
subjective expression, voicing individual interiority and vision. An interest
in manuscript around later lyric largely stems from urges better to understand a poet's singularity and unique authenticity of voice – a manuscript
is sought as an autograph validating an individual's creative virtuosity. In
contrast, verse manuscripts in sixteenth- and seventeenth-century England
reveal poetry undertaken as collective enterprises, allowing lyrics to be

employed in manners that fundamentally challenge perceptions of them as expressions of felt subjective experience.

Samuel Daniel's principal fear of the printing press is that it gives 'the vulgar' a sense of empowerment above their true station in life – 'with a self-presumption ouer-growne'.[14] Central to this anxiety is that they will be incapable of proper comprehension in reading printed matter, a problem that rests not simply with absorbing content but through understanding the medium. Print conveys a fixed sense to a written work, whereas manuscript celebrates textual fluidity. In the preface to his translation of Seneca's *Thyestes* published in 1560 Jasper Heywood considers the faults and errors in the play that transmission and translation introduce.[15] Heywood relates an imaginary dream in which Seneca appears and offers him a text of the play 'trewly wrote': 'For here hathe neuer prynters presse / made faute, nor neuer yet, / Came errour here by mysse of man.'[16] But Heywood recognises his dream is a fantasy; transmission inevitably involves error in the act of reading as much as in the act of transcription. Readers as well as authors should be wary of an illusionary textual stability. Shifting forms of interpretation as much as shifting forms of presentation are to be expected.

In a sonnet, Sir Thomas Wyatt proposes:

> Eche man me telleth I chaunge moost my devise
> And on my faith me thinck it goode reason
> To change propose like after the season[.][17]

Wyatt suggests that by altering his 'devise', or device (a word that conveys implications from straightforward intention, to legal testament, to heraldic or symbolic representation), he is departing from stability and, indeed, a sense of identity. Such a move is not 'wyse' in some understandings; yet Wyatt proposes it is the condition of his world in which 'dyvernes' is usual, and in which remaining constant is prone to curtailing life. Change is presented as natural. Wyatt's sonnet exploits the way 'oon' sounds both as 'one' and 'own', questioning whether individual uniqueness is desirable within his mutable social world: 'keep still oon gyse' (line 4); 'I shall not be variable / But alwaies oon' (13–14). This fluctuating environment is conveyed by the poem's shifting words. The aural insecurities (heightened in an environment where there was no educated 'standard' English), the limited punctuation that enables lines to be freshly recombined and newly stressed with each reading, the vocabulary that simultaneously allows immaterial states of virtue and visceral sexual innuendo within words and phraseology, create a sonnet – Wyatt's device – whose meaning fluctuates within its form's dictated structure. Such variability is heightened if we examine its shifting presence in early collections. This lyric contains some significant differences in two of the most important early manuscripts of Wyatt's writing: British Library, MS Egerton 2711 and the Devonshire manuscripts of early Tudor verse (British Library, MS Additional 17492), both contemporary with the poet and the former containing some poems copied in the poet's own hand. While the overall design in both versions is similar, differences in them further confirm Wyatt's own sense of alterability. For example, Egerton asserts, 'My word nor I shall not be variable' (line 13), while Devonshire has 'my wordes nor I shall never be variable'.[18] Wyatt's poem illustrates a literary environment that preferred the mutability of manuscript transmission to the constancy of print. The poets' crafting of their lyrics adopts strategies that collude with a transmission process that expects textual and interpretive instability.

Since the appearance of Harold Love's *Scribal Publication in Seventeenth-Century England*, Arthur Marotti's *Manuscript, Print and the English Renaissance Lyric*, and Henry Woudhuysen's *Sir Philip Sidney and the Circulation of Manuscripts*, scholars increasingly recognise that far more than print, let alone editions devoted to single authors, contemporary readers encountered English lyric verse of the sixteenth and much of the seventeenth century in handwritten manuscripts.[19] How lyrics appear in these manuscripts is astonishingly diverse and it would be misleading to propose that a simple print–manuscript dichotomy existed. Manuscript collections extend from single lyrics without any acknowledgment of the author, set among widely differing prose and poetic texts on a multitude of subjects, to carefully designed collections of a single author, commissioned from a professional scribe and fabricated to be presented to a patron or potential patron. Exceptionally, in some manuscripts lyrics can be identified with a reasonable level of confidence to be in a poet's own hand (or corrected by the poet in a manuscript prepared by another), though more generally poems have been copied from non-authorial sources, sometimes even from printed collections. Some manuscript collections reflect distinct coterie groups often emerging from the universities or the Inns of Court; others can be traced to family groupings. Many lyrics are copied in commonplace collections that emerged out of an educational training that required students to develop a store of *sententiae* or precepts to use in disputations. Some assemblages reflect a vibrant female literary society that is distinct from more male-oriented collections. In many collections the copyist has had no compunction to amend a lyric to accord with his or her own desired perspectives; in others, poems by established authors are intermixed with more amateur efforts composed either by the copyist or contemporaries in his or her circle. Notably, too, the dispersal of lyrics by particular authors in manuscripts is not particularly related to their reputations, either contemporary or subsequent. John Donne's poetry is currently found in around 250 surviving manuscript collections made both during his life and the 40 years or so after it. Given the generally low survival rate of such collections, this suggests a huge circulation (though of course in many cases the poem is not ascribed to Donne and there is no way of knowing whether the copyist knew who the author was). In contrast, George Herbert, who was hugely influential among contemporary devotional poets after the 1633 publication of his *Temple*, seems to have been known principally through print.[20]

The reluctance around print that Daniel articulates can also be observed when poems are printed. During their lifetimes both Sidney and Donne acquired substantial literary reputations; yet, given the uneasy social decorums around writers seeking print, their lyrics are printed almost entirely after their deaths. Their earliest editions, however, reveal printers' reluctance to depart from conventions associated with manuscript collections, emphasising links with coterie circulation among familiars. For example, neither Sidney's nor Donne's identity is fully evident on the title-pages of these early printed collections, and both indicate the authors being deceased, perhaps to legitimise the recourse to print: *Syr. P. S. His Astrophel and Stella. Wherein the excellence of sweete Poesie is concluded / To the end of which are added, sundry other rare Sonnets of diuers Noble men and Gentlemen* (1591, 1597); *Poems, by J.D. VVith elegies on the authors death* (1633, 1635, 1639, 1649, 1650, 1654). It is only in 1669 that an edition of Donne's poems distinctly announces the author's identity on the title-page, while Sidney's identity as the author of *Astrophil and Stella* is first made explicit in the 1598 edition of the *Arcadia* to which the sonnet sequence is appended.

To some extent, current editorial practices with sixteenth- and seventeenth-century lyric recognise that we should not assume the primacy of print in seeking to establish reliable editions. In the 1980s, editors of Elizabethan and Jacobean drama started to present variants in plays as representing different thoughts by authors, or a play's evolution among its varying contributors, whose later emendations were often made at dates substantially after first performances or even a principal author's death. This has prompted editors of lyrics, too, to recognise that methodologies founded on imagined attempts to recover verses as they dropped freshly from their authorial sources are in need of revision. Michael Rudick's 'historical edition' of Sir Walter Ralegh's poems sets out to develop a social and cultural collection. The authority of Rudick's texts derives from the contexts the poems were put into by their collectors instead of from 'substantive or accidental conformity with hypothesized "true original copies"'.[21]

If the implications of flexible texts shifting through manuscript transmission are increasingly acknowledged by editors, they appear less so among critical interpreters who often overlook variant or differing versions when considering a lyric's meaning. What alterations might occur in the ways that we read and understand sixteenth- and seventeenth-century lyrics if we acknowledge manuscript rather than print as the medium in which they were envisaged principally to exist? As Arthur Marotti notes about manuscript transmission: 'it was normal for lyrics to elicit revisions, corrections, supplements, and answers, for they were part of an ongoing social discourse. In this environment texts were inherently malleable, escaping authorial control.'[22] In approaching a lyric on a printed page our usual assumption is that it should lead us to an understanding that at least acknowledges authorial intention. What though of a cultural environment where authors assumed their lyrics would circulate in the malleable manner Marotti posits? Poets such as Wyatt or Donne are known for employing protean qualities of voice, elusive word-play, and generic teasing in their lyrics: facets that become more readily grasped if understood as emerging from the poet's anticipation that his lyrics will be regularly encountered by readers in shifting, copied texts where authorial identity appears of no concern. Donne's constantly varying stanzas, which can appear overly intricate and ill-suited to the expectations of standard visual patterns conferred in print, seem more appropriate to the less formalised and idiosyncratic presentations encountered in manuscripts. As Harold Love, citing Walter Ong's work on orality notes, 'A manuscript based culture preserves "a feeling for the book as a kind of utterance, an occurrence in the course of conversation" … Print "situates words in space" thus giving them the status of objects rather than experiences and separating off the apprehension of meaning from an awareness of presence.'[23]

II

Illustrations from John Donne's poetry elucidate how our interpretive practices may be reconsidered through acknowledging lyrics' textual variability. As editors have long recognised, 'The Canonization' in many manuscripts favours a reading in which the lovers 'extract' rather than 'contract' the world's soul:

> You, to whom love was peace that now is rage;
> > Who did the whole worlds soule contract, and drove
> > Into the glasses of your eyes
>
> > > > (39–41)

Contract, or a variant of it, is found in the 1633, 1635, and 1669 printed edition, whereas 'Who did the whole worlds soule extract' is a more familiar manuscript reading. Conventionally, an editor seeks to decide which is 'right', and the orthodox assessment is to give primacy to the printed editions. This textual crux may be approached differently, however. In the Houghton Library's O'Flahertie manuscript (completed in late 1632 and, with 440 leaves, the largest surviving early manuscript collection of Donne's poetry) the scribe decided to have it both ways:

> You to whome Loue was peace that now is rage
> con
> who did the whole worlds soule <u>extract</u>, and droue.[24]

While this may be a copyist attempting to replace 'extract' with 'contract', no attempt has been made to score through one to give precedence to the other. The copy allows that either, or both, of the two readings might function in the lyric – a flexible alternative that manuscript accommodates but that print conventions nullify. These alternatives may not fundamentally alter the sense of what Donne is seeking to convey; yet there are obviously nuanced differences: 'extract' takes up alchemical resonances frequently found in Donne, 'contract' equally familiar legal significances, while both words allow Donne's premise of intensification through reduction.

A different issue arises with the conclusion of Donne's *Holy Sonnet*, 'Batter my heart, three person'd God', with its final lines: 'Except you 'enthrall mee, never shall be free, / Nor ever chast, except you ravish mee' (13–14). This is how the lines appear in the 1633 edition and most manuscripts. In the 1635 and 1669 editions, 'chast' becomes 'chaste' and this is the spelling selected in most modern editions. In certain respects, 'chast' and 'chaste' appear broadly interchangeable in the sixteenth and seventeenth centuries until the latter becomes the standard spelling in the eighteenth century. Donne's lines employ a conventional association of pain and ecstasy acting to lead the soul towards the divine, a topos familiar in contemporary emblem practice – though Donne's startling conjoining of chastity with rape proposes carnal violence, licentiousness, and immorality, which disturb the narrator's craving for a euphoric incorporation into divine love.[25] But are 'chast'/'chaste' interchangeable? Interestingly, the likely current supposition that 'chast' emphasises a link with chastisement – particularly a Calvinistically inclined sinner's recognition of human unworthiness that returns us to the sonnet's opening plea for the heart to be 'battered' and theologically valorises the violence, physical or mystical, that the speaker's ravishment entails – seems less pronounced for early modern readers. It is 'chaste' as a verb meaning to punish or inflict discipline upon that appears more readily interchangeable with the form 'chasten' in Donne's era, with 'chasten' only becoming the dominant term later in the seventeenth century. Used as a verb, 'chaste' does not appear to be used to mean purify, refine, or make chaste until the eighteenth century. Rather, it is 'chast' that is more readily associated with sexual purity in early usage. Conceivably, 'chast'/'chaste' held slightly differing nuances for early readers of this sonnet: 'chast' accentuating the paradox that sexual purity and virtue are achieved through divine rape; 'chaste' a stress on the contradiction that the correction – the abusive beating – that the heart experiences is also its spiritual mending that provokes divine rapture. Both implications are potentially present within each spelling, but selecting one word or the other by compilers may reflect a poetic disposition similar to the interpretive preference of a musician who chooses to give a particular emphasis to a note or phrase in different performances so that it affects listeners subtly differently. This interpretive presumption around the use of 'chast'/'chaste' in different versions of Donne's sonnet is impossible to prove decisively. However, the textual fluidity familiar in manuscript transmission points to an aesthetic accommodation of such practices among readers and recorders untroubled by anxieties about a single authorial archetype. How 'chast'/'chaste' was articulated and how understood might desirably vary for a reader on different occasions.

Further implications for a critical practice that acknowledge textual variability within manuscript culture are raised by Donne's 'The good-morrow'. This lyric explores the spiritual and sensual awakening that ostensibly occurs when a couple experience genuine mutuality in love. The closing stanza asserts the immortality that such a relation confers:

> My face in thine eye, thine in mine appeares,
> And true plaine hearts doe in the faces rest,
> Where can we finde two better hemispheares
> Without sharpe North, without declining West?
> What ever dyes, was not mixt equally;
> If our two loves be one, or, thou and I
> Love so alike, that none doe slacken, none can die.
>
> (15–21)

Donne's anxiety about mortality is typically matched with an irreverent sexual playfulness. The resoundingly corporeal 'slacken' indicates that the lovers' ideal matching should theoretically prevent the inevitable consequence of male sexual orgasm, or 'little death', that has the penis shrivel. The physical reality of intercourse, however, will inevitably expose as false the poem's assertion about the lovers' perfect spherical balance, the geometric form associated with divine immortality. The male's carnal readiness will slacken; the poet's avowed achieving of perfect equilibrium with this lover is proved unfounded, empowering him to continue his quest for true love with another partner – a new morrow that his poem will equally serve to address anew. These lines may further hint at a same-sex possibility, since 'none do slacken' might suggest the mirror imaging of the two lovers is more apparent if they are the same sex. Of course, Donne is also using slackening in the paradoxical sense of delaying: proposing that the constant vigour associated with loving extends life, when usually, according to contemporary ideas surrounding sexuality, using up your sexual potency was envisaged as hastening the end of vitality (as illustrated in Marvell's appeal to his coy mistress: 'Now let us sport us while we may; / And now, like am'rous birds of prey, / Rather at once our time devour / Than languish in his slow-chapped power').[26] 'The good-morrow''s quest for, and celebration of, an ideal lover involves a recognition that this search will be futile: the 'waking soules' (8) of the lovers cannot escape their somatic actuality that will inevitably embrace change and decay. As frequently occurs in Donne's poetry, whether the sentiments are directed at God or at worldly lovers, much in the verse undermines the narrator's avowals, inviting an exploration of concerns underneath the poetry's surface declarations.

The stanza cited above appears in the 1633 print edition and is also found in many manuscripts containing Donne's work, including the St Paul's Cathedral manuscript that the Variorum Donne editors propose was prepared around 1620, speculating that it contains versions of poems written before Donne entered his Church of England ministry in 1615.[27] However, the carefully compiled O'Flahertie manuscript at Harvard records a different conclusion to the lyric:

> What ever dyes was not mixt æqually
> If our two loves bee one, both thou and I
> Love iust alike in all, none of these loues can dye.[28]

This reading is also found, sometimes substituting 'both' by 'or', in a number of other manuscripts, and significantly it is also the version used in both the 1635 and 1669 printed editions of Donne's poetry. No current reader is likely to prefer this finish to the bodily innuendos generated by 'slacken'; yet we should not dismiss this as a mistranscription from some stage in the poem's existence that was then further copied and altered in a variant-rich manuscript culture. The 1633 and 1635 printed editions, along with all editions of Donne until 1650, were undertaken by the publisher John Marriot at his shop in St Dunstan's churchyard off Fleet Street, so there can be little question that those preparing the second text would be unaware of the reading used in the 1633 edition. While broadly the sentiment in both versions of the stanza is similar, with the playfulness in the second version notably resting on the vagueness around 'just', the change transforms the overall poetic effect. The virtual removal of the sexual dynamics in the poem's conclusion may stem from social and cultural decorums with which Donne himself may have colluded; but the implications extend beyond the poet, or some of his admirers, seeking to underplay the lyric's carnality to accord with an image of the poet's sober dignity as a prominent churchman: a version of the Jack Donne/Dr John Donne evolution. It suggests more broadly that the brash sexual physicality (and its consequent heightened awareness of looming morality) that is registered by 'slacken' may have been uncomfortably challenging for some and that this was readily accommodated through altering the lines to a familiar, if anodyne, commonplace about love. As Moretti reminds us, manuscript culture prompted a poetics of 'ongoing social discourse' in which 'texts were inherently malleable'.[29] In this environment, we confront contemporary editorial processes that often show scant interest in pursuing, or even trying to imagine, what an author's original design might have been. Alternative versions allow the cultural preferences of compilers or editors to emerge, enabling adaptations of lyrics that do not decisively seek to supplant each other but that concede their mutual coexistence. As this example indicates, such textual enhancements may not be experienced as preferable among current readers. Just as Nahum Tate's sentimentalised version of *King Lear* was favoured by audiences after its appearance in 1681, replacing Shakespeare's on the stage until the mid nineteenth century and winning the approval of Dr Johnson over the Jacobean versions, the literary culture in which 'The good-morrow' circulated enabled its concluding lines to record either a tame affirmation about the longevity of love or a more socially challenging contention about sexuality. We cannot claim that either ending of this lyric is closer to Donne's original as we have no means to authenticate which was prior. The O'Flahertie manuscript may record an early version Donne later strengthened in revision just as readily as one changed later. What we possess in either may be an emendation by another hand. The critical interest, however, is generated by considering why the different versions of this lyric appear to have been preferred by different contemporary readers within the same cultural moment.

Many recent students of Donne will be familiar with his poetry arranged in an edition that begins with *Songs and Sonnets*. This convention follows the 1635 and subsequent early printed editions where various love lyrics are collected as *Songs and Sonets*, a title harking back to the Tudor printed verse miscellanies that begin with Tottel's *Songes and Sonettes* in 1557. There is no evidence that Donne ever imagined organising his miscellaneous shorter secular amatory lyrics as a collection. Only the O'Flahertie manuscript among the major manuscript compendia that group Donne's secular poetry together proposes such a dedicated and named organisation, one that is not followed in the 1633 first printed edition. Unlike the convention of placing *Songs and Sonnets* first in editions of Donne's poetry that the 1635 volume establishes, most of the larger manuscript collections of his verse begin either with his devotional poems (as both the O'Flahertie manuscript and the 1633 printed edition do) or with the satires. Increasingly, recent editors, including Robin Robbins in his 2010 Longman edition, arrange these poems in alphabetical order and group them generically as love lyrics, suppressing implications that they are designed to be read as an organised unit.[30]

In manuscript circulation readers encounter poems whose authors are frequently not cited. Further, compilers often show no inclination to try to group lyrics according to authorship, with poems by the same writer scattered throughout collections even when identified. If a contemporary reader wished to establish authorial identity in many verse miscellanies, there was rarely any secure way to do so; but concerns about authorship often were a matter of indifference. Recognising such contextual practices offers current readers a different perspective on sixteenth- and seventeenth-century love lyrics' declarations, notably providing enhanced ironic resonances to their narrators' proclamations about their love's longevity through their verse granting lasting reputation. The declaration of Donne's 'The Canonization' that its lovers' legend as written in sonnets will stand comparison with a historical reputation as recorded in chronicles strikes a more sardonic note if we envisage that these assertions were encountered in a collection where a reader had no sense about who these lovers might be. Though current readers usually acknowledge that the narrators of Donne's poems should in no respect be imagined as the actual John Donne, our sense that the poetic voice is a poetic 'Donne' addressing his lover acts to record an identity on the 'well wrought urne' as distinct as the names we expect to find inscribed upon the memorial stones of 'halfe-acre tombs' (29–34). Encountered in a collection where there is no guide that the narrator is 'Donne', the poem's avoidance of naming the lovers becomes noticeable, putting their anonymity into explicit contrast with the lyric's claim that 'Countries, Townes, Courts' (44) shall invoke them. Invoke whom? Though not always having a title in its manuscript copies, this lyric's irreverent application of the Roman Catholic practice of formally declaring exemplary individuals to be sainted (a process that since the late Middle Ages was known for its complex and lengthy inquiries into candidates' legitimacy) is more ironically tinged if Donne assumes that readers will be unable to fathom these lovers' identities.[31] The woman's silence has frequently been remarked upon in Renaissance love lyrics where the addressed female lover often has a shadowy presence, partly in keeping with courtly decorums surrounding not compromising a lover through identifying her. In contrast, as the male voice becomes identified with an author through printed editions, the poet's identity appears more visible. Later readers lose the perspective that in manuscript circulation a poetic narrator's identity was often as obscure as that of his addressed lover.

Correspondingly, Donne's 'A Valediction: of the booke' affirms that a study of its lovers' 'manuscripts' will enable a writing of 'Annals' that will produce such agreed records that no 'schismatique' will subsequently contest them (10–16), developing a similar type of fantasy as Jasper Heywood's dream of Seneca's delivering an uncorrupted manuscript of *Thyestes* as 'trewly wrote'. Donne's imagined book is both 'all-graved' (produced expensively) but written in 'cypher' or 'new made Idiome' (posing reservations about its intelligibility among its audience). While the lovers' book's indestructability and longevity are declared, readers are also reminded of the uncertainties surrounding textual continuance. It is not merely the cited ancient Vandals or Goths that were responsible for the destruction of learning; Donne's poem recalls the considerable loss of manuscripts, annals, and records in England as a result of the Reformation's religious divisions. Manuscript culture might have been more intimate than print, but it was also fragile, and the poem reflects this precariousness even as its narrator asserts how 'Learning were safe; in this Our Universe' (26): a cosmos where we are confronted with the lovers' anonymity, the condition that their being recorded in annals should deny. Even as the lyric asserts the lovers' uncorrupted reputation recorded throughout time, these poetic figures are rendered obscure and unknown.

A consideration of 'The triple Foole' further illustrates the trenchant quality to Donne's self-ironic displays that are posed when imagining his lyrics circulating in a manuscript culture that shows little regard for authorship. Usually untitled or simply called 'Song' in manuscripts, the poem expands upon the familiar theme that the lover is doubly ridiculous, first for loving per se because his desire will not be returned, and then for 'saying so' in poetry. However, the poet-lover justifies the wisdom of his composition because the lyric may convince his desired 'she' to reconsider the poet, admiring his qualities as a versifier (1–4). In Donne's poem, the narrator additionally emphasises the therapeutic qualities of poetry: 'Griefe brought to numbers cannot be so fierce / For, he tames it, that fetters it in verse' (10–11).

Unfortunately, for the poet what has been designed as a private exchange becomes public:

> Some man, his art and voice to show,
> Doth Set and sing my paine,
> And by delighting many, frees againe
> Griefe, which verse did restraine.
>   (13–16)

This act of adoption, in which the narrator's verse is utilised by another for his own purposes as a song set to music, and employs a musical idiom that he perceives as inappropriate, is a common facet of a culture where poetry featured as social exchange and where verse was redeployed to suit the occasion. As David Lindley's chapter in this volume argues, this poem illustrates the tension between a lyric's private and public functions. In 'The triple Foole', though, there is a good deal of self-mockery as the poem invites speculation as to whether 'some man' has gained access to the lyric through the addressed 'she'; or, indeed, whether 'some man' is the poet himself, the 'I' of the poem, now assuming his third 'foolish' identity in seeking to gain wider audience for his song. Sidney's *Astrophil and Stella* and Shakespeare's *Sonnets* are the best-known instances where poetic narrators in Renaissance love lyrics betray their absorption in, and preference for, creating accomplished poetry over successful amatory encounters, and much of Donne's work is similarly cleverly directed. However, in this 'song' Donne details a process whereby a lyric apparently originally conceived for private delivery becomes distanced from the poet and ultimately turned back upon him by his future encounter with it in a public performance or in published form. The art of setting that 'some man' undertakes is a placing of words to music that also gestures at fixing them in print type.

> To Love, and Griefe tribute of Verse belongs,
> But not so much as pleases when 'tis read,
> Both are increased by such such songs:
> For both their triumphs so are published[.]
>
> (17–20).

Donne's meditation on how love and grief are enhanced rather than restrained by being 'published' in this new song playfully echoes the anxieties Daniel articulates about printed matter being fundamentally misunderstood by vulgar readers. A private lyric designed to purge grief is transformed by being disseminated in public media, where the poem is now encountered sung to a different tune or appears in an altered printed context, becoming a vehicle for 'delighting many'. The consequence for the poet is that verses that were designed to function as a remedy enabling a purging of his 'paines' now operate as a toxin that increases his suffering. Slyly drawing attention to his poetic accomplishments that are adopted by others, Donne's narrator also concedes his foolishness in imagining that the poet has any control over his poem.

Donne's poetry circulated widely in manuscript and some of his poems are found in up to seventy separate copies. His elegy 'Going to Bed' – now frequently titled 'To His Mistress Going to Bed' – is found (copied either completely or partially) in more extant manuscripts than any other Donne poem. Yet it was not printed until 1669, perhaps reflecting a similar cultural hesitation around the printing of the more sexually explicit conclusion to 'The good-morrow'.[32] While it would be vastly over-simplistic to claim that this disparity between printed absence and manuscript abundance reflects a private permissiveness tolerated in manuscript circulation in contrast to a public prudishness around print, this elegy's history exemplifies how our understanding of Donne's poetry within the seventeenth century and subsequently must take account of its manuscript presence. As the illustrations considered above show, if we somehow presume that there might be a collection of Donne's poetry organised and presented so that it decisively reflects what he 'trewly wrote', we are misconceiving the character of sixteenth- and seventeenth-century lyric verse.

III

Unlike Donne, most contemporary readers encountered George Herbert's poetry in print. A few examples of his poems are found in manuscript commonplace books but these appear to have been copied from the printed *Temple*.[33] However, our understanding of Herbert's poetry, too, benefits from considering its links with scribal manuscript traditions. We possess two important manuscript collections that predate the first edition of *The Temple Sacred Poems and Private Ejaculations*, which was printed in Cambridge in 1633 about six months after Herbert's death. The Dr Williams Library manuscript (MS Jones B62) in London and MS Tanner 307 in the Bodleian Library, Oxford are both carefully prepared and have been linked with the Little Gidding community near Cambridge, which was led by Herbert's friend Nicholas Ferrar.[34] The Williams Library manuscript, while it lacks about seventy-five poems found in the larger Tanner collection which contains the whole of the printed *Temple*, nevertheless has corrections to poems that appear to be in the poet's hand (as well as a number of poems not found in the printed *Temple*). Greg Miller has detailed how both these manuscripts reflect important features of scribal publication associated with coterie groups, such as the Pembroke circle at Wilton House in Wiltshire, which Herbert visited frequently, as well as the Little Gidding community.[35] Miller proposes that the Williams manuscript, written in a visually unadorned secretary hand, rather than the more embellished italic hand usually used within aristocratic circles, was a conscious choice of Herbert and the Little Gidding community to express the devotional simplicity that the lyrics themselves celebrate. In contrast to both manuscripts, the printed *Temple* employs a range of visual signs – italics, capitalisation of words, printed borders – that affect readers' encounters with the poems. A good example is the use of italic and roman typefaces to separate the voices within a lyric. God frequently answers the poet in these poems. The manuscripts deploy a consistent hand for both 'speakers', reinforcing a perception that the godly voice emerges from within the narrator. In the printed texts the respondent's voice is designed to look independent of the poet, making God's replies to his dilemmas appear to emerge externally. With typefaces regularised by the printer, Miller suggests that the visual impact of the printed *Temple* acts like a contemporary catechism, presenting scriptural quotation in italics so that the reader readily sees how God – through Scripture – responds to human inquiry in 'a sanctioned, stable, more authoritatively self-authorizing text'. In contrast, in the manuscripts Herbert seeks to reveal the human impossibility of thoroughly achieving this divine dialogue.[36]

A good example of the implications of this presentational difference is 'Heaven', the penultimate lyric in the 'Church' section of the *Temple*:

O who will show me those delights on high?
　　　　　　Echo.　　　　　　*I.*
Thou Echo, thou art mortall, all men know.
　　　　　　Echo.　　　　　　*No.*
Wert thou not born among the trees and leaves?
　　　　　　Echo.　　　　　　*Leaves.*
And are there any leaves, that still abide?
　　　　　　Echo.　　　　　　*Bide.*
What leaves are they? Impart the matter wholly.
　　　　　　Echo.　　　　　　*Holy.*
Are holy leaves the Echo then of blisse?
　　　　　　Echo.　　　　　　*Yes.*
Then tell me, what is that supreme delight?
　　　　　　Echo.　　　　　　*Light.*
Light to the minde: what shall the will enjoy?
　　　　　　Echo.　　　　　　*Joy.*
But are there cares and buisnesse with the pleasure?
　　　　　　Echo.　　　　　　*Leisure.*
Light, joy, and leisure; but shall they persever.
　　　　　　Echo.　　　　　　*Ever.*

The print text's use of italics disembodies the echo from the questioner, creating a resonance that provides firmer spiritual assurance within the poem. When the echo answers 'I', the reader is aware that, as an echo, the 'I' must in some sense be the speaker. But Echo is also a well-known, if tragic, mythological figure in Ovid's *Metamorphoses*, condemned to lose her independent speech and only able to repeat what she hears. If Echo has migrated from being a forlorn figure in Classical mythology to a providential answering God in Herbert, this transformation provides enormous comfort to a poetic interlocutor struggling over whether promises of heavenly immortality apply to him. There is a greater disquiet within the lines, however, if Echo's reply of 'No' to the questioner's assertion about Echo's mortality is felt to emerge from the questioner himself, who is undeniably mortal as an embodied speaker. Without the alternating typefaces fashioning a determined separation of the speakers, this lyric expounds a less assured dialogue about how a human spiritual pilgrim may or may not discover the nature of divinity. As a separate speaker, Echo's responses command authority – true echoes, if you wish. When Echo is identified with the questioner, doubt is occasioned because the speaker may be said, in effect, to be 'mishearing' the echo's response: for example 'no' for 'know', 'holy' for 'wholly'. Echo's final answer of 'Ever' in the printed format proclaims certainty. In contrast, a possible alternative reverberation of 'persever' – 'sever' – is ignored, an unsettling possibility that readers might more readily acknowledge if they were less confident about the identity of the echo that is rebounding back, confronting a more variable aural experience than is offered by the concrete visual appearance of the printed text. The vexed question over reading Scripture properly – both through human understanding and through divine revelation – which was pronounced for Herbert's era, is displaced by a printed format that indicates intimacy between God and questioner. The narrator's initial question: 'O who will show me those delights on high?' is answered by a seeming authority who will lead the questioner effortlessly to 'Heaven'. The troubling issue about whether, through potentially mishearing the echo, the questioner is revealing his miscomprehension of what Scripture reveals is repressed by the poem's printed form.

As Samuel Daniel agonises, print in early modern England could 'a world of Pennes performe'; yet print offered versions of poems that were ultimately different from manuscript. Print acted to fix and contain a lyrical flexibility that many poets cherished, embracing the malleability that manuscript recording and circulation offered their poetic practice. Even a poet such as Herbert, who envisaged his lyrics grouped within a tightly structured framework, welcomed the different opportunities that the copying and scribal production of his poetry afforded.[37] Attending to lyrics' social and cultural transactions within a manuscript culture that was the dominant vehicle for the circulation of shorter poetic forms in England until the mid seventeenth century affords current readers opportunities to reassess our understanding of how these poems function and what they may mean.

Notes

1 Samuel Daniel, *The Ciuile Wars Betweene the Howses of Lancaster and Yorke* (London, 1609), VI.38 (p. 153).
2 *Ibid.* VI.37 (p. 153).
3 J. W. Saunders, 'The Stigma of Print: A Note on the Social Bases of Tudor Poetry' *Essays in Criticism* I (1951), 139–64.
4 John Foxe, *The Unabridged Acts and Monuments Online* (Sheffield: HRI Online Publications, 2011), Book IX, p. 1562, available online at www.johnfoxe.org/index.php?gotopage=1562&realm=text&edition=1570&gototype=modern&x=1&y=16 (last accessed 23 May 2013).
5 Richard Tottel, *Tottel's Miscellany*, ed. Amanda Holton and Tom MacFaul (London: Penguin Books, 2011), p. 3.
6 John Donne, 'Doctissimo amicissimoque v. D. D. Andrews', in *Donne's Poetical Works*, ed. H. J. C. Grierson, 2 vols. (London: Oxford University Press, 1913), Vol. I, p. 397, esp. lines 1–6. All Donne citations are to this edition.

7   A. F. Marotti, *Manuscript, Print and the English Renaissance Lyric* (Cornell University Press, 1995), p. 245.
8   Heather Dubrow, 'Neither here nor there: deixis and the sixteenth-century sonnet', above, pp. 33–4; *The Challenges of Orpheus: Lyric Poetry and Early Modern England* (Baltimore: Johns Hopkins University Press, 2008), pp. 15–53.
9   David Lindley, 'Words for music, perhaps: early modern songs and lyric', above, pp. 10–11.
10 Margaret Healy and Thomas Healy, 'Introduction', in *Renaissance Transformations: The Making of English Writing (1500–1650)*, ed. Margaret Healy and Thomas Healy (Edinburgh University Press, 2009), pp. 4–5.
11 Samuel Daniel, 'A Defence of Rhyme', in *Elizabethan Critical Essays*, ed. C. G. Smith, 2 vols. (London: Oxford University Press, 1904), Vol. II, p. 366.
12 Nigel Smith, 'Lyric and the English Revolution', below, pp. 71–91.
13 Cited in A. D. Wright and V. F. Stern, *In Search of Christopher Marlowe: A Pictorial Biography* (London: MacDonald, 1965), p. 63.
14 Daniel, *Ciuile Wars*, IV.38 (p. 153).
15 Seneca, *The Seconde Tragedie of Seneca Entituled Thyestes*, trans. Jasper Heywood (London, 1560), pp. 5–17.
16 *Ibid.*, p. 16.
17 Sir Thomas Wyatt, *Collected Poems of Sir Thomas Wyatt*, ed. Kenneth Muir and Patricia Thomson (Liverpool University Press, 1969), p. 11, lines 1–3.
18 British Library, MS Egerton 2711, fo. 11v; MS Additional 17492, fo. 75v. See Sir Thomas Wyatt, *The Canon of Sir Thomas Wyatt's Poetry*, ed. Richard C. Harrier (Harvard University Press, 1975), p. 112.
19 Harold Love, *Scribal Publication in Seventeenth-Century England* (Oxford: Clarendon Press, 1993); Marotti, *Manuscript, Print*; H. R. Woudhuysen, *Sir Philip Sidney and the Circulation of Manuscripts, 1558–1640* (Oxford: Clarendon Press, 1996).
20 Richard Todd and Helen Wilcox, 'The Challenges of Editing Donne and Herbert', *Studies in English Literature 1500–1900* 52 (2012), 187–206.
21 Michael Rudick, in Sir Walter Ralegh, *The Poems of Sir Walter Ralegh: A Historical Edition*, ed. Michael Rudick, Medieval and Renaissance Texts and Studies 209 (Tempe, AZ: Arizona Center for Medieval and Renaissance Studies, 1999), pp. lxxv–lxxviii.
22 Marotti, *Manuscript, Print*, p. 135.
23 Love, *Scribal Publication*, p. 142.
24 O'Flahertie manuscript of Donne's poems, Harvard University, MS Eng.966.5, available online at *DigitalDonne: The Online Variorum*, www.digitaldonne. tamu.edu/DisplayText, p. 259 (last accessed 23 May 2013).
25 See for example Herman Hugo, *Pia Desideria Emblematis, Elegiis & Affectibus* (Antwerp, 1624); many of Hugo's emblems are used by Francis Quarles in his *Emblems Divine and Moral* (London, 1635).
26 Andrew Marvell, 'To His Coy Mistress', in *The Poems of Andrew Marvell*, ed. N. Smith, Longman Annotated English Poets (Harlow: Pearson Education, 2003), p. 83, lines 37–40.

27 Bibliographical description of St Paul's Cathedral Library. MS 49.B.43, available online at *DigitalDonne*.

28 O'Flahertie manuscript, p. 291.

29 Marotti, *Manuscript, Print*, p. 135.

30 John Donne, *The Complete Poems of John Donne*, ed. Robin Robbins, Longman Annotated English Poets (Harlow: Pearson Education, 2010).

31 Donne's employment of canonisation is less heretical within an English religious context than many currently assume. The Calendar of the Elizabethan (1559) *Book of Common Prayer* that Donne's early English readership would be familiar with records various saints' days; but while technically allowing the idea of 'canonisation', the English Church has only ever proclaimed Charles I as a saint.

32 Todd and Wilcox, 'The Challenges of Editing Donne and Herbert', pp. 188, 192.

33 George Herbert, *The Works of George Herbert*, ed. F. E. Hutchinson (Oxford: Clarendon Press, 1941), p. lvi.

34 George Herbert, *The English Poems of George Herbert*, ed. Helen Wilcox (Cambridge University Press, 2007), pp. xxxvii–xl. All citations to Herbert are from this edition.

35 Greg Miller, 'Scribal and Print Publication: The Case of George Herbert's English Poems', *George Herbert Journal* 23 (1999/2000), 14–34.

36 *Ibid.*, pp. 24–6.

37 Herbert, *English Poems*, pp. 39–40.

CHAPTER FOUR

Lyric and the English Revolution

Nigel Smith

I

There are very many different ways of describing lyric change and innovation during the mid seventeenth century, as Alastair Fowler has shown with typical acuteness and authority.[1] Change also applies to longer verse forms, such as epic and satire, and was to some degree part and parcel of them. These changes relate in different ways to widespread and sometimes drastic social and cultural transformation. Few pieces of poetry were written in the 1640s and 1650s that were not explicitly touched by the Civil War and the political revolution that followed it. The impact of the 'scientific revolution' was widespread and triggered a revival of a non-lyric genre most associated with agricultural improvement: the Georgic. Jonson's classicism released the epigram (which though short was not considered a type of lyric by every authority at the time) as a fashion, but it also subsequently became a universal building block, a smaller Roman-sized brick that could be used with great flexibility in many different larger configurations. Jonson himself thought that those that relied on 'tuneing and riming' were shallow and in fact 'have no composition at all'.[2] As we have seen in the previous chapter, he claimed to base his poetry in prose. Those who looked back into the mid-century from the vantage point of the Restoration noted the rise then of a certain kind of 'smooth' and easy verse, a civilised painlessness that allegedly took poetry in various genres to the advantageousness of being like prose. This was where the verse of Sir John Denham and Edmund Waller in particular was held responsible for the kind of line that would make the high Augustanism of Alexander Pope possible. Yet Francis Atterbury's claim in 1690 that the poets of the previous age and before wrote 'down-right Prose tagg'd with Rhymes', only in monosyllables – especially Donne – can easily be refuted, while many other qualities can be discerned in innovative seventeenth-century lyric that those praising the rise of 'Augustan verse' simply did not consider.[3]

Lyric poetry and its history had been discussed with no little originality in Elizabethan and early Jacobean critical discourse. Despite the enormous variety and creativity of mid-seventeenth-century lyric there is by contrast little or no significant discussion of lyric in the criticism of mid-seventeenth-century England, or in the two decades that preceded it. J. E. Spingarn, editor of an influential collection of seventeenth-century critical writings, saw this as a consequence of the rise of neoclassical priorities, and added the lofty Baconian principles that were reorganising knowledge at the time. In Bacon's view, poetry should only represent the outer world in an imaginatively heightened way; lyric poetry, with its focus on the inner emotional life, was as an aspect of philosophy and rhetoric and had no place in this world.[4] Everyone claimed to know what lyric was – short poetry that was usually set to music, as opposed to heroic verse, sometimes associated with dance, often gentle or sweet in manner, often with complex and varying metre, and which had descended from the ancient Greeks (including the famous trio of Alcaeus, Anacreon, and Sappho). This was a given, not something to be discussed and redefined. Thus, writing in 1622, Henry Peacham praised Horace as the greatest and unsurpassable lyric poet for his acuteness, sweetness, and fluency, where 'his Stile is elegant, pure, and sinewie'.[5] There are 210 instances of the word 'lyric' (usually spelled 'lyrick') in 114 separate texts between 1630 and 1660 in the searchable part of the *Early English Books Online* website (about one quarter of the total corpus), almost all of them describing the short and often sung poem.[6] Going further than Bacon, however, in 1650 Thomas Hobbes denied lyric any status as a discrete verbal entity, while assuming that poetic genres were naturally produced by their corresponding nurturing environments: heroic (epic and tragedy) by courts, comic (comedy and satire) by cities, and pastoral (bucolic verse, pastoral comedy) by the country. He claimed that most lyrics were in fact parts of longer poems (he was repeating the views of earlier Italian writers like Robortello): 'but essayes and parts of an entire poem' such as epics (and there is plenty of evidence of this in Milton's *Paradise Lost*).[7] Otherwise lyrics count for very little indeed. The focus in criticism is on poetry as a form of philosophy: one that, through its formal qualities, is particularly well suited to keeping the insights of antiquity (such as those of Plato) alive. In an age dominated by civil crisis, military violence and the dissolution of Church and state, it is not surprising that epic and the heroic, as they were addressed in the tradition of literary criticism, should become the central focus.[8]

Contemporary Continental discussions of verse, most of them influential in England, took a similar view. Lyric verse was to be associated with 'charm and sweetness', and the term 'lyric' should be interchangeable with 'melic' because 'melos' means 'song', although not from the Greek name for honey.[9] The term was once applied generally to poetry and was then restricted to lyric because of its special focus on harmony, and the same was true of other terms applied to lyric: 'eide', 'ode', and 'carmen.' Complex catalogues of lyric types in antiquity, distinguished by formal metrical characteristics and by the many different occasions for which they were designed, were established. Mastery of the form of a given lyric was not considered a guarantee of success: only when the poet is moved, even if he departs from what is expected, is the audience pleased.

All this sense of the given status of lyric is true in so far as it was a subject of literary discussion. The scene is very different the moment music becomes involved. G. J. Vossius, the influential and capacious literary historian and theorist, is clear that lyric took its name from the instrument that accompanied it: the lyre.[10] The use of poetry to make song lyrics was a central part of Elizabethan cultural achievement, as David Lindley's chapter in this volume amply makes clear, not least in his treatment of Thomas Campion, at once both poet and composer. Elizabethan lutesong – the madrigal – marked by strong, drawn-out, tuneful melodic lines and polyphonically conceived accompaniment, was being replaced in the earlier and mid seventeenth century by the 'continuo' song, a single declaimed voice accompanied by a single bass line or chords on lute or theorbo.[11] By the middle decades of the century English song had evolved to the point where the impact of new kinds of musical composition and performance was beginning to be felt. Thus, while, as we have seen, Elizabethan poets wrote words for pre-existing music (this was called *contrafacta*), Henry Lawes (1585–1662) conversely set other people's poems to music, possibly under the influence of the rise of opera in Italy, and certainly showing a new preference for speech over melody and rhythm. In this evolved arena of composition the pitch changes of melody and the rhythms of the music had to be subservient to speech. Henry Lawes' music itself has been analysed as exhibiting an interim state: still obeying the principles of earlier song-setting, but allowing an emphasis on declamatory style to intrude into the composition:

> Modern scholars … now refer to songs in the half-declamatory half-melodic style denounced by Burney [in the eighteenth century] as 'declamatory ayres' and find much more to admire. Rhythmic distortion is a 'characteristic feature' undoubtedly – 'at first sight [this] seems at odds with the principles of good prosody' – but it had an aesthetic basis in the 'new principles of text delivery' adopted by professional stage singers, rhetorically exaggerated rather than naturalistic.[12]

The first instances of declamatory style in England seem to have been in songs written by Alfonso Ferrabosco for Jonson's court masques in 1608–9 and by Nicholas Lanier in 1613, but it would take a while for the style to become dominant. Robert Johnson expanded declamatory style for the stage and is usually thought to have most influenced Lawes. Lawes too registered the change in dominant rhythmic conventions, replacing conventional duple time with the triple time brought by the new French fashion in lute music. This meant that somehow a language that was very and naturally happy with the iambic foot had to be accommodated to the three-part foot in 3/4 and 6/8 time.

In his comments on song Lawes was also quite sure that English was not too clumsy a language, too full of syllables, to be very worthily set to music; he maintained that visiting foreign musicians regarded English musical culture as highly as any other in Europe.[13] He spoke much of the attention he gave to fitting music to words, and others felt that his settings surpassed punctuation in rendering both the sense and the proportion of the verbal edifice: 'No pointing Comma, Colon, halfe so well / Renders the Breath of Sense; they cannot tell / The just Proportion how each word should go, / To rise and fall, run swiftly or march slow; / Thou shew'st 'tis Musick only must do this.'[14] What is now appreciated as the 'unique charm' of the songs of Lawes and his contemporaries – 'the best affective settings in the English language before Purcell' – has to be seen as part of the history of lyric in this period.[15]

The total effect of a Lawes setting is overwhelming, arresting melancholy, exemplified in the Lady's opening song, 'Sweet Echo', from Milton's *Comus* (1634), lines 230–43. The rhythm of the melody is matched to that of the words so that it does indeed feel like musical speech as opposed to song. The Lady's concern at being lost and the purity of her own soul are signalled in the modulating chord changes, which suggest moments of unsettled surprise when they resolve in an unexpected way. The melody meanwhile stays high or descends only to go higher in accordance with the Lady's beautiful state. Liberation from the dark woods and this life is registered by the change from minor to major key. There is something 'ravishingly' beautiful about the poised simplicity of these songs. This is equally true of Lawes' setting of Edmund Waller's comparably famous 'Go lovely rose', even when, as is the case with this song, Lawes failed to make every musical phrase match the words in accentuation and quantity. Here the chord progressions suggest the complexity of mood on the speaker's part: that desire cannot be left unrequited without pain on the lover's part. That quality is carried well, although the music is more challenged by the *carpe diem* element emphasised in the last stanza, and the music seems here altogether too melancholy to be a successful persuasion to love. The rising presence of recitative was registered forcefully by Lawes' setting of William Cartwright's 'Ariadne's Lament' (*c.* ?1633–9), 195 bars long and taking 10 minutes to perform. It feels like a musical narrative, despite the persistence of lyrical musical elements (for example formal cadences) that interrupt narrative flow.

Thomas Carew's *Poems* of 1640 contain some of the most innovative love lyrics of the era, and his verse was very frequently copied into miscellanies: nearly forty surviving collections contain ten or more poems; one has more than eighty.[16] Lawes put more lyrics of Carew to music than of any other poet, and they were copied in one sequence in his manuscript songbook; he himself was acknowledged as the collaborating composer on the title-page of the third edition of Carew's *Poems* in 1651. The volume's frank articulation of sexual desire is matched by an easy *sprezzatura*, seen in the balance of caesurae against rhyme and, in the second poem, 'To *A. L. Perswasions to love*', in the deliberate mixture of different metres, even in the opening poem 'The Spring', which sets the scene for the speaker to persuade 'A. L.' to love in the next poem. Carew signals that he is too grand to be slavishly brilliant: he is very much his own man, loving and writing as he pleases. A poem like '*A cruell Mistris*' is notable for its crude treatment of the iambic metre and the rhyme: 'WEE read of Kings and Gods that kindly tooke, / A pitcher fil'd with water from the brooke; / But I have dayly tendred without thankes / Rivers of teares that overflow their bankes.' The poem is redeemed by the classical imagery that follows, when an earlier time is evoked in which sacrifices in the name of love were honored: '*Vesta* is not displeas'd if her chast vrne / Doe with repayred fuell ever burne.'[17] Perhaps too the dactylic line 4 is a signal of that world and Carew's power to evoke it. The awkwardness of the beginning suggests the manner of a petulant poet-lover, less than his best in the moment of frustration. The prosody may indeed be rough in the sense of being relatively unrefined and unlearned, but it does have the advantage of some dramatic energy, conveying the sense that the author had seen some plays:

> When you returne, pray tell your Soveraigne
> And mine, I gave you courteous entertaine;
> Each line receiv'd a teare, and then a kisse,
> First bath'd in that, it scap'd vnscorcht from this:
> I kist it because your hand had been there
> But 'cause it was not now, I shed a teare.[18]

This immediacy gave Carew the ability and the freedom to evoke sexual excitement, for which his verse is justly famous and his contemporary reputation not a little tainted. The exposure to French libertine verse may have been a help along the way as the poetry celebrated intemperance: 'Give me a storme; if it be love, / Like Danae in that golden showre / I swim in pleasure.'[19] The step to Carew's crowning achievement in 'A Rapture' is short. This poem is not anthologised in two of the best recent collections, and perhaps this points to an uncertainty of tone that is absent in Carew's brilliant elegy on his teacher Donne, whose influence on Carew's erotic verse is obvious.[20] Its witty frankness and bravado are nonetheless remarkable:

> Yet my tall pine shall in the *Cyprian* straight
> Ride safe at anchor and unlade her fraight:
> My Rudder, with thy bold hand, like a tryde,
> And skilfull Pilot, thou shalt steer, and guide
> My Bark into love's channel, where it shall
> Dance, as the bounding waves do rise or fall.[21]

Carew's poetry was of the court and the city, with its theatres and inns, where the men of letters gathered, and where what Andrew Marvell called the 'candid age' flourished.[22]

Lawes, however, was challenged by the demands of Carew's longer lyrics. Declamatory style was appropriately deployed, but the view has been that these settings lose direction in too much detail and would have needed simpler harmonic variation over a longer period of time, together with a stronger sense of flow that could accommodate rhythmic variation; in other words the qualities of true recitative.

A very different kind of verse, verse practice, and understanding are evident in the poetry of Hester Pulter (1605–1678), unknown until 1996 when her one surviving manuscript was discovered in the Brotherton Library at Leeds University.[23] Her poetry is defined by her role as mother and mistress of a household in Hertfordshire: she was mother to fifteen children, of whom only one survived her, and she thought of herself as a kind of secular anchoress, keeping watch over the rhythm of birth and mortality in a confined community. This did not stop her tackling national themes, but the quality to note about her verse is its lack of the prosodic discipline that would have been provided by a regular humanist education, even though she is no less wellborn than Carew. Her verse seldom stands up to Carew's, even at his weaker moments, if we judge quality in these conventional terms. It has rather an expressive integrity that looks forward to

modern stream-of-consciousness writing, and perhaps has more in common in its own time with prose conversion narratives. The poem on the
death of her daughter Jane – she of the 'sparking Diamond eyes' – in 1646
is a case in point, where the arresting attention to Jane's diseased skin suggests the dappled skin of a hunted deer, itself marked again by blood, a
connection that works of course against the hunt as a well-known emblem
of the courtly love quest:

> E'ne soe the spots upon her faire skin shows
> Like drops of blood upon unsoiled snow
> But what a heart had I, when I did stand
> Holding her forehead with my Trembling hand
> My Heart to Heaven with her bright spirit flyes
> Whilst shee (ah mee) closed up her lovely eyes
> Her soule being seated in her place of birth
> I turnd a Niobe as shee turn'd earth.[24]

The master of metre, however, was Ben Jonson, and everyone knew it,
especially Jonson himself. He cast a huge shadow over succeeding generations, having died aged sixty-five in 1637. Jonson's scholarship; his facil-
ity with ancient languages; and his ability to make effective, appropriate,
and imaginative transitions from Latin to English, meant that he gave to
English lyric a taut, urbane solidity that it had lacked. Few could equal him
though he was much imitated, and perhaps he was the dominant poetic
genius of the kind of line we find in the mid-century miscellanies, even
though he wrote 'Not of Love': so dominant in fact that he was commonly
evoked in poetry as a character, an avatar of standards made to live as a
guiding literary presence long after his death.[25] As he said of another: 'so
ample, full, and round, / In weight, in measure, number, sound'.[26] Jonson's
ambition took him to write in later 1629 'To the Immortal Memory, and
Friendship of that Noble pair, Sir Lucius Cary, and Sir H. Morison' the
first proper Pindaric ode in English, achieved by a very strict adherence
to metrical patterns, as opposed to the looser 'imitation' of Pindar that
would come with Abraham Cowley in the 1650s. Jonson's encomium to
a friendship severed by an untimely death keeps the business of imitation
firmly in the reader's mind, with English names for the formal division of
the triads (originally called strophe, antistrophe, and epode; now 'turn',
'counterturn', and 'stand'). This has seemed too formal and inauthentic
for some, showing a literary ambitiousness inappropriate for the occasion
of grief. But in its own terms, terms that were recognised by contemporaries, the poem sustains the famous energy of Pindar, achieved by a very
particular prosodic discipline, while exercising an appropriate intelligence.

In the third 'Stand', lines 85–96, a word-split across lines 92–3 signals the
separation of the heavenly twins Castor and Pollux, who never appear
together as stars (and in myth this was explained by Jupiter half-permit-
ting Pollux's request that the dead Castor be restored to life, alternately
living and dying every day):[27]

> Jonson, who sung this of him, ere he went
> Himself to rest,
> Or taste a part of that full joy he meant
> To have expressed,
> In this bright asterism:
> Where it were friendships schism,
> (Were not his Lucius long with us to tarry)
> To separate these twi-
> Lights, the Dioscuri;
> And keep the one half from his Harry.
> But fate doth so alternate the design,
> Whilst that in heaven, this light on earth must shine.

Other members of Jonson's circle, such as Robert Herrick, with similar
inroads at court but also enjoying city life, for some periods at least, built
on his tonal surety and made an art of fine description, albeit description
driven by the relationship of what one can see and how one is aroused by
it. 'When as in silks my *Julia* goes, / Then, then (me thinks) how sweetly
flowes / That liquefaction of her clothes' (lines 1–3, half the entire poem),
is not merely sexual, and leads to John Creaser's well-seen affirmative
judgement: Herrick, he claims, 'is not with Julia in the imagined moment
of uttering the poem, but thinking with a connoisseur's rapture at how
she enthralls him. The experience is recreated with conscious virtuosity, a
voluptuary yet deliberate pleasure in the language used to recall her erotic
allure.'[28] Since poetry and drinking went together, Herrick ominously saw
potential for too much intoxication and loss of control in an imitation
of the bibulous Greek poet Anacreon. Here too a reference to the satirist
Petronius might be concealed in the poem.[29] Herrick built careful parallels in his verse between Ovid and Jonson, Tibullus or Propertius and
himself; or rephrased Dante, placing Jonson in the radiant glow that surrounded Homer, Horace, Ovid, and Lucan in the *Inferno*; or like Ovid,
projected himself as an already dead author.[30] Thomas Randolph was no
less a 'Son of Ben' than Herrick, and his poems took from Jonson's ease of
tone, just as Randolph allegedly drank himself to death, taking due note
no doubt of Jonson's love of wine.[31] Both Herrick and Randolph accepted
Jonson's retraction of the poetic line; the tightening of syntax; the refusal
of the pentameter's liberty, with its valve-like, regulatory caesura. Henry

Lawes' settings of Herrick's lyrics are noteworthy, not least for the contrast between the 'graceful air and rhythmic spice' in tuneful triple time for most of the lyrics, and the striking declamatory ayres such as 'Amaryllis, by a spring', where the music is subtly attached to the delicate words, and where there is a high instance of intense vocal ornamentation that is intended to be descriptive of the content of the words.[32]

II

The business of writing lyric verse was undoubtedly most seriously inflected by the Civil War, the regicide, and the eleven years of experiment with non-monarchical forms of government that followed. Although much of his verse was written in the twenty-five years before the wars, it was Herrick's lot to let his subtle symposiastic verse speak for compromised Royalism when his major printed collection *Hesperides* first appeared in 1648, dedicated to the future Charles II. That context includes many things, such as the association of Royalism with bucolic pastoral: a poetry dedicated to defending the culture of maypole dancing, Sunday sport, and Christmas celebration, much of which had been abolished by the Puritans.[33] Early performances of William Lawes' (brother of Henry) plangent setting of Herrick's 'To the Virgins, to make much of Time' would have been tinged with an incendiary spirit of resistance: it was a Cavalier anthem.[34] William Lawes himself, especially venerated as a musician and composer by the king, was shot dead in the rout of Royalists at Rowton Heath, near Chester, on 24 September 1645, which disgrace the poet Henry Vaughan managed to survive.[35]

Hester Pulter felt the same trauma deeply:

> if the sun should lose his heat and light
> Wee should invaded bee with Death and Night
> Soe since our Martred sovere'ngs [*sic*] spirits fled
> Our light, and life; our hopes, and Joyes, are dead
> Nay should the Poles or Axes of the skie
> Their Raidient luster unto us denie
> Or Cinthia cease to wane or to increase
> Wee should subsist, t'wold not disturb our Peace
> But should we loose the influence of the sun.[36]

This poem interestingly ends with a section on the death of her daughter Jane repeated from the other poem quoted just above, and suggests that Pulter was thinking through the two deaths conjunctly and through exactly the same poetry. The regicide poems (there are several) come at the end of a series of longer meditations on the plight of Charles I, as he lost his cause. 'The complaint of Thames 1647 when the best of Kings was imprisoned by the worst of Rebels at Holmbie' is the poet overhearing the river talk of her despair and lost pride at the king's gradual failure. The anger and frustration of Royalist writers is often expressed in an imaginative revenge on the king's enemies:

> Below this curssed Earth \t/would hide my head
> And run amongst the ~~cavers~~ \Caverns/ of the Dead
> Where my pure Wave with Acharon should mix
> With Leathe, Phlegethon, Cocîtus, Stix;
> Then would I waste them to the Stigian shade
> Examples unto Reybels to be made.[37]

The worse things became, the more Royalist manuscript verse acknowledged the pain of the situation as a community of loyalists felt utterly outrun.[38] It is hard to underestimate the extent to which the verse partook of and embodied a widespread cultural trauma. An English monarch had not been put to death by his subjects since the Middle Ages, and back then it had been a matter of dynastic change, not a proclaimed systemic transformation. It is no surprise that the Royalist mourning elegy has been seen as a long-term cause of the Romantic-period elegy.[39]

Even a subject as seemingly impersonal as political service has been associated intimately with amorous lyric development in this period. Cowley's much admired collection *The Mistress* (1647) has been seen as a covert response to the need for secrecy during the Civil War and the consequences of secrecy's violation. Cowley was a secretary for the Royalist forces, and he would have witnessed at first hand the shocking revelations and political capital generated by Parliament when, after the king's baggage train had been seized, sensitive documents were published as *The King's Cabinet Opened* (1645) to the king's great disadvantage. This is a strong insight, but to go on and claim that this context was particularly suited for *The Mistress* because its poems were a dying or declining form is very problematic.[40] That is only a judgement that can be made with considerable hindsight. Cowley and his followers and imitators did not think sonnets and associated love poetry were dying, so much as the required duty of the poet, and a place where imagination had great free range on the topic of love and in poetic inventiveness. His biographer Thomas Sprat liked his deft fusion of feminine (smooth) and masculine (rough) tones, and saw throughout his works a common 'unaffected modesty, and natural freedom, and easie vigour, and natural passions, and innocent mirth'.[41] Moreover: 'If his verses seem in some places not as soft and flowing as some would have them, it was his choice not his fault. He knew that in diverting men's minds, there should be the same variety observ'd as in the Prospects of their Eyes.'[42]

Cowley's 1650s poetry, his engagements with Pindar and his translations of Horace, his praise of solitude, his participation in poetry's Georgic revolution, are important and usually preferred today, but the lyrics in *The Mistress* must also be included in the objects of Sprat's praise. Tinged with the Epicurianism Cowley had encountered in Paris, *The Mistress* at its best is in Sprat's terms both rough and smooth, as in 'The Request':

> Come; or I'll teach the world to scorn that Bow:
>   I'll teach them thousand *wholesome arts*
>   Both to resist and cure thy darts,
> More then thy skilful *Ovid* ere did know.
>   *Musick* of sighs thou shalt not hear,
> Nor drink one wretched *Lovers* tasteful *Tear*:
>   Nay, unless soon thou woundest me,
> My Verses shall not onely *wound*, but *murther* Thee.[43]

The tone is abrupt, suggesting sharp male dissatisfaction with perhaps a hint of ironic presentation of the libertine speaker on Cowley's part, but on the other hand, the verse is perfectly iambic, with unbending metrical regularity, thereby making a fine contrast with the disgruntled sentiments of the speaker. We do not value this bravura discipline in numbers today, and have not for a very long time, but Cowley's contemporaries made much of it.

The process of shoring up civilisation's resources, seen by many Royalists as necessary for any kind of recognisable future, had been begun long before the king was in any danger of being tried and executed. The brilliant young gentleman scholar Thomas Stanley, poet, translator, intellectual historian, had installed himself in Gray's Inn and instituted a semi-secret literary patronage circle whereby he enabled like-minded poets to live at this inn of court and keep writing the verse that was so vital, as they saw it, to national virtue.[44] Stanley's poetic agenda is to use ancient and Continental exemplars to take English verse to an even more refined but productive place. He did not hesitate to write in French, or render the distinctive poetics of other versions of courtliness in his own vernacular: Montalvan, Ronsard, Guarini, Marino, Lope de Vega, and St Amant. Here he is in lyric mode, but not translating:

> This silent speech is swifter far,
> Then the ears lazy species are;
> And the expression it afford
> (As our desires) 'bove reach of words

Thus we (my Dear) of these may learn
A Passion others not discern;
Nor can it shame or blushes move,
Like Plants to live, like Angels love:
Since All excuse with equal Innocence
What above Reason is, or beneath Sence.[45]

This is certainly 'smooth', although flawed by the awkward definite article in line 19, yet helped by the deft parentheses that add a higher degree of self-aware reflection on the narrator's part. One manuscript copy associated with the author contains annotations to lines 1, 9 and 10 that are allusions to Catullus lyrics.[46] The final poem in the 1651 edition of his *Poems* is attributed to Pythagoras, followed by a long scholarly note in which Stanley explains that Pythagoras' poems must have been an assemblage of fragments gathered by his former students. It is clear that Stanley greatly respected the even younger scholarly and poetic prodigy John Hall of Durham, whom he also supported, and John Milton, but by the time his circle was fully constituted both Hall and Milton were Parliamentarian apologists and would soon become Republican journalists, although their shared dislike of the Presbyterians gave them common cause with the Royalists at this point in the course of events. Like Stanley, Milton had been learning his art from Continental as well as ancient verse, and, as is well known in literary history, achieving real success – especially with the poems written during the 1630s, published in collected form in 1645. To judge by poetic allusions to it, serious men of letters noted Milton's extraordinary talent and insight into the very business of writing poetry and being a poet.[47] Where Stanley, like Marvell, goes to contemporary European verse, Milton impresses by having such a long, bold reach back in time. Milton himself was caught at this point in the chasm that opened as society divided and took sides. The best measure of this is his sonnet on Henry Lawes, who had written the music for Milton's *Comus* and who may have played the part of the Attendant Spirit in the first performance at Ludlow Castle.[48] As we have seen, no less an integral part of court music than his brother, Lawes stood for Royalism. Milton had been embattled with his apparent co-religionists, the Presbyterians, for their attacks on his divorce tracts and his tolerationist views, and here Milton crosses back for the length of a sonnet to the other side of the cultural divide, in prefatory verse printed in Lawes' *Choice Psalmes* (1648), dedicated to the by-then imprisoned Charles I and published to commemorate Henry's fallen brother William. Line 11 is glossed in this volume with a reference to Lawes' setting to music of the 'Complaint of Ariadne' by another ardent and influential Royalist poet-playwright, William Cartwright, fellow of Christ Church, who was involved in the defence of Oxford and who died of camp fever in 1643.[49] Milton praises Lawes' respect for words in his musical settings, never matching short notes with long syllables – a quality that, as we have seen, was often praised in Lawes' settings. It is perhaps a piece of Miltonic egotism to compare himself silently with Dante, and Lawes with Casella, the singer whom the poet meets, singing his own canzone, in *Purgatorio* II.76–117. Compared with Stanley, Milton's phrasing is far more rhythmically assured. He rhymes superbly (*pace* Dryden's notorious later judgement), echoing the principles by which Lawes set words to music:

> Thou honour'st Verse, and Verse must lend her wing
> To honour thee, the Priest of Phœbus' Quire
> That tun'st their happiest lines in Hymn, or Story.
> Dante shall give Fame leave to set thee higher
> Then his Casella, whom he woo'd to sing
> Met in the milder shades of Purgatory.[50]

III

Poetry was also associated with the new regime, and here we see one of the major functions of poetry as a tool in diplomacy, public deliberation, and, indeed, as a device in the working of appointments within a world that still depended on patronage. A presentation poem in a diplomatic context was part of the way in which international relations took place, while myriad other functions required the writing of poetry. Andrew Marvell wrote some of his most well-known verse to celebrate occasions within Puritan households, and Latin verse for important embassies abroad.[51] Situating Horatian echoes and ethos within Petrarchan form, Milton made the English Republican sonnet a reality, while Marvell's meticulous ear caught echoes from the poetically virtuous cavalier poets, including Carew, Cartwright, Sandys, and Waller, in order to build a Protectoral literature, with a refined prosodic competence but one that was also in tune with Puritan ideals.[52] Before then he had managed to write what many now feel is the greatest political poem in the language, 'An Horatian Ode upon Cromwell's Return from Ireland' (June 1650), precisely so because of its ability to capture the complexity of historical flux in a particular, very important moment while also revealing the importance of highly significant events to different points of view, even as the poem is ostensibly in praise of the new free state's chief military commander, Oliver

Cromwell. This is achieved by what has been called its 'remarkable thinking form', the shorter couplets in each group of four commenting on the
two longer lines preceding them, and the contraction of syntax facilitating
appropriate ambiguity, with puns operating between English and Latin:

> So restless Cromwell could not cease
> In the inglorious arts of peace,
> > But thorough advent'rous war
> > Urged his active star.
>
> And like the three-fork'd lightning, first
> Breaking the clouds where it was nurst,
> > Did through his own side
> > His fiery way divide.[53]

Does Cromwell urge his star, or vice versa? The poem is deeply allusive, to
ancient literature and its political resonances, and to contemporary journalism and political pamphlets. In this respect the vast energies claimed
in Lucan and Lucretius' epics are relocated within a tightly controlling
Horatian analysis machine. Complexity and enormity are reduced to sharp
points where the reader is made aware of the truth in history. Did Oliver
Cromwell's fellow MPs, officers, and Puritans enjoy his cutting through
them powered by his own ambition, as Marvell depicts? Marvell's associate John Hall translated Longinus' treatise on the sublime in 1650 (it is ful-
somely echoed in Marvell's 'Ode'), an act that has been seen as distinctly
anti-tyrannical (since Longinus says that poets flourish best in a free state).
In making the translation he is also the first translator of Sappho into
English, quoted by Longinus, and praised for her ability to intimate the
passions. Marvell's use of Horace is well attested, as is his implicit response
to other English Horace imitators (like Sir Richard Fanshawe), but since
he appears to have seen Hall's translation one wonders if Sappho's ability to express the passions found its way too into Marvell's head: a stanza
that was both highly expressive and facilitated huge artistic control. Says
Longinus (in Hall's English): '*where* appears this great *skill?* she knew
how to call out the *greatest* and *bravest* things, and then to *mould* them
into *proportion* and *correspondencie*':

> How did his *pleasing* glances dart
> *Sweet* languors to my *ravish'd* heart!
> At the *first* sight thou so *prevail'd*
> That my voice *fail'd*.
>
> I'me *speechlesse*, *feav'rish*, fires assail
> My *fainting flesh*, my *sight* doth fail,

> Whilest to my *restlesse* mind my *ears*
> Still *hum* new *fears*.

The translation goes on:

> *Wonder* you not at this? The *soul*, the *body*, the *tongue*, the *ears*, the *eyes*, the *complexion*, things so widely *different* are here by a strange *artifice* brought *together*, and according to her severall contrary *agitations*; how she *burns*, how she *freezes*, how she *raves*, & how she *deliberates*! for either she's in *fear* or at the point of *death*; so that it appears not a *single passion*, but a *conflux* and general *rendezvouz* of them *all*.[54]

It was such a fusion of control and energy, a kind of 'raving', that attracted Cowley to imitate Pindar (whom he thought close in some ways to Alcaeus): 'harsh', 'uncouth', 'irregular' in form and yet still with 'Sweetness and Numerosity'.[55]

In their different ways, Marvell, Thomas May, George Wither, Lucy Hutchinson, Marchamont Nedham, James Harrington, John Hall, and Henry Marten all wrote Republican lyrics. A good amount of verse partook of the articulation of the different viewpoints in pamphlets and journalism, by no means all of it Royalist, and many times in Latin as well as in English. Is it possible that 'An Horatian Ode' was originally planned for newsbook publication? The role of cited verse in religious and political controversial prose remains significantly understudied. In this respect Marvell was able to exceed the aesthetic dimensions of the by-now elderly George Wither's commonwealth verse, faithful to the Parliamentarian and Puritan causes, but focused on a free verse that few are able to read with pleasure today.[56]

I have already quoted Marvell's insightful verse letter to Richard Lovelace that prefaced Lovelace's landmark volume *Lucasta* (1649). Does Lovelace's plangent lyricism, suited both to poems (where he intrudes speech by way of metrical irregularity) and songs; his bitter sense, perhaps even at a very early stage, that the king's cause was fatally damaged; his careful use of veiled political and religious expression; earn him the title of greatest cavalier? If that were the case, we could turn to the famous 'To Althea, from Prison: Song', with its insistence that enforced confinement is no denial of freedom: 'Stone walls do not a prison make, / Nor Iron bars a cage / … / If I have freedom in my love, / And in my soul am free; / Angels alone that soar above, / Enjoy such liberty.'[57] We might also turn to 'The Grasshopper' – also in *Lucasta*, in the manner of Anacreon, Jonsonian in subject matter – but even more acutely oblique is one of the two poems called 'The Snail' ('Wise emblem of our politic world'), published in 1659, the year after Lovelace died in a garret dressed only in rags – also Anacreontic, a riddle, emblematic, and where several allegories are pitched together in a meditation light and dark on the meeting of observation, description, and interpretation:

> Now hast thou chang'd thee saint; and made
> Thy self a fane that's cupola'd;
> And in thy wreathed cloister thou
> Walkest thine own grey friar too;
> Strict, and lock'd up, th'art hood all o'er,
> And ne'er eliminat'st thy door.
> On salads thou dost feed severe,
> And 'stead of beads thou dropp'st a tear;
> And when to rest, each calls the bell,
> Thou sleep'st within thy marble cell,
> Where in dark contemplation plac'd,
> The sweets of nature thou dost taste;
> Who now with time thy days resolve,
> And in a jelly thee dissolve,
> Like a shot star, which doth repair
> Upward, and rarify the air.
>
> (51–66)

Lovelace's admirers still compared him to Sidney and Jonson: Lovelace reminded people of the former's fusion of fierce chivalry and poetic brilliance. Inside Lovelace's poetry Sidney's writing remains the arbiter of excellence: 'Heav'nly Sidney', 'Caelestial Sidney'. Lovelace might not have been quite so ostentatiously innovative as Sidney, and his verse is much changed from that of the 1560s and 1570s, but he thought he was deploying a line and an ethos that went straight back to the high Elizabethan era.

The shaping of history belongs to the victors; if it had not been for the fame that quickly gathered about *Paradise Lost* after it was first published in 1667 it would have been a much harder task to recover Milton's views and full literary achievements from obscurity and contempt, and that of other Republicans and Puritans. The verse that was increasingly influential after 1660 (for instance as fuel for Samuel Butler's very popular burlesque *Hudibras*) was in many ways a fugitive poetry during the Commonwealth. It was a crude poetry that began in drinking clubs and that became the emblem of cavalier suffering and the will to survive. Devoid of its scurrilous subject matter, and when the city or the scene of Civil War and exile has been replaced by the study and extended retirement, as in the case of Charles Cotton, the result is a lyric poetry that, all in all, is every bit as 'light' as the thin garments worn by Herrick's Julia. No less learned than Stanley (Cotton was the son of a famous literary patron, also called Charles; he translated Montaigne) although perhaps more influenced by French libertine verse than any other English poet, Cotton manages to free English poetry from the contexts and prosodic or lexical elements that make for complexity:

> Hark, the cock crows, and yon, bright star
> Tells us the day himself's not far;
> And see where, breaking from the night,
> He gilds the Western hills with light.
> With him old Janus doth appear,
> Peeping into the future year
> With such a look, as seems to say,
> The prospect is not good that way.[58]

The speaker then finds good cause to welcome the year as day breaks to a clear sky and despite the adversity that will probably arrive, as it did the year before. The contrast with Henry Vaughan's 'Cock Crowing' (1650), a poem that embodies rich Hermetic symbolism, makes Cotton's strategy stand out, and justifies the aptness of Lamb's judgement that these lines contained 'the purging sunlight of pure poetry'.[59] The drive to 'empty' lyric is paralleled by the 'downsizing' that was involved in Cotton's very popular travesty of Virgil, although this work was apparently preceded in the 1650s by Reginald Forster's innovative salty parody of 'Sappho to Phaon' (Ovid, *Heroides* XV), a mini-me to Ovid:[60]

> This note, for which my muse I bang'd,
> What? if thou canst not reade, be hang'd.
> What? know'st thou not my style, although
> I had not under-writ Saph-o?
> Jugg, Jane, Doll's company I shun,
> At flatts, for thine at the long-run.
> For—
> Phaon, thou hast a face, o face
> Moving mine eyes out of their place!
> Thou, of discretion art beside
> At yeeres, to make thy whore, thy bride.
> Take to thee courage, and a quiver,
> Thou art Apollo, the verse-driver.

Through the unhappy years of Civil War and gloomy defeat, the Royalists could only escape from history in bucolic fantasy or confront it in plangent tenderness, bolstered by the state of refinement to which they had brought the lyric as poem and as song. This mode could convert readily into triumphalist abandon after 1660. The Republicans and Commonwealthsmen made the lyric do innovative work in keeping tyrants at bay while paying court to the awing energy that the times had released. And even the defeated saw that lyric offered powerful windows of awareness in a time of deep perplexity. That was their song.

Notes

1 Alastair Fowler, 'Introduction', in *The New Oxford Book of Seventeenth-Century Verse*, ed. Alastair Fowler (Oxford University Press, 1992), pp. xxxvii–xliii.
2 J. E. Spingarn, ed., *Critical Essays of the Seventeenth Century*, 3 vols. (Oxford: Clarendon Press, 1908–9), Vol. I, p. 21.
3 Francis Atterbury, 'The Preface', in Edmund Waller, *The Second Part of Mr. Waller's Poems* (London, 1690), pp. 3, 7.
4 Spingarn, *Critical Essays*, Vol. I, pp. xii–xiii.
5 Henry Peacham, 'The Compleat Gentleman' (1622), in *ibid.*, Vol. I, p. 126.
6 *Early English Books Online*, http://eebo.chadwyck.com/home/ (last accessed 25 May 2013).
7 Peacham, 'The Compleat Gentleman', Vol. I, p. xxxi. See Francesco Robortello, *In librum Aristotelis poeticam explicationes* (Florence, 1548).
8 Nigel Smith, *Literature and Revolution in England, 1640–1660* (London and New Haven: Yale University Press, 1994); Christopher R. Orchard, 'Politics and the Literary Imagination, 1642–1660' (unpublished D.Phil. thesis, University of Oxford, 1994).
9 Gerardus Joannes Vossius, *Poeticarum institutionum libri tres* (1647), ed. and trans. Jan Bloemendal, 2 vols. (Leiden and Boston: Brill, 2010), Vol. II, p. 1057.
10 *Ibid.*, Vol. II, p. 1059.
11 Ian Spink, *Henry Lawes: Cavalier Songwriter* (Oxford and New York: Oxford University Press, 2000), p. 6.
12 Andrew Pinnock and Bruce Wood, 'A Mangled Chime: The Accidental Death of the Opera Libretto in Civil War England', *Early Music* 36.2 (2008), 265–84 (p. 267).
13 Henry Lawes, *The Second Book of Ayres, and Dialogues* (London, 1655), sig. [A1v].
14 John Cobb, 'To my ever honour'd Friend & Father, Mr. *HENRY LAWES*, on his Book of *Ayres* and *Dialogues*', lines 17–20, in Lawes, *Ayres and dialogues, for one, two, and three voices*, 3 vols. (London, 1653–8), Vol. I (1653), sig. [A1r].
15 Robert Eisenstein, album cover note (p. 6), in The Folger Consort with Rogers Covey-Crump, *When Birds Do Sing: Music of 17th-Century England* (Bard Records, 1992).
16 I cite and quote from the standard edition of Carew's works: *The Poems of Thomas Carew, with His Masque 'Coelum Britannicum'*, ed. Rhodes Dunlap (Oxford University Press, 1949).
17 Thomas Carew, 'A cruell Mistris', lines 1–4, 9–10.

18 Thomas Carew, '*My mistris commanding me to returne her letters*', lines 15–20.

19 For temperance and intemperance in verse, see Joshua Scodel, *Excess and the Mean in Early Modern English Literature* (Princeton University Press, 2002).

20 Fowler, *Seventeenth-Century Verse*; and Robert Cummings, ed., *Seventeenth-Century Poetry: An Annotated Anthology* (Oxford and Malden, MA: Blackwell, 2000).

21 Carew, 'A Rapture', lines 85–90.

22 Andrew Marvell, 'To His Noble Friend Mr Richard Lovelace', line 5, in Andrew Marvell, *Poems*, ed. Nigel Smith, rev. edn (Harlow: Longman, 2007), p. 21.

23 University of Leeds, Brotherton Library, MS Lt q 32.

24 Hester Pulter, 'Upon the Death of my dear and lovely Daughter J. P.', lines 41–8. Connections with Marvell's 'A Nymph Complaining for the Death of Her Fawn' are noted in Marvell, *Poems*, pp. 67, 71.

25 Ben Jonson, 'Why I Write Not of Love', in Cummings, *Seventeenth-Century Poetry*, p. 84.

26 Ben Jonson, 'To the Immortal Memory, and Friendship of That Noble Pair, Sir Lucius Cary, and Sir H. Morison' (composed *c.* late 1629), lines 49–50, in *ibid.*, p. 98.

27 See Ovid, *Fasti*, 5.715–20; Cummings, *Seventeenth-Century Poetry*, p. 100.

28 Robert Herrick, '*Upon* Julia's *Clothes*'; John Creaser, '"Jocund his Muse was": Celebration and Virtuosity in Herrick', in *'Lords of Wine and Oile': Community and Conviviality in the Poetry of Robert Herrick*, ed. Ruth Connolly and Tom Cain (Oxford University Press, 2011), p. 63.

29 Petronius calls a thin garment 'woven air': *Satyricon*, line 55; see Cummings, *Seventeenth-Century Poetry*, p. 161.

30 Syrithe Pugh, 'Supping with Ghosts: Imitation and Immortality in Herrick', in Connolly and Cain, *'Lords of Wine and Oile'*, p. 245.

31 Thomas Randolph, *Poems: with the Muses looking-glasse: and Amyntas* (Oxford, 1638); see also aspersions cast in the name of another bibulous cavalier poet, Sir John Suckling: anon., *The Sucklington faction or (Sucklings) roaring boyes* (n.p., 1641).

32 Spink, *Henry Lawes*, p. 27.

33 The classic case for this interpretation is made by Leah S. Marcus, *The Politics of Mirth: Jonson, Herrick, Milton, Marvell, and the Defense of Old Holiday Pastimes* (University of Chicago Press, 1986); later rebutted by Marcus herself and reaffirmed by Achsah Guibbory in Connolly and Cain, *'Lords of Wine and Oile'*, pp. 65–82, 300–16.

34 See Stacey Jocoy, '"Touch but thy Lire (my Harrie)": Henry Lawes and the Mirthful Muse of *Hesperides*', in Connolly and Cain, *'Lords of Wine and Oile'*, pp. 250–75 (p. 275).

35 For further evidence of Civil War damage to musical/literary culture, see Pinnock and Wood, 'A Mangled Chime'.

36 Hester Pulter, 'On that Unparraleld Prince Charles the first. his Horrid Murther', lines 21–9, in Brotherton Library, MS Lt q 32, fo. 15v.

37 Hester Pulter, 'The complaint of Thames 1647', lines 107–12, in Brotherton Library, MS Lt q 32, fo. 10r.

38 See also University College London, MS Ogden 42; Peter Beal, *In Praise of Scribes: Manuscripts and Their Makers in Seventeenth-Century England* (Oxford University Press, 1998), p. 148; John McWilliams, 'A Storm of Lamentations Writ': Lachrymae Musarum and Royalist Culture after the Civil War', *YES* 33 (2003), 273–89.

39 J. W. Draper, *The Funeral Elegy and the Rise of English Romanticism* (New York University Press, 1929).

40 Tim Morris, 'Cowley's Lemmon: Secrecy and Interpretation in *The Mistress*', *English* 60 (2011), 21–41. The classic study of Royalist secrecy is Lois Potter, *Secret Rites and Secret Writing: Royalist Literature, 1641–1660* (Cambridge University Press, 1990).

41 Thomas Sprat, 'An Account of the Life of Mr. Cowley', in Abraham Cowley, *Works* (London, 1668), sig. b[1]r.

42 *Ibid.*, sig. B [1]v.

43 Cowley, 'The Request', lines 17–24, 49–56, in Abraham Cowley, *Collected Works*, ed. Thomas O. Calhoun, Laurence Heyworth, and Allan Pritchard, 2 vols., Vol. II: *Poems (1656)*, Part I: *The Mistress* (Newark: University of Delaware Press, 1993), 21.

44 See Nicholas McDowell, *Poetry and Allegiance in the English Civil Wars: Marvell and the Cause of Wit* (Oxford University Press, 2008), especially Chapters 1–3.

45 Thomas Stanley, 'Love Innocence', lines 18–26, in *Poems and Translations*, ed. Galbraith Miller Crump (Oxford University Press, 1962), p. 382.

46 Cambridge University Library, MS 7514.

47 Nicholas Von Maltzahn, 'Death by Drowning: Marvell's "Lycidas"', *Milton Studies* 48 (2008), 38–52.

48 See above, p. 74.

49 See above, p. 75.

50 John Milton, 'Sonnet XIII: To Mr. H. Lawes', lines 9–14. Text taken from John Milton, *Complete Shorter Poems*, ed. John Carey, 2nd edn (Harlow: Longman, 1997).

51 Nigel Smith, *Andrew Marvell: The Chameleon* (New Haven and London: Yale University Press, 2010), pp. 113–15, 121–2, 239.

52 See the commentary on Milton's sonnets on Fairfax, Cromwell, and Vane in *Complete Shorter Poems*, pp. 324, 328–9; Marvell, *Poems*, pp. 54–8, 246–56, 266–312, 316–19. See also Edward Holberton, *Poetry and the Cromwellian Protectorate: Culture, Politics and Institutions* (Oxford University Press, 2008).

53 Marvell, 'An Horatian Ode', lines 9–16.

54 Longinus, *Peri hypsous; or, Dionysius Longinus of the height of eloquence*, trans. John Hall (London, 1652), pp. xxi–xxiii.

55 Abraham Cowley, 'The Preface', in Abraham Cowley, *Poems* (London, 1656), sig. b[1]r–v.

56 David Norbrook, 'Levelling Poetry: George Wither and the English Revolution, 1642–1649', *ELR* 21 (1991), 217–56.

57 Richard Lovelace, 'To Althea, from Prison', lines 25–6, 29–32, in Richard Lovelace, *Poems*, ed. C. H. Wilkinson (Oxford: Clarendon Press, 1953), p. 79. I have regularised the spelling. Further citations of Lovelace poems are to this edition.

58 Charles Cotton, 'The New Year', in Charles Cotton, *Poems*, ed. John Beresford (London: Cobden-Sanderson, 1923), p. 71.

59 See commentary in Henry Vaughan, *The Complete Poems*, ed. Alan Rudrum (Harmondsworth: Penguin, 1974), pp. 597–9.

60 Reginald Forster, *Scarronides; or, Virgile travestie A mock-poem. Being the first book of Virgils Æneis in English, burlesque* (1664); a unique copy of Forster's poem survives in British Library, MS 61744. See James Harmer, 'Reginald Forster's Burlesque Ovidian Epistle', *Translation and Literature* 16 (2007), 193–204.

CHAPTER FIVE

Modulation and expression in the lyric ode, 1660–1750

David Fairer

> Begin the SONG! your Instruments advance!
>   Tune the Voice, and tune the Flute;
>   Touch the silent, sleeping Lute,
> And make the Strings to their own Measures dance.
> Bring gentlest Thoughts, that into Language glide,
> Bring softest Words, that into Numbers slide …

In these subtle lines, which open *For an Anniversary of Musick on St Cecilia's Day*, John Oldham readies himself and us for the performance that is beginning.[1] The instrumental ensemble are finding their voice, as are the singers; but it is clear that human language also is attuning itself, relaxing into metrical arrangement. Music is simply happening: it is not a divine spirit being invited to descend and inspire, but something being heard here and now, emerging from silence. The emphasis is on the skill of the human participants, who include the poet himself and his own instrument of words.[2] In these opening lines Oldham's emphasis is on the power of poetry to sing and dance, not to be either the master or the slave of its sister art.

As the performance continues, the audience begins to participate too, and the affective language conveys how much their responsiveness is integral to the whole experience. The stringed instruments explore the air, and as they do so the language conveys a sense of being moved and touched simultaneously, both spiritually rapt and physically aroused:

> Hark! how the waken'd Strings resound,
>   And sweetly break the yielding Air!
> The ravish'd Sence, how pleasingly they wound,
>   And call the list'ning Soul into the Ear!
> Each Pulse beats Time, and every Heart
> With Tongue and Fingers bears a part.

This goes beyond the old topos of music's harmony drawing out the soul.[3] Here Oldham not only engages the senses directly but insists on turning the strings into a seductive lover who exploits the language of wounds, ravishment, and beating heart. Such a palpable physical response sees the *Pulse* and *Heart* of the listeners as an emotional accompaniment to the *Tongue* and *Fingers* of the performing singers and players. Each *bears a part*: the rhythms of the music and the rhythms of the audience's pumping blood quickening the heartbeat. No-one can be immune from the emotional atmosphere, which is palpable. The air itself is not only the medium of arousal but the first victim, broken and yielding.

We may think we are a long way here from the print lyric poem, dealing rather with words for music, not with an independent text, and that as readers we are limited to imagining our presence at a performance. From this viewpoint it is easy to say that the ode assumes an aural dimension whose absence is felt by anyone who merely reads the words; and that a criticism which ignores the specific musical setting – the melody, harmonisation, scoring, rhythm, dynamics – will fall short. But it is possible to think of the poem as having not just a public character (the ode in performance) but a more direct one, in which the poet has knowingly made the transition to the page and the act of reading, is conscious of the potential independence of his words, and incorporates elements of performance into his own text. Oldham does so here: the 'flute' exists only in his lines, since Blow's scoring is for strings and keyboard and includes no wind instruments. It would therefore be too simple to assume that a verbal 'reading', such as is being done here, must be inadequate, its meaning somehow limited by the lack of the musical dimension.[4] We might conversely say that Oldham's deliberate staging of the event in his text; his awareness of tuning, rhythm, and tone; the timed entry of the voices and the strings; and audience response; is in fact to privilege the reader of the poem and leave the audience at a musical performance conscious of being given a commentary on what they should be experiencing, on the state of their pulse and their required ravishment.

In talking about the modal character of some formal lyric poems during the Restoration and early eighteenth century, including several odes that were written for public performance, I want to work along the tricky borderline between verbal text and music/sound and look at ways in which the poets negotiated it, some making use of the idea of lyric eloquence without thought of any musical setting. My contention is that poets, acknowledging the ancient roots of lyric in the lyre,[5] were aware of a defining expressiveness in lyric verse, and of an interplay of technical skill and audience response. During a period when the staging of music (Chapel Royal anthems, court odes, subscription concerts, opera, etc.)

was to become increasingly popular, they might introduce performative elements into their poems, not just looking for specific aural effects but finding equivalents for some of the techniques of the ancient lyrists. In default of a lost original music, this was a way of exploiting modal and expressive features that could make the transition to modern lyric poetry and become a defining aspect of it.[6]

The Greek citharode or lyrist could achieve varied, subtle, and dramatic effects on his instrument. His fingers could press or pluck individual strings, or touch a string gently while it vibrated and thus raise the note slightly; or stop a string to sound a large interval; or by selective dampening 'allow different notes to dominate the tone cluster at different moments'.[7] The character, the *ethos*, of the music was conveyed by the modes (*harmoniai*) – literally the 'attunements' – with their distinctive series of intervals and rhythmic motifs, encompassing most famously the manly and dignified Dorian, the more varied Phrygian, and the softer, youthful Lydian.[8] In the first half of the fifth century BCE the favoured enharmonic scale, which Pindar exploited, made use of quarter-tones and allowed for the slightest of modulations.[9] A notoriously innovative citharode of the next generation, Timotheus, specialised in modulating between all three of the scales – enharmonic, diatonic, and chromatic – within the same piece, sometimes with flamboyant vocal and physical effects.[10]

The principles and techniques of ancient Greek music were well known during the seventeenth and eighteenth centuries through the treatise *De musica*, which was attributed to Plutarch and included in his *Moralia* throughout this period,[11] and British musical theorists of the seventeenth century specifically linked music's varied 'moods' to the 'modes' of the Greeks.[12] Charles Butler wrote in 1636: 'Musik is the Art of modulating Notes in voice or instrument, the which having a great pouer over the affections of the minde, by its various Moodes produceth in the hearers various effects. These Moodes ar five: *Dorik, Lydian, Æeolik, Phrygian*, and *Ionik*.'[13]

Given the complexity and subtlety of ancient lyric performance, it is not surprising that the poets of the 1660–1750 period recognised that ancient Greek poetry posed a musical challenge, and that English verse could not hope to reproduce the sounds of the original lyrics (in the words of one translator) 'without that additional Beauty of the Attuning Harp, which was customary in those days'.[14] Metrically also, as Chambers' *Cyclopædia* (1728) pointed out, the Greeks with their 124 named metrical feet (comprising from two to six syllables) could achieve effects denied to English poets. Because of 'the shortness and uniformity of our Feet … our Poets are fetter'd … it's no wonder they can make no extraordinary Motions'. Set against the ancients' metrical scope and variety, 'our Quantities make such poor Music, that we are forced to call in the *Gothic* Aids of Rhyme to distinguish our Verse from Prose'.[15] Daniel Webb wrote in 1769: 'We cannot, it must be confessed, pretend to equal the sweetness of sound or dignity of motion of the Greek measures.'[16]

English poets who worked in the tradition of Greek lyric tended to show a raised awareness of 'sound' and 'motion', of both cadence and rhythm, and some bravely tried to widen the dynamic range and capture the boldness that seemed to be denied them. A sense of musical challenge is rarely absent, and references to the modern poet's own 'lyre' are a frequent reminder of what they knew was missing. Sometimes the effect could be an awkward one: 'Here pause, my Muse! and wind up higher / The Strings of thy Pindarick Lyre!'[17] The link between lyre and lyric remained so strong that by the mid eighteenth century the word 'lyrick' could still be considered an adjective ('pertaining to an harp') rather than a noun.[18] With this in mind, poets tried to find an equivalent of that responsiveness between voice and hand which the Greek lyrist showed, and to catch what James Thomson characterised as 'that deep-searching Voice, and artful Hand, / To which respondent shakes the vary'd Soul'.[19] Lyric had to that degree become something of a 'lost' art. A few ancient Greek lyrics of course survived, notably Pindar's forty-five *epinikia*, each of which is metrically different; but these great victory odes were regarded less as generic models (they were, after all, celebrations of victorious athletes) than as tokens of what might be done if a poet could tune language to the appropriate pitch.

Rather than regarding 'lyric' as a formal genre, poets of the post-1660 period tended to see it as an instrument of range and power that was flexible and capable of a wide variety of music. They were interested in recovering a classic genealogy that consisted of a mixture of lyric modes, each of which might imprint a different character. The key to lyric lay in its adaptability. The question, 'How can my Muse with animating Fire / Adapt her Numbers to the sounding Lyre?', was one that Horace had famously confronted.[20] The skill of adapting one's numbers, of finding the right notes and a suitably expressive tone, was the key challenge to a modern lyric poet of this period.

The precedents were set by the four canonical lyrists of ancient Greece: Pindar's finely tuned 'trembling string', Anacreon's relaxed conviviality, Sappho's passionate strains, and Alcaeus' martial exhortations.[21] Each spoke with a different accent. This range meant that the notion of a generic 'model' was more fluid and adaptable, and indeed much of the poetic skill lay in adapting moods and tones in appropriate ways. What was being handed over to one's successors in the lyric line was less a text or genre than the lyre itself, with the unspoken encouragement: 'here, see what you can do'. Lyric was in that sense itself an instrument. In his 'Ode on Lyric Poetry' (1745) Mark Akenside stages an imaginary scene in which those four Greek poets successively take up the lyre and, inspired by the Muse, 'By turns her melody repeat', each playing in their own style.[22] First we hear the pleasure-loving Anacreon who banishes cares with his jaunty mood of 'kind laughter and convivial joy'.[23] This is followed by the voice of patriot liberty, Alcaeus, who 'With louder impulse and a threatening hand / … smites the sounding chords'.[24] After those warlike notes on the lyre, Sappho's 'plaintive measures' turn the instrument towards the sorrows of love. And finally it is the turn of the daring Pindar, whose verses soar to the heights 'as eagles drink the noontide flame'. In Akenside's ode we hear in succession the notes of pleasure, freedom, love, and fame. For the young eighteenth-century poet, the 'Queen of the Lyre' could touch all emotions: 'Thy strings adapt their varied strain / To every pleasure, every pain.'[25]

The adaptiveness of lyric, its ability to turn in a moment from one passion to the next, was both a challenge and an opportunity. It was common for poets to combine passages of a contrasting character, so that a single ode might, on Akenside's model, display a repertoire of effects, with the poet showing his/her eloquence in handling the instrument. In a self-conscious parade of skill, the poets allude repeatedly to their ability to produce different sounds and moods. Modern poets had precedent for this in Horace, whose awareness of 'the sound of a lighter plectrum' (*modos leviore plectro*), his searching for words 'to be modulated to the Latin lyre' (*fidibus modulanda Latinis*), is one feature of his notable tonal flexibility.[26] At moments like these Horace is playing with expectation, consciously shifting the *modus*: a term that in music and poetry can mean rhythm, measure, metre, or mode, but which also, of course, marks a change of mood, a *mod*ulation within the verse form.[27] Handling the plectrum in a lighter way sets a different tone – to use a term that bridges words and music – and the lyric artist is aware of the skill this needs. In the eighteenth century Horace himself could be celebrated for being a responsive voice of shifting moods and reactions. Particularly in his odes he seemed to contain in himself all the different strands of the Greek lyric tradition:

> This poet … made himself master of whatever was excellent of that kind in the Grecian lyrics, every one of which he appears to have read. He has,

according to the respective subjects, the gravity and dignity of Alcæus … the sublimity and heat of Pindar, the fire and vivacity of Sappho, and the softness and sweetness of Anacreon.[28]

Horace might embody the full range of lyric, and he in turn offered poets of the 1660–1750 period a congenial example of how the ancient Greek lyric tradition could enliven the sophisticated and civilised voice of an Augustan poet.[29]

All these precedents lie behind the poem that more than any other established the full possibilities of the so-called 'higher' lyric for the next century: Dryden's *Alexander's Feast; or, The Power of Musick* (1697). Written for public performance on St Cecilia's Day,[30] this irregular Pindaric works not only as a public ode but as a tour de force for the individual reader, who is given an atmospheric description – what amounts to a private staging – of Alexander's triumph. The lyrist for the occasion, Timotheus, holds his audience spellbound from the moment he takes up his instrument (he '[w]ith flying Fingers touch'd the Lyre: / The trembling Notes ascend the Sky'),[31] and the poem follows his performance through all its virtuoso turns. Dryden's Timotheus is an all-round performer who sings, plays the lyre and the flute, and displays the full range of lyric modes.[32] But the modern English lyrist is also very much on show. By focusing on the banquet celebrating Alexander's conquest of the Persian Empire, Dryden is able to create a scene that combines the four elemental topics of Greek lyric – fame, wine, love, and war – those subjects mastered in turn by Pindar, Anacreon, Sappho, and Alcaeus.

At first Timotheus welcomes the emperor's victory; but the mood begins to shift with the varied stanzas, and it becomes clear that the ruler himself is being ruled by the music. His godhead is loudly proclaimed:

> The list'ning Crowd admire the lofty Sound,
> A present Deity, they shout around:
> A present Deity the vaulted Roofs rebound.
> 　　With ravish'd Ears
> 　　The Monarch hears,
> 　　Assumes the God,
> 　　Affects to nod,
> 　　And seems to shake the Spheres
> 　　　　　　　　(34–41)

The lines are repeated by the full chorus, but as they reverberate sublimely, the moment of glory slips over into *hubris* and becomes a challenge to the gods. It may seem like predictable 'Pindaric' flattery, but Dryden, with masterly suggestiveness, is giving us a distortion of the Greek poet's nuanced celebrations of mortal glory. Pindar's athletic champion briefly knows the radiance of the gods, 'the glory of his desire'; but in capturing such moments of brilliant illumination Pindar always seems conscious of a darker track of fate shadowing his human actors. The power of his imagery, drawing god, hero, and human momentarily into the same context, is the awareness that the unbridgeable boundaries remain: 'Seek not to become Zeus! / You have everything, if a share / Of these beautiful things comes to you. Mortal ends befit mortal men.'[33] The true Pindaric epiphany is gained in the face of failure, divine disfavour, and destiny. The successful athlete, a kingly one included, can inherit renown (κλέος) but it is also his, as a man, to lose.[34] Dryden's Alexander needs to remember this.

Underneath the modern lyric celebration, therefore, a potentially political subtext begins to make itself felt. Dryden's ode was performed, to the music of Jeremiah Clarke, two months after the Treaty of Ryswick had finally made William III's throne secure, ending eight years of war with France. Clarke's setting was given two further performances within a few weeks, and at the second of these it was paired with his Ode on the Peace of Ryswick ('Tell All the World'), a setting of an anonymous poem celebrating the treaty.[35] In the ostensible triumph of *Alexander's Feast* the national mood of celebration is evident, but the poet's strings repeatedly quiver to hints of excess, indulgence, and instability. As Timotheus displays the 'many-toned range' of the lyric repertoire, his rapid shifts suggest how quickly the political tune can alter and the dynamics of power go out of control.

Dryden manages this through modal shifts in the character of his ode. After the opening Pindaric flourish, the next section gives us the pulse of intoxication with an anacreontic on the joys of wine: '*Bacchus* Blessings are a Treasure; / Drinking is the Soldiers Pleasure; / Rich the Treasure, / Sweet the Pleasure; / Sweet is Pleasure after Pain' (56–60). The reader can hear the hands pounding the tables. Alexander is fired up and responds like a drunken soldier wanting to fight all his old battles again. Fearing the consequences Timotheus (now 'The Master') immediately adjusts his music:

> The Master saw the Madness rise;
> His glowing Cheeks, his ardent Eyes;
> And while He Heav'n and Earth defy'd,
> Chang'd his hand, and check'd his Pride.
> (69–72)

The telling phrase, 'Chang'd his hand', catches the essential lyric skill of *modulation*: the fingers instantaneously reset themselves to bring a different mood, a fresh sound from the instrument. The monarch's pride needs checking. With a masterly touch Timotheus now laments the fall of the Persian enemy Darius, and draws responsive tears from Alexander's eyes. Having achieved this effect of pathos, the lyrist takes his opportunity to transpose the song towards love – after all, moving from pity to love requires, he says, no more than the minimal adjustment of a single note (a 'degree'), perhaps just a semitone, or even a quarter-tone:

> The Mighty Master smil'd to see
> That Love was in the next Degree:
> 'Twas but a Kindred-Sound to move;
> For Pity melts the Mind to Love.
>   Softly sweet, in *Lydian* Measures,
>   Soon He sooth'd his Soul to Pleasures.
>   (93–8)

In response to this modal shift ('Lovely *Thais* sits beside thee') Alexander now becomes the pained lover, his heart softened into a mood that recalls the frustrations of Sappho: 'The Prince, unable to conceal his Pain, / Gaz'd on the Fair / Who caus'd his Care, / And sigh'd and look'd, sigh'd and look'd, / Sigh'd and look'd, and sigh'd again' (109–13). But such effeminate vacillation will not do, and the monarch, whose head has now sunk on his consort's breast, has to be roused to action. The mode changes to the warlike Phrygian, and with the words, 'Revenge, *Timotheus* cries!' (131), memorably set by Handel in 1736,[36] the poet finally introduces the stirring, martial tones of Alcaeus, which quicken the pulse and bring the ode to its high-decibel climax as Alexander, swept up by anger, hurries off to put Persepolis to the flames.

As a performance, *Alexander's Feast* exploits the full gamut of Greek lyric poetry, evoking Pindar, Anacreon, Sappho, and Alcaeus in turn. At the same time Dryden is aware of the particular nervous energy of Pindaric writing, the sense of being on a knife's edge, with lines risking a satiric inflection, brilliance teetering towards madness. Abraham Cowley famously declared that '[if] a man should undertake to translate *Pindar* word for word, it would be thought that one *Mad man* had translated *another*'.[37] The emotional ebb and flow of the scene is conveyed through a dramatic poetry that exploits the expressiveness of lyric rhythms and tonal variations. Not only is the lyric instrument a virtuoso thing in itself but it mimics the ways the human being can also be an instrument played on by the passions: 'Timotheus, to his breathing Flute, / And sounding Lyre, / Cou'd swell the Soul to rage, or kindle soft Desire' (158–60).[38]

The mechanisms of human passion were of experimental interest at this period. The Royal Society was chartered in 1662, and in an intriguing way the concerns of lyric poetry and scientific observation can be seen momentarily to coincide. The mind's responses to stimuli, and the intimate processes of action and reaction within the brain, were seen as underlying an individual's emotions, and the process naturally expressed itself through musical analogies. Describing the complex fibres of the nervous system in his ground-breaking work on the anatomy of the brain in 1664, Thomas Willis (FRS 1663) saw them as attuned like the sounding strings of the lyric instrument: 'In Sensation the Fibres receive first of all and immediately the impressions of sensible things, and *express* the same (as musical strings do the strikings of a quill or fingers) by an intrinsecal *modification* of the Particles.'[39] In explaining the intricacies of sensation Willis reaches for two of the defining concepts of the lyric art, expression and modification. For him they together form a single responsive movement. In 1699 Lord Shaftesbury developed the idea:

> It is the same with the Passions in an animal Constitution, as with the Cords or Strings of a musical Instrument ... the same degree of strength which winds up the Cords of *one*, and fits them to a Harmony and Consort, may in *another* burst both the Cords and Instrument it self. Thus men who have the liveliest and exquisitest sense, and who are in the highest degree affected with Pleasure or Pain, have need of the strongest ground ... It would be agreeable enough to inquire thus into the different *tunings* (if one may speak so) the different structures and proportions of different men, with respect to their passions ...[40]

It is possible to locate here the beginnings of a concept of Sensibility that would develop into a cultural phenomenon during the eighteenth century, but that in embryo had already found a natural home in the fine 'tunings' of lyric poetry.

Lyric poets tapped into this kind of exquisite responsiveness, and in the notion of the tuned string they were able to claim the power of their verses to express every shade of human emotion. The language of the lyre became a kind of shorthand through which to set or adjust the tone of a poem. Searching through the many odes of the 1660–1790 period, it is fascinating to discover that *strings* are, on various occasions, *sounding, tuneful, trembling, nervous, untry'd, obedient, according, plaintive, mournful, tender, sweetly-sounding, softer, swelling, vocal, indignant, bolder, nobler, martial, applausive, joyful, deep-ton'd, high-set, lighter, sympathetic, grateful, conscious, living, bounding, speaking, tinkling, undulating, twanging, dancing,* and (not least) *enchanting.* We have here the full spectrum of emotional possibilities, with the poet sometimes indicating a change of dynamics (*softer, lighter, swelling, bolder, nobler*), or a specific tone (*deep-ton'd, high-set, tinkling, twanging*), an individual character (*indignant, sympathetic, plaintive, mournful, tender, martial, joyful*), or a pronounced rhythm (*bounding, undulating, dancing*). Simply through this adjectival vocabulary it is possible to gauge how lyric poets thought of themselves as playing skilfully on an instrument and also playing on the responses of a hearer.

The ability of the lyrist simultaneously to *convey* an emotion and to *arouse* it takes us to the heart of the complex notion of expressiveness, which at this period brought the arts of poetry and music together.[41] For the influential Shaftesbury the expressive and responsive were interdependent: 'Nothing affects the Heart like that which is purely *from itself*.' For him, the term 'Men of Harmony' encompassed both poet and musician, and they were similar in their artistic powers 'in vocal Measures of Syllables, and Sounds, to express the Harmony and Numbers of an inward kind; and represent the Beautys of a human Soul, by proper Foils, and Contrarietys, which serve as Graces in this Limning, and render this Musick of the Passions more powerful and enchanting'.[42]

The 'Musick of the Passions', in which the poet becomes a composer in words, is nowhere better represented than by William Collins' ode, 'The Passions', set to music for public performance in the Sheldonian Theatre, Oxford, in 1750.[43] Collins locates his poem in the days when the human passions were in their primal state, 'When Music, Heav'nly Maid, was young, / While yet in early *Greece* she sung' (1–2), and he creates from the start an unruly scene in which the passions try to outdo each other and show off their virtuoso powers. They are adolescent and combative, each snatching their favourite instrument in turn and performing on it, as if finding a voice for the first time: 'Each, for madness ruled the hour, / Would prove his own expressive power' (15–16). But it is soon clear that there is a parallel competition for expressiveness going on in the ode, with poetry challenging music to what it can do. 'The Passions' might seem an ideal example of a poem that needs performance to be fully appreciated; and a recent recording (the first) of William Hayes' setting shows a composer who revels in every opportunity the poet has given him.[44] But throughout the piece it is words that lead the way, and music's role becomes one of brilliant translation. With his virtuosic language Collins makes a pre-emptive strike on expressiveness, and in response to the verbal challenge Hayes' music cannot avoid onomatopoeia, with every phrase, occasionally each word, being individually painted in sound. In the opening passage, for example, Collins compresses into just eight words the wide emotional range of what is to come: 'Exulting, trembling, raging, fainting' (5) is followed three lines later by 'Disturb'd, delighted, rais'd, refin'd' (8). In the score each of these words is given its own appropriate phrase where the melody trembles and faints, becomes disturbed and raised on cue. Hearing the sparkling music confirms that its inventiveness is more truly ingenuity, and its expressiveness a mode of imitation. Indeed it was this that Charles Avison criticised in his ground-breaking *Essay on Musical Expression* (1752) when he wrote disparagingly of composers who 'seem to think they have exhausted all the Depths of Expression, by a dextrous Imitation of the Meaning of a few particular Words'. For Avison this is 'trifling *Mimickry*', not true 'Expression', which lies primarily in the shaping and harmonising of a melody, avoiding pyrotechnics of performance and looking for something 'beyond the Power of Words to express'.[45]

Collins, however, revels in his verbal powers, confident that he can shift the mood instantaneously without the need for instruments.[46] He even plays tricks on any potential composer, giving him directions, challenging him to capture a complex rhythmic effect or a modulation of tone:

> Thy Numbers, *Jealousy*, to nought were fix'd,
>   Sad Proof of thy distressful State,
> Of diff'ring Themes the veering Song was mix'd,
>   And now it courted *Love*, now raving call'd on *Hate*.
>   (53–6)

The words offer a restless scenario that invites the composer to stray out of his comfort zone of form and harmony. Throughout the poem there are echoes, contrasts, modulations, mixtures, and turns. The poet is aware of the variable tuning of the passions and gives his own indications of dynamics, phrasing, etc., which are the equivalent of a composer's key and time signatures, and markings of staccato, crescendo, andante, or vivace ('the brisk awak'ning Viol' (83)). Alongside these are the stage directions, indications of movement, gesture, facial expression, and the character of the voice. Anger rushes in and 'In one rude Clash he struck the Lyre, / And swept with hurried Hand the Strings' (23–4); Despair vocalises 'a solemn, strange, and mingled Air, / 'Twas sad by fits, by Starts 'twas wild' (27–8); Hope enjoys playing with echoes: 'A soft responsive Voice was heard at ev'ry Close' (37); Revenge and Pity are brought on stage together in order to heighten the power of each ('Dejected Pity at his Side, / Her Soul-subduing Voice applied, / Yet still He kept his wild unalter'd Mien, / While each strain'd Ball of Sight seem'd bursting from his Head' (49–52)).

In this way the ode employs what Shaftesbury refers to as expressive 'Foils, and Contrarietys'. This is evident also in the move from Pale Melancholy to her contrary Chearfulness. Collins envisages this dramatic change of mood at the centre of his poem as being carried by a single instrument, the horn, which alters its character from the Penseroso figure, who 'pour'd thro' the mellow Horn her pensive Soul' (61) to the Allegro of the bus-kined huntress Chearfulness, who 'blew an inspiring Air, that Dale and Thicket rung' (73).[47]

The combination of expressive features in Collins' ode can be seen in Melancholy's scene:

> With Eyes up-rais'd, as one inspir'd,
> Pale *Melancholy* sate retir'd,
> And from her wild sequester'd Seat,
> In Notes by Distance made more sweet,
> Pour'd thro' the mellow *Horn* her pensive Soul:
>> And dashing soft from Rocks around,
>> Bubbling Runnels join'd the Sound;
> Thro' Glades and Glooms the mingled Measure stole,
>> Or o'er some haunted Stream with fond Delay,
>>> Round an holy Calm diffusing,
>>> Love of Peace, and lonely Musing,
>> In hollow Murmurs died away.
>
> (57–68)

Collins's word-music goes beyond onomatopoeia to explore the possibilities for mingling different elements of his scene. Aware of the visionary tradition of melancholy, he thinks spatially, imagining a far-off horn combining sadness and sweetness; then closer at hand he hears the lively stream *dashing soft*, with the rocks softening the water into playful 'bubbling Runnels' and giving a new timbre to his subtle orchestration of nature. With the words *join'd*, *mingled*, and *diffusing* Collins imagines sinuous interwoven harmonies blending together elements of the furtive (*stole*) and the ghost-like (*haunted*), then moving to calmness, loneliness, and finally slipping into tenuous *hollow Murmurs* that *die away* to nothing (as they do in Hayes' extraordinarily responsive setting). What comes across is Collins' sensitive conducting of the performance, varying the mood, tone, and tempi, and shaping the material into an emotional architecture.

A poet's own lyric performance could in that way use modulated tones and eloquent phrasing to animate the writing – almost literally. A well turned line of verse could be shaped into an air or melody that took on the qualities almost of a human breath. One of the most advanced musical theorists of his age, Roger North, advised performers to 'Learn to fill, and soften a sound … so as to be like a gust of wind, which begins with a soft air, and fills by degrees to a strength as makes all bend, and then softens away again into a temper, and so vanish.'[48] This heightened sense of lyrical phrasing was something else that brought music and poetry together. The young Alexander Pope, in his 'Ode for Musick' (c. 1708), seems to be striving for an expressive effect of just this kind:

> Hark! the Numbers, soft and clear,
> Gently steal upon the Ear;
> Now louder, and yet louder rise,
> And fill with spreading Sounds the Skies;
> Exulting in Triumph now swell the bold Notes,
> In broken Air, trembling, the wild Musick floats;
> Till, by degrees, remote and small,
> The Strains decay,
> And melt away
> In a dying, dying Fall.[49]

Pope is confident of his ability to express emotions through metrical variation, slipping from iambic into the anapaestic and then to a final echoing trochee. He is like a conductor guiding the orchestra over a single sweeping arc of sound: in only ten lines his numbers steal, rise, fill, spread, exult, swell, break, tremble, float, decay, melt, and die.

Roger North's comparison of the expressive phrasing of a musical performance to a gust of wind swelling and subsiding conveys how the lyric art, in the hands of skilled poets like Pope and Collins, could mimic the dynamics of Nature. It was an idea taken to an extreme by Anne Finch in her ambitious irregular ode, 'Upon the Hurricane'.[50] Her subject is the Great Storm of November 1703, when southern England was ravaged by hurricane-force winds not matched again till 1987. In Finch's vision the storm is also a reminder of God's power to destroy, and a terrible warning to the British nation – the culmination of sixty years of bad faith and disturbance in the State. The poem is packed with cameos of accidental death, of sudden shifts in fortune, elemental uncertainties, and suspensions of the laws of Nature:

> All Rules of Conduct laid aside,
> No more the baffl'd *Pilot* steers,
> Or knows an Art, when it each moment veers,
> To vary with the Winds, or stem th'unusual Tide.
> Dispers'd and loose, the shatter'd Vessels stray …
>   (263–7)

In Finch's disturbing poem the storm challenges human *Art*. Both the perplexed mariner and the poet are confronting an experience of Nature that seems to make no coherent sense. In response, the lyric art becomes one of veering and varying, unpredictably pulling, loosening its hold on the lines. The fluid dynamics animate the scenes of destruction, not by way of mimicry (sound echoing sense) but as the reaction of the poem itself, its consciousness of how things can unpredictably turn, slip, fall. The shock of this elemental instability is reflected in the unstable elements of the irregular Pindaric. Finch offers an expressive lyric 'now' in which nothing is directed and certain. The elements of the verse become almost instrumental, conveying the remarkable power of mere weightless air, once set in motion, to convulse and destroy:

> Now find, that even the lightest Things,
> As the minuter parts of Air,
> When Number to their Weight addition brings,
> Can, like the small, but numerous Insects Stings,
> Can, like th'assembl'd Winds, urge Ruin and Despair.
> (182–6)

There is a sense in which the metre ('Number'?) has become part of the impetus of the storm with its bluster and unpredictable gusting and swirling. Solid words collapse by their own weight ('Now down at once comes the superfluous Load' (73)). Throughout 'Upon the Hurricane' the verse weighs things in its own terms, and has a capacity to turn things round, turn heavy to light, as if the character of the verse itself is challenging the foundations of law and regularity: 'Thus! have thy Cedars, *Libanus*, been struck / As the lythe Oziers twisted round' (51–2). Huge solid trunks become basket willow. Things are torn from their moorings, wrenched away from their foundations ('that awful Fabrick bow'd, / Sliding from its loosen'd Bands' (102–3)). The Almighty has spoken in the whirlwind, and as the lines stretch, turn, and break, the poet is finding her own lyric equivalent of '[t]hese furious Shocks of hurrying Air' (46).

In a telling allusion to the language of lyric inspiration, the music is here anarchic and jarring. The unruly winds have become a discordant ensemble:

> And in the loud tumultuous Jar
> Winds their own Fifes, and Clarions are.
> Each Cavity, which Art or Nature leaves,
> Their Inspiration hastily receives;
> Whence, from their various Forms and Size,
> As various Symphonies arise,
> Their trumpet ev'ry hollow Tube is made …
> (130–6)

Behind the tumult of the hurricane is the anarchic noise of civil discord. We sense the bitter tone here as Finch sees how fissures in the state have been widened and exploited by unruly elements. Every empty vessel has a noise to make, the hollower the noisier, all disturbing the peace and stirring up contention.[51] The passage mimics a badly performed St Cecilia ode: it is an extraordinary performance, like an ill-disciplined school rehearsal for the Last Day. In Finch's ode the language of modulation and transposition has slipped towards anarchy.

'Upon the Hurricane' shows how the lyric winds could change, and a reader of that ambitious and striking poem would immediately realise that if it was set to music it would not make the sound an audience would enjoy. The poetry reaches for a music never yet heard. It shows how far the expressive range of lyric might stretch, and how a modern poet could offer a performance that, simply through words on the page and its own tumultuous silent music, taps into the expressive power of the ancient lyric tradition.[52] Here it merges with the inspired music of the Psalmist, in which the passionate human voice is swept up into the voice of the Lord.[53] That sacred tradition demands its own story; but its elements of praise and prophecy are not discontinuous with the Greek lyric achievement. Whether writing for musical setting or not, poets of the 1660–1750 period drew on the imagined music of the ancient lyre, and they found in the voices of the Classical tradition a tonal and emotional range that encouraged them to be expressive and adaptable. The poets exploited the ability to move between modes, and achieve subtle, varied, and eloquent effects. They exploited turns and modulations, appreciating the fluid handling of tempo, dynamics, and rhythm to capture changing moods, sometimes for quite dramatic effect.

Choosing the lyric instrument involved testing oneself in performance against a range of poets who between them had shown the full scope of the lyre; and the idea of competitive performance was still there, whether in Akenside's *alpha* lyrists, or Collins' wrangling passions. The old music may have been lost, but the poets found fresh opportunities in the baroque ensemble of their own time, and in new writings on science and aesthetics, which saw links between the strings of an instrument and the mechanisms of the human mind. Even when poets offered texts for musical setting they did so in a challenging spirit, seeing what their words could do by way of expressive melody, modulation, and tone, and even to some degree pre-empting the composer. The poets could discover their own 'musicality' without waiting for musicians to bring their words to life.

Notes

1 Text from the earliest printed edition, John Oldham, *A Second Musical Entertainment Perform'd on St. Cecilia's day. November XXII. 1684* (London: John Playford, 1685). The 22 November celebrations, featuring the performance of an ode set for instruments, soloists, and chorus (i.e., members of the royal violin band, the Private Musick, and the Chapel Royal, sometimes augmented with male singers attached to the London theatres), were organised by the Musical Society of London, and held regularly until 1700. See David Hopkins, 'The London Odes on St Cecilia's Day for 1686, 1695, and 1696', *Review of English Studies* 45 (1994), 486–95; and Giovanni Battista Draghi, *From Harmony, from Heav'nly Harmony: A Song for St Cecilia's Day, 1687*, ed. Bryan White, Purcell Society Companion Series 3 (London: Stainer and Bell, 2010), pp. ix–xvii.

2 Oldham's commissioned ode was set to music by John Blow (1649–1708), scored for four-part strings, continuo, soloists (countertenor, tenor, bass), and chorus (with boy trebles). The first performance almost certainly included a theorbo (long-necked lute), but no flute. I am grateful to Dr Bryan White of the School of Music, University of Leeds, for his help and advice with this chapter.

3 See Gretchen L. Finney, 'Ecstasy and Music in Seventeenth-Century England', *Journal of the History of Ideas* 8 (1947), 153–86.

4 For a perceptive analysis of the engagement of verbal with musical elements of the St Cecilia odes of Dryden and Pope, see Clifford Ames, 'Variations on a Theme: Baroque and Neoclassical Aesthetics in the St Cecilia Day Odes of Dryden and Pope', *ELH* 65.3 (1998), 617–35.

5 The general reader was familiar with the etymology: Chambers' *Cyclopædia* from its first edition in 1728 defined *lyric* as 'something sung, or play'd on the Lyre or Harp', and added: 'The Word is particularly applied to the antient Odes and Stanza's; which answer to our Airs or Tunes, and may be play'd on Instruments' (Ephraim Chambers, *Cyclopædia; or, An Universal Dictionary of Arts and Sciences*, 2 vols. (London, 1728), Vol. II, p. 477, s.v. 'Lyric').

6 For a discussion of the creative use of contrasting lyric modes in the lyric and satiric poetry of the 1660–1740 period, see David Fairer, '"Love was in the next Degree": Lyric, Satire, and Inventive Modulation', *Journal for Eighteenth-Century Studies* 34 (2011), 147–66. The essay develops further some of the points made here.

7 On the playing technique of the Greek lyre, see M. L. West, *Ancient Greek Music* (Oxford: Clarendon Press, 1992), pp. 64–70 (the quotation is on p. 68). My account is indebted to West's discussion.

8 On the scales and modes of ancient Greek music, see West, *Ancient Greek Music*, pp. 160–89. The classic study of the modes is D. B. Monro, *The Modes of Ancient Greek Music* (Oxford: Clarendon Press, 1894). See also W. R. Johnson, *The Idea of Lyric: Lyric Modes in Ancient and Modern Poetry* (Berkeley: University of California Press, 1982). Dryden's use of the Greek modes in 'A Song for St Cecilia's Day, 1687' is shown by Douglas Murray, 'The Musical Structure of Dryden's "Song for St Cecilia's Day",' *Eighteenth-Century Studies* 10.3 (Spring 1977), 326–34.

9   See West, *Ancient Greek Music*, p. 164. Dionysius of Helicarnassus wrote that 'The dithyrambic poets used to change the *modes* also, introducing Dorian and Phrygian and Lydian modes in the same song; and they varied the melodies, making them now enharmonic, now chromatic, now diatonic; and in the rhythms they showed the boldest independence' (Dionysius of Helicarnassus, *On Literary Composition*, ed. W. Rhys Roberts (London: Macmillan, 1910), Chapter 19, p. 197).

10 On Timotheus and the 'new music' (late fifth century BCE), see Andrew Barker, *Greek Musical Writings*, 2 vols., Vol. i: *The Musician and His Art* (Cambridge University Press, 1984), pp. 96–8; West, *Ancient Greek Music*, pp. 361–4; and Timotheus of Miletus, *The Fragments of Timotheus of Miletus*, ed. J. H. Hordern (Oxford University Press, 2002), pp. 7–8. A public performance by Timotheus is reconstructed by John Herington, *Poetry into Drama: Early Tragedy and the Greek Poetic Tradition* (Berkeley: University of California Press, 1985), pp. 151–60.

11 See Barker, *Greek Musical Writings*, Vol. 1, pp. 205–49. In Plutarch the primal link between the lyre and lyric poetry is emphasised: '*Amphion* … was the first that invented playing on the Harp and Lyric Poesie' (*Plutarch's Morals: Translated from the Greek by Several Hands*, 5 vols., 4th edn (London: Thomas Braddyll, 1704), Vol. 1, p. 99).

12 The etymology of a mental 'mood' is of course from the Germanic *mod* (*Oxford English Dictionary*, s.v. 'Mood', sb.1), not from *modus*. See below, n. 27.

13 Charles Butler, *The Principles of Musik* (London: John Haviland, 1636), p. 2. A later example is John Playford's much reprinted work, *An Introduction to the Skill of Musick* (London, 1654), pp. 17–20, where he describes the 'five Græcian Moods' and their different musical characters.

14 'S. B.', 'Preface' to *Anacreon Done into English Out of the Original Greek* (Oxford: L. Lichfield, 1683), sig. A2^v.

15 Chambers, *Cyclopædia*, Vol. ii, p. 935, s.v. 'Quantity'.

16 Daniel Webb, *Observations on the Correspondence between Poetry and Music* (London: J. Dodsley, 1769), p. 54.

17   John Hughes, *The House of Nassau: A Pindarick Ode* (London: D. Brown and A. Bell, 1702), p. 7. A more modest gesture could be awkward too: 'I quit my Needle, string my Lyre, / And boldly dare the mighty Theme' (Jane Brereton, 'To the Author of the foregoing Verses', in *Poems on Several Occasions by Mrs Jane Brereton* (London: Edw. Cave, 1744), p. 24).

18 Johnson's *Dictionary* (1755) defines the *adjective* 'Lyrick' as 'Pertaining to an harp, or to odes or poetry sung to an harp', whereas the *noun* 'Lyrick' is simply 'a poet who writes songs to the harp'. But 'Lyrick', meaning 'lyric poem', occurs in John Gay's *The Shepherd's Week* (1714; see *Oxford English Dictionary*, s.v. 'Lyric', *n*. 3), an instance Johnson overlooked.

19 James Thomson, *Liberty, A Poem*, Part 2, lines 289–90. James Thomson, *Liberty, the Castle of Indolence, and Other Poems*, ed. James Sambrook (Oxford: Clarendon Press, 1986), p. 65.

20 Horace, *Epistles*, 2.2.84–6, trans. Philip Francis, in *A Poetical Translation of the Works of Horace*, 4 vols., 2nd edn (London: A. Millar, 1747), Vol. IV, p. 195.

21 A full canon of nine lyric poets, including these four, was established by the Alexandrian critics during the Hellenistic age. The additional five were Alcman, Stesichorus, Ibycus, Simonides, and Bacchylides, none of whose works were known in the eighteenth century beyond scattered fragments.

22 Mark Akenside, *Poetical Works of Mark Akenside*, ed. Robin Dix (Madison and Teaneck: Fairleigh Dickinson University Press; London: Associated University Presses, 1996), pp. 284–9. The poem was first published as the final item in Akenside's *Odes on Several Subjects* (London: R. Dodsley, 1745), pp. 39–44.

23 Anacreon's texts survive only in fragments, and until the nineteenth century 'Anacreon' tends to mean the *Anacreontéa*, a collection of short poems on love and joviality dating from centuries later and written in his style. See Stuart Gillespie, 'The *Anacreontea* in English: A Checklist of Translations to 1900 with a Bibliography of Secondary Sources and Some Previously Unpublished Translations', *Translation and Literature* 11 (2002), 149–173; and Patricia A. Rosenmeyer, *The Poetics of Imitation: Anacreon and the Anacreontic Tradition* (Cambridge University Press, 1992).

24 Alcaeus' eighteenth-century reputation rested on the celebrated freedom hymn, 'In a myrtle branch I will carry my sword', which was erroneously attributed to him at this period. See Thomas Gray, William Collins, and Oliver Goldsmith, *The Poems*, ed.Roger Lonsdale (London: Longman, 1969), pp. 442–3.

25 Akenside, 'Ode on Lyric Poetry', 75–6.

26 Horace, *Odes*, II.1.40 ; *Epistles*, II.2.143.

27 *Oxford English Dictionary*, s.v. 'Mode', sb. See n. 12 above.

28 Charles Batteux, *A Course of the Belles Lettres; or, The Principles of Literature*, 4 vols. (London: B. Law, etc., 1761), Vol. III, p. 42.

29 Speaking of Horace's lyric skill, Dryden remarks that 'there is nothing so delicately turn'd in all the Roman Language' (Preface to *Sylvæ; or, The Second Part of Poetical Miscellanies* (London: Tonson, 1685), sig. A6^v).

30 *Alexander's Feast* was first performed on 22 November 1697 to the music (now lost) of Jeremiah Clarke. For a full account of the poem with detailed notes, see John Dryden, *The Poems of John Dryden*, Vol. 5, ed. Paul Hammond and David Hopkins. (Harlow: Longman, 2005), pp. 3–18.

31 Dryden, *Alexander's Feast*, 22–3. John Dryden, *The Poems and Fables of John Dryden*, ed. James Kinsley (London: Oxford University Press, 1962), p. 504. All quotations from Dryden are from this edition.

32 Dryden's Timotheus is a conflation of two figures of that name who had become identified: Alexander the Great's flute-player, and the fourth-century citharode Timotheus, famed for his wild lyric performances (see n. 10 above). See Dryden, *Poems*, ed. Hammond and Hopkins, pp. 6–7.

33 Pindar, Fifth Isthmian Ode, lines 8, 14–16, in *The Odes of Pindar*, trans. Maurice Bowra (Harmondsworth: Penguin, 1969), p. 47. See David A.

Campbell, *The Golden Lyre: The Themes of the Greek Lyric Poets* (London: Duckworth, 1983), pp. 242–8.

34 See Simon Goldhill, *The Poet's Voice: Essays on Poetics and Greek Literature* (Cambridge University Press, 1991), pp. 135–41.

35 As reported in the *London Gazette* for 13 December 1697. I am grateful to Bryan White for this information.

36 Handel's setting of *Alexander's Feast* was first performed at Covent Garden, 19 February 1736.

37 Abraham Cowley, preface to *Pindarique Odes* (London, 1668).

38 On the long tradition of music's power to raise and quell the passions, see John Hollander, *The Untuning of the Sky: Ideas of Music in English Poetry 1500–1700* (Princeton University Press, 1961), pp. 162–244.

39 Thomas Willis, *Cerebri anatome, cui accessit Nervorum descriptio et usus* (1664); English translation ('by S. P. Esq.') in *Dr Willis's Practice of Physick, Being All the Medical Works of That Renowned and Famous Physician* (London: T. Dring, etc., 1681), p. 128 ('The Anatomy of the Brain'; my italics).

40 Anthony Ashley Cooper, third earl of Shaftesbury, *An Inquiry Concerning Virtue* (London: A. Bell, etc., 1699), pp. 97–8.

41 In his cognitive analysis of musical expression, Peter Kivy distinguishes between 'to express' and 'to be expressive of'. He offers, he says, 'an account of how it is that music can be expressive of the emotions … not a theory of how music can express them'. He therefore maintains that 'sadness is a quality of the music, not a power of the music to do things to the listener' (*The Corded Shell: Reflections on Musical Expression* (Princeton University Press, 1980), pp. 14, 23).

42 Shaftesbury adds: 'Let Poets, or the Men of Harmony, deny, if they can, this Force of *Nature*, or withstand this *moral Magick*' (Anthony Ashley Cooper, third earl of Shaftesbury, 'An Essay on the Freedom of Wit and Humour', in his *Characteristicks of Men, Manners, Opinions, Times*, 3 vols. (London, 1711), Vol. I, pp. 135–7).

43 Collins' 'The Passions' was published in his *Odes* (1747) and first performed as part of the annual Oxford Encaenia celebrations on 2 July 1750, to the music of William Hayes (1708–77), the University's Professor of Music. See Gray, Collins, and Goldsmith, *Poems*, pp. 477–85. For a detailed discussion of 'The Passions' see Richard Wendorf, *William Collins and Eighteenth-Century English Poetry* (Minneapolis: University of Minnesota Press, 1981), pp. 135–54. Wendorf sees Collins' volume of *Odes* as organised on 'a principle of diversity and modulation' (p. 105).

44 Performed by Schola Cantorum Basiliensis and La Cetra Barokorchester, Basel, dir. Anthony Rooley (Glossa, 2010).

45 Charles Avison, *An Essay on Musical Expression* (London: C. Davis, 1752), pp. 59, 90, 3. William Hayes responded with his *Remarks on Mr Avison's Essay* (1753), which drew a further reply from Avison. See Charles Avison and William Hayes, *Charles Avison's Essay on Musical Expression, with Related Writings by William Hayes and Charles Avison*, ed. Pierre Dubois (Aldershot and Burlington, VT: Ashgate, 2004).

46 Collins did not write his ode for Hayes to set and was not present at the Oxford performance, news of which came to him second-hand. In a letter of thanks Collins told Hayes: 'I have another more perfect copy of the Ode; which, had I known your obliging design, I would have communicated to you'; William Seward, *Anecdotes of Distinguished Persons*, 3 vols. (London: Cadell and Davies, 1798), Vol. II, pp. 384–5.

47 A contrast well caught by Hayes. On the early development of the horn and its versatility, see Henry Raynor, *The Orchestra: A History* (New York: Scribner's, 1978), pp. 29–30.

48 North was the author of *The Musicall Grammarian and Theory of Sounds* (1728), which has been edited, with introduction and notes, by Mary Chan and Jamie C. Kassler (Cambridge University Press, 1990). The advice, from his *Autobiography*, is quoted by Robert Donington, *A Performer's Guide to Baroque Music* (London and Boston, MA: Faber and Faber, 1973), p. 292.

49 'Ode for Musick', lines 12–20, in Alexander Pope, *The Poems of Alexander Pope*, ed. John Butt (London: Methuen, 1963), p. 139. Pope's ode seems not to have been set to music until 1730, when Maurice Greene's setting was performed at the official opening of the new Senate House in Cambridge on 6 July.

50 First published in Anne Finch, *Miscellany Poems* (London, 1713), pp. 230–47. It is included in *Eighteenth-Century Poetry: An Annotated Anthology*, ed. David Fairer and Christine Gerrard, 2nd edn (Oxford: Blackwell, 2004), pp. 26–33.

51 Cf. the imagery of Aeolist 'inspiration' in Jonathan Swift's *A Tale of a Tub* (1704), Section 8.

52 Thomas Gray's ode 'The Progress of Poesy' (1757), charts the tradition of the Greek 'lyre divine', culminating in himself. See Marcus Walsh's chapter in this volume (pp. 112–34). For a concise discussion of how eighteenth-century lyric poets thought of themselves as continuing the ancient tradition, see Dustin Griffin, *Patriotism and Poetry in Eighteenth-Century Britain* (Cambridge University Press, 2002), pp. 63–7.

53 In Finch's *Miscellany Poems*, the ode 'Upon the Hurricane' is immediately followed by a paraphrase of Psalm 148 ('Winds and Storms fulfilling his Word'). On Smart's *A Song to David*, see Marcus Walsh's chapter, pp. 124–6.

CHAPTER SIX

Eighteenth-century high lyric
William Collins and Christopher Smart

Marcus Walsh

Lyric has always been a fluid and evolving genre, and a variable set of practices. Eighteenth-century conceptions, taxonomies, and hierarchies of lyric are no doubt at least as various as those of any other period, and as unfamiliar to a modern reader. David Fairer's chapter has already pointed out the compelling taxonomy of Greek lyric models set out in Mark Akenside's 'Ode on Lyric Poetry' (1745): the convivial Anacreontic, the patriotic Alcaic, the erotic Sapphic, the sublime Pindaric (p. 96). Such lyric exercises thronged the eighteenth-century magazines. Other forms used by eighteenth-century British lyric poets included, especially, the Horatian, and (most voluminously and vitally) the Christian hymn, which itself derived from centuries of English Psalm versification. Some at least of these distinct lyric practices, the Pindaric in particular, were underwritten by their own sophisticated theoretics. There was not, however, and there could not have been, a theory of the lyric as a unified genre. Some eighteenth-century lyric sub-genres, the hymn most notably, would flourish and continue. Many, including the eighteenth century's flagship lyric form, the Pindaric ode, did not outlive their moment. Some of the most significant later lyric forms were barely conceived by the eighteenth century. The extended Romantic nature lyric, dependent on a subjective epistemology, did not exist at all. In this chapter I shall focus on a generic tendency associated with the circumstances and pressures of a particular literary historical moment: the attempt in the middle decades of the century to find, in ancient Classical and Hebrew poetry, and in some more recent English forms and modes, a credible way of writing an imaginative high lyric poetry that might assume a prominent position in the national literary culture.

It is a familiar truism that at the death of Alexander Pope in 1744 a younger generation of poets sought not merely to rival his achievement, but to turn poetry into new formal and generic channels, away from the moral and satiric modes considered characteristic of Pope, and towards a poetry of imagination and natural description. One of the best known and most representative statements of that ambition, and the anxieties associated with it, was made by Joseph Warton in the prefatory Advertisement to his *Odes on Various Subjects* (December 1746). Insisting that 'Invention and Imagination' are 'the chief faculties of a Poet', Warton complained: 'The Public has been so much accustom'd of late to didactic Poetry alone, and Essays on moral Subjects, that any work where the imagination is much indulged, will perhaps not be relished or regarded. The author therefore of these pieces is in some pain least certain austere critics should think them too fanciful and descriptive.'[1] In seeking adequate form for a modern poetry of imagination, Warton turned to the high lyric, more specifically the ode. He was one of a number of poets of his moment to do so. Mark Akenside's *Odes on Several Subjects* had already appeared in 1745. The *Odes on Several Descriptive and Allegoric Subjects* of William Collins would be published a mere fortnight after Warton's *Odes*, and were clearly driven at least in part by the same ambitions. Thomas Gray's Pindaric 'sister odes', 'The Progress of Poesy' and 'The Bard', followed in 1757, in *Odes by Mr. Gray*. Christopher Smart, a more needy and a more prolific poet than any of these, explored the possibilities of the ode throughout his career, from the 1740s onwards. This concerted attempt to reconstitute the high lyric as a leading genre for British poetry involved a variety of developments and experiments, not always successful or coherent, in lyric form, figure, method, and language. I shall explore some of the formal, figurative, and epistemological tendencies and possibilities of the printed ode in the mid eighteenth century, but I shall focus on two odes that exploit and develop those tendencies and possibilities in remarkable and distinct ways: Collins' 'Ode on the Poetical Character' (published in his *Odes* in 1746), and Smart's *A Song to David* (1765).

Powerful authority and vital formal models were available, for writers of the high lyric in the seventeenth and eighteenth centuries, in the writings of the Greeks especially. Plato permitted in his ideal state only hymns and encomia, poems in praise of gods and famous men; Aristotle specified these two forms of poetry as the first serious poetical kinds.[2] The epideictic ode praises, celebrates, and commemorates gods and heroes. It belonged with the epic at the highest point of the hierarchy of genres. The chief practitioner of the epideictic ode in Greek antiquity was Pindar, whose Olympian and Pythian odes, using for the most part an elaborate, repeated tripartite structure of strophe, antistrophe, and epode, are characterised by a rhetoric of amplification and sublimity, by metrical boldness and suddenness of transition. The vogue for the Pindaric ode was established in England by Abraham Cowley's *Pindarique Odes* (1656). Cowley characterised the form as obscure, daring, metaphorical: 'The digressions are many, and sudden, and sometimes long … The figures are unusual and bold, even to *Temeritie* … the *Numbers* are various and irregular.'[3] Though Cowley himself was aware of the regularity of Pindar's measures, his own odes are variable and unpredictable in line length, rhyme pattern, and stanza form. His powerful practical example, and the nearly simultaneous rediscovery of Longinus and the Longinian sublime, gave rise to a vogue that produced at least in John Dryden's hands some of the late seventeenth century's greatest lyric verse: the ode to the memory of Anne Killigrew (1686), 'A Song for St Cecilia's Day' (1687), and *Alexander's Feast* (1697). In the eighteenth century much 'lax and lawless versification' (to use Samuel Johnson's phrase) was licensed by the Cowleian example of 'Pindars unnavigable song'. However, a broader awareness of the regularity of Pindar's regular form had been early established by William Congreve's 'Discourse on the Pindaric Ode', prefaced to *A Pindaric Ode, Humbly Offered to the Queen* (1706). Congreve's poem should be read, he claimed, as 'an attempt towards restoring the regularity of the ancient lyric poetry … there is nothing more regular than the odes of Pindar, both as to the exact observation of the members and numbers of his stanzas and verses, and the perpetual coherence of his thoughts'.[4] Later writers of high lyric followed Congreve's pursuit of regularity either by adopting the strict Pindaric triad of strophe, counter-strophe and epode (as in Collins' 'Ode on the Poetical Character' and Gray's 'The Bard' and 'Progress of Poesy'), or by turning to monostrophic forms. Unlike the triadic ode, the monostrophic ode has no inherent formal principle, and poets who employed the form addressed that problem by such means as mid-point symmetry (in Gray's 'Ode on the Spring' (1748) and *Ode on a Distant Prospect of Eton College* (1747)), or by the use of balanced blocks of stanzas (in Gray's *Elegy Written in a Country Churchyard* (1751) and, more elaborately, in Smart's *Song to David*).[5]

The eighteenth-century high ode, amongst other characterising linguistic and rhetorical features, was regularly distinguished by prosopopoeia (more simply but less significantly, 'personification'), a figure of speech that would seem undesirable to Romantic writers, and which has been perceived by modern readers as both artificial and alien.[6] It was not, however, a mere historical poetic aberration. It emerged as poets began to turn to the models provided by *L'Allegro* and *Il Penseroso*, poems in which Milton was understood to have 'personified almost every object in his view, raised a great number of pleasing images, and introduced qualities and things inanimate as living and rational beings'.[7] William Collins and his near contemporaries recognised prosopopoeia both in theory and in practice as one of the most powerful of resources, in terms of emotional power, representational effectiveness, and mythopoeic creativity. Prosopopoeia was especially associated with strong feeling. 'Personification is natural to the human mind', James Beattie would write; 'some violent passions are peculiarly inclined to change things into persons'.[8] It was seen as having a particularly powerful mimetic effect, appealing to the sight – that sense understood by Addison, and almost all his theorising successors, to be imaginatively most effective. It was thought of as equivalent to such visually representative forms as medals, history paintings, and sculpture. Henry Home, Lord Kames (1696–1782) insisted that 'an allegory' (he uses the word here, as many did, as a synonym for personification) 'is in every respect similar to an hieroglyphical painting, excepting only, that words are used instead of colours. Their effects are precisely the same … The representative subject is described; and it is by resemblance that we are enabled to apply the description to the subject represented.'[9] The visually mimetic effect of personification was thought to give it an inherent emotional power. As Beattie insisted, in the course of his discussion of the figure, the keenness of our emotions 'is in proportion to the vivacity of the perceptions that excite them. Distress that we see is more affecting than what we only hear of … Of descriptions addressed to the fancy, those that are most vivid and picturesque will generally be found to have the most powerful influence over our affections.'[10] Personification, conceived as prosopopoeia, was a figure that, for those who admired its use by such forerunners as Spenser and Milton, as well as those who employed it poetically, allowed scope not only for convincing and affective mimesis, but also for the imagination, the fiction-making power. John Hughes, pioneering editor of Spenser, speaks of this in terms that, in invoking a divine or quasi-divine power for the poet as maker, echo Philip Sidney's *Apology for Poetry*:

> in Works of this kind there is a large Field open to Invention, which among the Ancients was universally look'd upon to be the principal Part of Poetry. The Power of raising Images or Resemblances of things, giving them Life and Action, and presenting them as it were before the Eyes, was thought to have something in it like Creation.[11]

The title of William Collins' *Odes on Several Descriptive and Allegoric Subjects* makes clear his claim to both the prosopopoeic and the mimetic aspects of personification, daring the 'austere critics' to think his new lyrics, as Joseph Warton had done in the Advertisement to his own *Odes*, 'too fanciful and too descriptive'. Certainly the great majority of Collins' odes are insistently descriptive, exploiting the specifically pictorial and mimetic. Some of the odes in the collection, notably 'The Manners' and 'The Passions', narrate pageants or dramas enacted by personified human emotions as they function in the musical, dramatic, and literary arts. The characters of 'The Manners' include Humour, recognisable from 'The comic sock that binds thy feet!', and 'young-eyed healthful Wit', wearing 'jewels in his crispèd hair'.[12] Some of the odes apostrophise the passions, as features of imaginative literature. So, Fear is addressed as

> Thou, to whom the world unknown
> With all its shadowy shapes is shown;
> Who see'st appalled the unreal scene,
> While Fancy lifts the veil between.
>   ('Ode to Fear', 1–4)

These visual personifications are generally presented as vignettes, not in full detail, but with brief characterising physical attributes such as the 'red arm, exposed and bare' of Vengeance, or with single identifying properties, such as the 'Attic robe' of the 'decent maid' Simplicity. Collins' use of such brief visual clues was a normal technique in his time, and the picture-forming faculty of eighteenth-century readers was evidently equal to such elided depictions.[13]

Though Collins used so extensively a rhetorical mode that was understood to exploit the affective power of the visual, these are poems about the depiction of feeling, not poems expressive of feeling. They are poems primarily about poetics. Fear and pity are discussed not as emotions in themselves, but as the emotions aroused and purged by *catharsis* according to the tragic theory of Aristotle, whose *Poetics* Collins evidently knew sufficiently well.[14] The 'Ode to Pity' celebrates Euripides and Otway; the 'Ode to Fear' Aeschylus, Sophocles, and Shakespeare. The 'Ode to Simplicity' identifies Simplicity as a specifically literary property:

> Though taste, though genius bless
> To some divine excess,
> Faints the cold work till thou inspire the whole.
>   (43–5)

In these odes Collins is less a poet of sensibility than a student of the mechanisms and uses of poetic affect. If personification represents in these poems the powerful emotional states and transitions that writing can evoke, the use of the figure is not itself the product of psychic distress. The 'Ode to Fear', like other odes, is written in the first person:

> I know thy hurried step, thy haggard eye!
> Like thee I start, like thee disordered fly.
>
> (7–8)

That first person, however, is that of the thinking poet, not an expressive and historical individual William Collins.[15]

Amongst Collins' odes on poetry and poetics, the 'Ode on the Poetical Character', while certainly embodying some of the same positions and employing some of the same methodologies, stands out in its formal originality, intellectual ambition, figurative complexity, and mythopoeic aspirations. This short Pindaric ode presents an extraordinary allegory that appeals to Spenser and Milton as poetic models, associates the inauguration of imaginative art with God's primal act of creation, and concludes with a declaration that poetic vision and prophecy are gifts no longer available to the modern poet. It is both a major and original creative achievement and a major work of theory, at the same time articulating and exemplifying Collins' visionary poetics.

The opening strophe of the 'Ode on the Poetical Character' works through a simile, which is figurative on both sides of the comparison. On one side is the girdle of chastity described and competed for in *The Faerie Queene*:

> That girdle gave the virtue of chaste loue,
> And wiuehood true, to all that did it beare;
> But whosoeuer contrarie doth proue,
> Might not the same about her middle weare,
> But it would loose, or else a sunder teare.

Spenser's summary of the competition for the emblematic girdle identifies the true Florimel as its one fit wearer, though at the competition itself the chaste Amoret is the only lady it fits.[16] For this idea of the magical girdle of chastity Collins invents an equivalent, providing the other side of his simile: that the gift of poetic creativity, 'the cest of amplest power', was given to a personified Fancy, who

> To few the godlike gift assigns
> To gird their blest prophetic loins,
> And gaze her visions wild …
> ('Ode on the Poetical Character', 20–2)

In the second part of the ode, structured unconventionally as a mesode, Collins invents a myth of the origin of Fancy's magical band.[17] The myth figuratively combines biblical creation account, Spenserian 'fairy legend',

and the Greek pantheon. Fancy, the 'loved Enthusiast', is seated alone with
God at the creation. 'The sainted growing woof' takes shape as God calls
into being earth, sky, and sun ('thou rich-haired youth of morn', a personification of the sun that resonates with an imagery associated with the
poet-god Phoebus Apollo).[18] The weaving of Fancy's cestus is attended by
personifications of qualities associated with ideal poetry, 'ecstatic Wonder',
'Truth, in sunny vest arrayed', and the intellectual and imaginative 'powers', whose intertwinings mimic the band's texture:

> All the shadowy tribes of Mind
> In braided dance their murmurs joined.
>
> (47–8)

'[T]he shadowy tribes of Mind' is itself a brilliant poetic phrase for the
intellectual personifications that enact this ode's allegoric drama. The
mesode concludes with a question that brings us back to the privileged
and exclusive nature of the cest of poetic fancy mooted in the opening
strophe:

> Where is the bard, whose soul can now
> Its high presuming hopes avow?
> Where he who thinks, with rapture blind,
> This hallowed work for him designed?
>
> (51–4)

This extraordinary prosopopoeic pageant has generally been perceived as
the most troubling section of the poem.[19] Anna Laetitia Barbauld, in the
course of a brilliant Prefatory Essay to Collins' poems, complains that:

> it is difficult to reduce to any thing like a meaning this strange and by
> no means reverential fiction concerning the Divine Being. Probably the
> obscure idea that floated in the mind of the Author was this, that true
> Poetry being a representation of Nature, must have its archetype in those
> ideas of the supreme mind, which originally gave birth to Nature.[20]

Barbauld here recognises both the allegorical and the mimetic in the mesode. Her objection is to the impertinence of the construction of a complicated and obscure metaphoric fiction around God's divine creative act.

The poem's concluding strophe returns to more local and more immediate matters. The poet locates himself in a scene redolent of Milton's
Eden, gazing on 'that oak' beside which Milton might hear his own celestial music.[21] Disavowing an Augustan tradition initiated in '[Edmund]
Waller's myrtle shades', the poet seeks to follow the footsteps of the poet
of *Paradise Lost*; but just as only one lady could wear Fancy's cest, just
as mankind irrevocably fell in the Garden of Eden, just as (a Spenserian

image that doubly reminds us of this ode's other hero) Guyon destroyed forever the Bower of Bliss,[22] so Milton alone could achieve the heights of divine and imaginative verse:

> In vain – such bliss to one alone
> Of all the sons of soul was known,
> And Heaven and Fancy, kindred powers,
> Have now o'erturned the inspiring bowers,
> Or curtained close such scene from every future view.
>
> (72–6)

So an ode that has announced the writer's commitment to the model of imaginative and prophetic verse associated with Milton and Spenser concludes with the most resonant of statements of poetic loneliness, belatedness, and disinheritance.[23]

Like many another poem that articulates voicelessness and celebrates failure, however, Collins' 'Ode on the Poetical Character' might paradoxically be considered to achieve its own kind of triumph. If the collection as a whole is concerned with 'the nature of the True Poet, as Collins conceived it',[24] the 'Ode on the Poetical Character' represents its mythopoeic thematic summation. It is a poem that rises to quite new levels of figurative, formal, and intellectual ambition (on the part of the poet) and demand (on the part of the reader).

By the mid-century it was certainly not new to use the extended Pindaric strophic form. Many poets however preferred shorter strophes, whose metrical shape could be more easily grasped. Thomas Gray wrote to Thomas Wharton, in 1755, that:

> I am not quite of your opinion with regard to Strophe & Antistrophe. setting aside the difficulties, methinks it has little or no effect upon the ear, wch scarce perceives the regular return of Metres at so great a distance from one another. to make it succeed, I am persuaded the Stanza's must not consist of above 9 lines each at the most. Pindar has several such Odes.[25]

The 'Ode on the Poetical Character' is made up of strophe and echoing antistrophe, each of twenty-two lines, and a mesode of thirty-two lines. Many of the other odes in Collins' collection use shorter stanzaic units, such as the romance-six stanzas of the 'Ode to Pity'. Where longer Pindaric strophes are used, as in the 'Ode to Fear', metrical elements are synchronised with short, clear, syntactical units; typically the sense is completed within two or four, at most within six, lines. In the 'Ode on the Poetical Character', in stark and dramatic contrast, syntactical closure is deliberately, even wilfully, refused and deferred over virtually the extent of the stanza. The opening strophe begins by stating the first element of its highly elaborated simile:

> As once, if not with light regard
> I read aright that gifted bard,
> …
> One, only one, unrivalled fair
> Might hope the magic girdle wear …
>
> (1–6)

We expect the sense to be completed by the naming of the second element of the simile, but that does not arrive until line 17, and even that longed-for resolution is delayed, to line 20, by two intervening relative phrases and one relative clause:

> Young Fancy thus, to me divinest name,
> To whom, prepared and bathed in heaven,
> The cest of amplest power is given,
> To few the godlike gift assigns …
>
> (17–20)

This is all a stretch for the construing mind, for (as Gray insisted) the ear, and for the eye. A reader of the ode as first printed in 1746, in its generously sized octavo format, had to read to halfway down the ode's second page in order completely to parse the syntax in which this opening metaphor is conveyed. And indeed, what is offered in the opening line as a simile will persist as one of the poem's several involved conceits: cest, music, dance, weaving, Garden of Eden, fall, prophecy, all of them developed through imaginative prosopopoeia.

Such metrical and syntactical complexity, such figurative and intellectual energy and stamina, set the 'Ode on the Poetical Character' apart from the rest of its volume. Collins moves away in this poem from the clear, discrete, visual personifications typical of his other odes, and the relatively controlled and self-contained syntax in which they are presented. If he could imply that his other odes were 'descriptive',[26] the 'Ode on the Poetical Character' is 'allegorical'. It deals not, even briefly, with the visual, but with vision, specifically with 'the Visions wild' available only to the privileged followers of Fancy.[27] Its personifications function less as empirical representations of human experience than as symbolic articulations of ideas.[28] More than any poem in his collection, arguably more than any poem of his time, the 'Ode on the Poetical Character' bears out the argument that Edmund Burke would make a decade later: that, so far from creating, or encouraging the formation of, visual equivalents for the world, 'so little does poetry depend for its effect on the power of raising sensible images, that I am convinced it would lose a very considerable part of its energy, if this were the necessary result of all description'. Descriptive poetry, for Burke, works not by imitation, but 'by *substitution*'. Burke argues for a verbal sublimity that presents 'no distinct image to the mind', where the affections are powerfully moved by ideas that are 'not presentable but by language'.[29] The 'Ode on the Poetical Character' exemplifies, I would suggest, this Burkean sublime before Burke himself stated the precept.

In its failure, or rather its refusal, to offer brevity, clarity, and simplicity, the 'Ode on the Poetical Character' was at odds with a general, if not universal, contemporary critical preference for a poetry of distinct and apprehensible imagery. Even Collins' colleague Joseph Warton insisted on the vital importance of the visual in poetic epistemology: 'The use, the force and the excellence of language, certainly consists in raising *clear, complete,* and *circumstantial* images, and in turning readers into spectators.'[30] Lord Kames deprecated the mixing of metaphors for this very reason, that they deprive the reader of clear images: 'It is difficult to imagine the subject to be first one thing and then another … the mind is distracted by the rapid transition; and when the imagination is put on such hard duty, its images are too faint to produce any good effect.' In a warning that certainly would apply to the extended figurative arguments that carry Collins' ode, Kames warned that:

> a metaphor drawn out to any length, instead of illustrating or enlivening the principal subject, becomes disagreeable by overstraining the mind. Cowley is extremely licentious in this way … long allegories … never afford any lasting pleasure: witness the *Fairy Queen*, which with great power of expression, variety of images, and melody of versification, is scarce ever read a second time.[31]

It is pertinent that Kames resents the conceit that fails to illustrate its subject and 'overstrains' the mind; that the sinner he cites is Abraham Cowley, Pindarist; and that his key example of the distasteful in literature is the great poem of one of Collins' great heroes, Edmund Spenser.

In another conception of lyric poetry, however, the strenuous work to which such writing puts the reader's mind could be more highly valued. Anna Laetitia Barbauld, in her Prefatory Essay to Collins' poems, distinguishes the 'moral painting of men and manners' such as we find in the

Essays and Epistles of Pope, from the poetry of imagination that Collins had undertaken:

> The other class consists of what may be called pure Poetry, or Poetry in the abstract. It is concerned with an imaginary world, peopled with beings of its own creation. It deals in splendid imagery, bold fiction, and allegorical personages. It is necessarily obscure to a certain degree; because, having to do chiefly with ideas generated within the mind, it cannot be at all comprehended by any whose intellect has not been exercised in familiar contemplations; while the conceptions of the Poet (often highly metaphysical) are rendered still more remote from common apprehension by the figurative phrase in which they are clothed. All that is properly *Lyric Poetry* is of this kind.[32]

This praise is aimed at Collins' odes in general but arguably has a special propriety to the 'Ode on the Poetical Character'. Barbauld celebrates a 'pure Poetry' that is not primarily or straightforwardly mimetic. She is prepared to countenance (as Johnson famously was not[33]) a poetry that deals in fictions, and represents those fictions through allegorising prosopopoeia. She concedes that such a poetry may be *necessarily* obscure, as it deals with mental abstractions, and presents those abstractions figuratively, in a manner that may be beyond 'common apprehension'.[34] She understands that, having to do with idea, it requires a degree of intellectual engagement that profoundly challenges the reader's abilities and knowledge. She acknowledges that (to use Thomas Gray's phrase, itself translated from Pindar) such a poetry may be '*vocal to the intelligent alone*'.[35] And she makes a yet larger, and in literary-historical terms more challenging, claim: that a poetry of such a formal, epistemological, and figurative character is constitutive, or should be constitutive, of the lyric itself: 'All that is properly *Lyric Poetry* is of this kind.'

Christopher Smart, Cambridge college fellow, hack writer, journalist, comic poet, bankrupt, translator, pantomimist, transvestite, committed evangelical Christian, hymnodist, religious obsessive, children's writer, and drunk, was an altogether more various, and variously productive, literary figure than William Collins. He was also, however, a deeply serious poet. He was a writer of epideictic high lyric (amongst many other genres of verse) almost throughout his career. As much of a formal experimenter as any eighteenth-century poet, he tried his hand at almost all possible formal models for the ode. In his early years, he thought the irregular or Cowleian version of the Pindaric an appropriate form for the expression of 'arbitrary grief, that will not hear of bounds', in his ode 'On the

Sudden Death of a Clergyman';[36] and an appropriate form for celebration, in his 'Secular Ode', of the 1743 Jubilee at Pembroke College, Cambridge. Like Collins and Gray (in 'The Bard' and the 'Progress of Poesy'), Smart attempted the regular Pindaric triadic form (in 'To the King', published in *Gratulatio academiae cantabrigiensis*, 1748). Far more frequently, he turned to long stanzas, in his ode 'On an Eagle confined to a College Court', the 'Ode to Lord Barnard', and the odes 'To Admiral Sir George Pocock' and 'To General Draper'.[37] Here Smart might have found forerunners in Pindar's own occasional use of a regular monostrophic form. He might have found, too, a more obvious and congenial lyric model in the stanzaic odes of Horace. Horatian odes appeared from the early years of the English literary Renaissance. Henry Howard, earl of Surrey (1517–1547), wrote a version of the tenth ode of Horace's second book. Milton wrote a version of Horace's 'Ode to Pyrrha'. Marvell's 'Horatian Ode upon Cromwell's return from Ireland' uses a short, Horatian stanza form, and approximates the epideictic mode of the 'Roman' odes, in praise of Augustus and the Roman state, of Horace's third and fourth books. Horace's poems, more especially the odes, were hugely popular in translation, imitation, and paraphrase throughout the eighteenth century.

Smart's mature work, the poetry published after his release from the madhouse in the early 1760s, is predominantly and characteristically written in a wide variety of shorter stanzas. He was a self-conscious experimenter in and exploiter of stanzaic form, perhaps most distinctively in the *Hymns and Spiritual Songs for the Fasts and Festivals of the Church of England*, in the *Translation of the Psalms of David, Attempted in the Spirit of Christianity* (both 1765), and in *The Works of Horace, Translated into Verse* (1767). He appended to his *Translation of the Psalms* a set of metrical variations upon the Gloria Patri, in the twenty-five different measures that he had used. Such an exercise was not a unique practice, but neither was it a regular practice in English metrical Psalm books; if Smart undertook it primarily as an aid to the use of his Psalms in devotion, he no doubt intended also to draw attention to his own metrical virtuosity.

Smart's verse translation of Horace was similarly, and self-consciously, ingenious in its use of various stanza forms. Smart included, in Volume II, a list of Horace's odes arranged by their twenty-two different Latin metres. Where the Horatian original is stanzaic, so is Smart's translation (though the carelessly printed 1767 text does not employ vertical leading to demarcate each stanza from the next). For some odes, particularly the Sapphics (e.g., I.38), he insists that he has employed 'the original metre exactly'.[38]

His verse translation attempts throughout to emulate the *curiosa felicitas* of Horace's odes, and in his preface Smart goes so far as to nominate in which odes he believes he has succeeded in doing so (*Horace*, p. 5). It is in the preface to the verse Horace that Smart makes one of his two statements on 'the beauty, force and vehemence of *Impression* … a talent or gift of Almighty God, by which a Genius is impowered to throw an emphasis upon a word or sentence'. Impression is identified as peculiarly a property of epideictic verse: 'the force of impression is always liveliest upon the eulogies of patriotism, gratitude, honour, and the like' (*Horace*, pp. 6–7).

The verse Horace ranks amongst Smart's most forceful and inventive writings, both metrically and linguistically. Nevertheless, the Horatian lyric fell short, in Smart's own estimation, of the sublime verse of the Hebrew Bible: 'there is a littleness in the noblest poets among the Heathens when compared to the prodigious grandeur and genuine majesty of a *David* or *Isaiah*' (*Horace*, p. 9). It is in *A Song to David*, Smart's ode in praise of the Psalmist, that his major achievement in the exploitation of the internal resources, and architectonic possibilities, of the stanza are to be found.

The stanza used in *A Song to David*, the tail-rhyme stanza or romance-six, is made up of two tetrameter couplets, each followed by a trimeter, rhyming *aabccb*. It was used in religious and secular verse through the seventeenth century, and persisted through the eighteenth century as a popular form. It appears in much magazine poetry; in the hymns of Watts, Charles Wesley, and others; in Gray's 'Ode on the Death of a Favourite Cat'; in Johnson's 'Upon the Feast of St Simon and St Jude'; and in poems by Akenside and Collins.

The romance-six, then, was a common form, but it was also distinctively Smart's favourite lyric stanza.[39] The form suited his habit of expression just as the heroic couplet suited Pope. The extended compass of its six lines allowed for syntactical variation and ingenuity. Its short lines, closely successive rhymes, and two-part structure, connected by the tail rhymes, enabled the exploitation of a range of powerful rhetorical mechanisms, and encouraged the pointed, elliptical expression that is a signature of Smart's most impressive and characteristic later poetry.

All poetry is more or less distinct from prose in lexis or in syntax, but *A Song to David* makes denser use of syntactical and verbal peculiarity than most, almost all of it aimed at poetic concentration and pointedness within the stanza. This is what a linguist would call the use of 'deictic lenses': the tendency of instances of lexical rarity, novelty, or obsolescence, and of syntactic strain and distinctiveness, to draw attention to the texture of the writing and the articulation of meaning. Smart uses a wide range of such lenses throughout the *Song*; here are some instances. Apposition, in various forms, is a recurrent feature. Appositional noun phrases allow parallel gnomic statements of the subjects of David's singing:

> Of man – the semblance and effect
> Of God and Love – the Saint elect
> For infinite applause –
>> (stanza 20)[40]

Main verbs are regularly absent or implied:

> Good – from Jehudah's genuine vein,
> From God's best nature good in grain,
> His aspect and his heart;
>> (stanza 8)

Transitive verbs are used intransitively, avoiding (as often in the verse Horace[41]) needless prepositions or passive constructions:

> The crocus burnishes alive
>> (stanza 61)

At some points, parallel syntactical structures use the boundaries of the line and stanza to make points in brief:

> In armour, or in ephod clad,
> His pomp, his piety was glad;
>> (stanza 15)

Elsewhere chiasmus allows a similar emphasis:

> Controul thine eye, salute success,
> Honour the wiser, happier bless
>> (stanza 48)

The romance-six falls naturally into two halves, providing perfect frames for separate vignettes:

> For ADORATION, beyond match,
> The scholar bulfinch aims to catch
> The soft flute's iv'ry touch;
> And, careless on the hazle spray,
> The daring redbreast keeps at bay
> The damsel's greedy clutch.
>> (stanza 65)

Sometimes, however, Smart binds the stanza together, for example, in the concluding *amplificatio*, by repetition of the initial word of the line:

> Sweet is the dew that falls betimes,
> And drops upon the leafy limes;
>   Sweet, Hermon's fragrant air:
> Sweet is the lilly's silver bell,
> And sweet the wakeful tapers smell
>   That watch for early pray'r.
>   (stanza 72)

Elsewhere Smart surprises expectation by carrying the sentence over the stanza's third-line break, often with a peculiarity of syntax:

> Constant – in love to God THE TRUTH,
> Age, manhood, infancy, and youth –
>   To Jonathan his friend
> Constant, beyond the verge of death;
>   (stanza 14)

The sense here at first appears complete after the third line, but as we read on we find a changed structure. The inversion, and the appearance of the word 'constant' at the start of the fourth line, lend a metrical as well as a syntactical emphasis to this virtue. Often poeticism is used as an instrument not of vague verbosity but of concision. In *Jubilate agno* Smart invites Thomas to 'rejoice with the Sword-Fish, whose aim is perpetual and strength insuperable' (B129); in the *Song*, in the rather different poetic mode of high formal lyric, he writes:

> Strong thro' the turbulent profound
>   Shoots xiphias to his aim.
>   (stanza 75)

Here the periphrasis 'turbulent profound' gives the sea, home to a part of God's creation, a sublimity of wildness and extent, and the Greek name for the swordfish, 'xiphias' (borrowed from Spenser, *Faerie Queene*, II. xii.214), lends poetic strangeness (Smart thought an explanatory footnote necessary here). Smart used alliteration regularly, binding and emphasising sense units, underlining rhythms, creating parallelisms: 'keep from com-mixtures foul and fond'; 'wise are his precepts, prayer and praise' (stanzas 45, 16). Finally, a possibility whose implications I shall wish to explore later in this chapter: the structure of Smart's chosen stanza allows the con-struction of many lists. There are lists that set up the terms of a developed subsequent *anaphora*:

> Great, valiant, pious, good, and clean,
> Sublime, contemplative, serene,
>   Strong, constant, pleasant, wise!
>
> (stanza 4)

Other lists set out in themselves the infinite riches of the divine creation:

> The world – the clust'ring spheres he made,
> The glorious light, the soothing shade,
>   Dale, champaign, grove, and hill;
> The multitudinous abyss …
>
> (stanza 21)

The omission or implying of main verbs of course enables or encourages this cataloguing tendency.

Smart's use of the romance-six has a fundamental effect too on overall organisation. Stanzaic parts are related to the architectonic whole, as statement is accommodated to stanzaic form. Smart insisted (in the Advertisement printed in *Poems on Several Occasions*, 1763) on 'the exact Regularity and Method' of his poem. 'Regularity' is a word that answers to the long-standing English debate about the form of the ode. In engaging in this debate, Smart had adopted for his greatest epideictic lyric a more elaborated solution. As the list of contents he provided carefully sets out, the poem is divided into a series of thematic stanza blocks, organised by symbolic numbers, including twelve stanzas on the virtues of David, nine on the subjects of David's verse, seven on the pillars of knowledge, ten on the Decalogue, three on each of the four seasons, five on the senses (together making up the ADORATION passage), and a concluding 'amplification in five degrees' amounting to fifteen stanzas. Each of these internal frames makes up a subordinate part, and argument, of the poem.

Smart's uses of formal rhetoric within the poem, almost always in support and delineation of these larger architectonic structures, are no less striking. In the contents list he draws attention to what is perhaps the most dramatic instance of such a rhetoric: the concluding 'amplification in five degrees'. For each of these five degrees Smart provides three stanzas. In each degree the first two stanzas give instances of what is sweet, strong, beautiful, precious, and glorious, in the natural world (the instances are virtually all made up of allusions to the Bible, and especially from the sublime book of Job), in man's world, and in the man-made world. Each degree concludes with a stanza finding David is sweeter, stronger, more beauteous, more precious, and more glorious, as man of praise, man of prayer, poet, man after God's own heart, and type of and believer in Christ's salvation. In each stanza of each degree Smart makes use of *anaphora*, the repetition of a word at the beginning of a line. The poem's climax is effected in part by a movement from relatively varied and light use of *anaphora* in the first four degrees, to a drum-beat insistence in the fifth and last:

> Glorious the northern lights astream;
> Glorious the song, when God's the theme;
>   Glorious the thunder's roar:
> Glorious hosanna from the den;
> Glorious the catholic amen;
>   Glorious the martyr's gore
>
>   (stanza 85)

Indeed, though Smart, keen that his reader should understand the Classical rhetorical motives of his poem, calls this an 'amplification', it is also, in its intensification from stanza to stanza, an instance of *gradatio*. Such a use of *gradatio* may again more easily be paralleled in the sixteenth and seventeenth centuries – for instance in the fifth song of Sidney's *Astrophil and Stella*, which combines *gradatio* and *anaphora*, or in Herbert's 'Sighs and Grones' – than in the eighteenth. No doubt the most significant other use of *anaphora* in the *Song* is in the 'exercise upon the senses' (stanzas 65–70), where the repetition of the phrase 'For ADORATION' at the beginning of the first line of each stanza serves particularly to distinguish this passage from the 'exercise upon the seasons', in which the capitalised word ADORATION is cycled through the stanzas. Finally, an instance of *enumeratio*, a type of *amplificatio* in which each detail of the subject is taken up and expanded: David's twelve virtues are listed in one half of a single stanza:

> Great, valiant, pious, good, and clean,
> Sublime, contemplative, serene,
>   Strong, constant, pleasant, wise!
>
>   (stanza 4)

Each of these virtues is then elaborated by twelve single stanzas, opening with the name of each virtue in turn.

I have already spoken of Smart's creation of lists within the boundaries of the stanza. Lists also operate throughout the poem above the level of the stanza, not only in the account of David's virtues, but also in the subjects of which he sang (God, angels, man, 'trees, plants and flow'rs', fowl, fishes, beasts, gems), in the seven pillars, or in the natural vignettes of the Adoration passage. The *Song*, like the *Jubilate*, though in a different poetic mode, presents us with a series of catalogues. I want to argue that, as in the *Jubilate*, this is a matter both of meaning and of formal method.

In the *Jubilate* Smart claimed that 'the philosophy of the times evn now is vain deceit'. His particular target was Sir Isaac Newton, whose natural science, because mathematical rather than scriptural, is 'more of error than of the truth'. Newton was αλογοσ, because in his anti-Trinitarianism he denied Christ the Word; because he denied the power of the creating Logos; and because he questioned the authority of the Scriptures. Smart, on the other hand, congratulated himself on defending 'the philosophy of the scripture'.[42] He drew his philosophy of the Scripture in part (as Karina Williamson and Albert J. Kuhn have shown)[43] from the writings of the Hutchinsonians. He drew it in part from St Paul, whose exhortation to the Colossians, as Karina Williamson has pointed out, Smart echoes: 'Beware lest any man spoil you through philosophy and vain deceit, after the tradition of men, after the rudiments of the world, and not after Christ' (Colossians 2: 8). And he drew it in part no doubt, as Albert Kuhn suggests, from the analogical thinking of such evangelical physico-theologians as James Hervey: 'we should always view the visible System; with an Evangelical *Telescope* … and with an Evangelical *Microscope*: Regarding CHRIST JESUS, as the great Projector and Architect; that planned, and executed the amazing Scheme … Whatever is magnificent or valuable; tremendous or amiable; should ever be ascribed to the Redeemer. This, is the Christian's *Natural Philosophy*.'[44] Smart similarly insists, in the first stanza of the pillars passage, on Christ as creating logos: 'His WORD accomplish'd the design' (stanza 30). The first and last of the pillars are alpha and omega, which are Christ. The pillars passage is immediately followed by the ascription of just such a natural philosophy to David: 'O DAVID, scholar of the Lord! / Such is thy science' (stanza 38). David's knowledge is of the infinite life of the creation, a universe 'FULL of God's works' (*Jubilate*, B185): that is, a plenum rather than Newton's vacuum. *Jubilate agno* insists on the infinity of the creation: 'For the names and number of animals are as the name and number of the stars' (B42). Infinite or enormous number or extent are common themes of the *Song*: the Archangel Michael bows in heaven with 'his millions', the 'Saint elect' offer up 'infinite applause', the sea is 'the multitudinous abyss', David's science earns him 'infinite degree' (stanzas 19, 20, 21, 38). This, rather than the terrible, is Smart's characteristic sublime, a sublime of the ineffable, of a divine creation whose scale and number are beyond mortal apprehension or mathematical description, 'For nature is more various than observation tho' observers be innumerable (*Jubliate*, B53). As Umberto Eco puts it in his recent study of the list in verbal and visual art, 'Faced with something that is immensely large, or unknown, of which we still do not know enough or of which we shall never know, the author tells us he is unable to say, and so he proposes a list very often as a specimen, example, or indication, leaving the reader to imagine the rest.'[45] Such lists may be found in the Middle Ages, in litanies, or in lists of the attributes of Christ or the Father. They may be found even earlier, for example in Homer's list of the Greek ships in the *Iliad* (Book XVIII). It may be true, as Smart writes in his hymn on Christ's Ascension, that:

> The song can never be pursu'd
> When Infinite's the theme –
> (*Hymns and Spiritual Songs*, XIV.56–7)

Nevertheless, when the issue is the infinity of the creation, rather than the mystery of the divine, the poet may attempt a representative list, as Smart does in the alphabetical and numerical series of *Jubilate agno*, and in the poetically structured representative catalogues of *A Song to David*. These lists have a different motive than those of natural philosophy. They are symbolic and allusive, rather than complete or taxonomic. The hierarchies of Smart's concluding *amplificatio*, and of the list of David's poetic subjects, are not the taxonomies of science, but the hierarchies of God.

The history of the eighteenth-century ode was in part a struggle for adequate form and answerable style. To the high lyric poets of the mid eighteenth century may be applied with especial and particular force T. S. Eliot's broader-ranging comment that English poets between Pope and Wordsworth were faced with the problem, and too often failed to solve the problem, of finding 'a style of writing for themselves, suited to the matter they wanted to talk about and the way in which they apprehended this matter'.[46] Collins and Smart had rather different things to talk about. They had different understandings of the world, and represented it in different ways. Both found, and exploited in their greatest lyrics, appropriate form and language. The extended strophes of the regular triadic Pindaric ode gave Collins scope for the ambitious development of a fundamental figurative method of his time, in a consciously sublime account of the divine origins of imaginative poetry, of the achievements of the two prophets of English verse, and the inevitable inadequacy of their contemporary disciples. The romance-six afforded Smart not only a hospitable internal discipline but also the technical resources to articulate, thematically and rhetorically, his extended ode to the Psalmist who had celebrated the order and the fullness of the creation, and in doing so had provided Smart with a model for sacred lyric verse. These two odes are innovative and specific exercises in particular lyric sub-genres, strenuously and ingeniously adapting Greek, Hebraic, and English models. They answer powerfully to their respective writers' emergent expressive needs. They were little valued in their own time, and they left scarcely a rack behind.

Notes

1 Joseph Warton, *Odes on Various Subjects*, 2nd edn (London: R. Dodsley, 1747), p. xi.

2 Plato, *Republic*, 10.606E–607; Aristotle, *Poetics*, 4.1448b 24ff.

3 Abraham Cowley, preface to *Pindarique Odes* (1656), sigs. b1^{r-v}.

4 For an account of knowledge in England of the organising principles of the Pindaric triad, see Norman Maclean, 'From Action to Image: Theories of the Lyric in the Eighteenth Century', in *Critics and Criticism*, ed. R. S. Crane (University of Chicago Press, 1952), pp. 408–60 (p. 425 and note).

5 For a persuasive account of Gray's methods, see Thomas Gray, William Collins, and Oliver Goldsmith, *The Poems*, ed. Roger Lonsdale (London: Longman, 1969), p. 114.

6 For a thoroughly documented study, see Chester E. Chapin, *Personification in Eighteenth-Century Poetry* (New York: Octagon, 1974); and for a significant article, see Earl R. Wasserman, 'The Inherent Values of Eighteenth-Century Personification', *PMLA* 65 (1950), 435–63.

7 John Newbery, *The Art of Poetry on a New Plan*, 2 vols. (London, 1762), Vol. I, p. 137.

8 James Beattie, *Essays: On Poetry and Music, as they Affect the Mind* (Edinburgh, 1776), pp. 277, 279.

9 Henry Home, Lord Kames, *Elements of Criticism*, 3 vols. (London and Edinburgh, 1762), Vol. III, p. 113.

10 Beattie, *Essays*, pp. 277–8.

11 Edmund Spenser, *Works of Mr. Edmund Spenser*, ed. John Hughes, 6 vols. (London, 1715), Vol. I, p. xxxi.

12 William Collins, 'The Manners', lines 50–1, 54–5, in Gray, Collins, and Goldsmith, *Poems*, p. 474. All citations of Collins' poetry are from this edition.

13 William Collins, 'Ode to Fear', lines 20–1, 'Ode to Simplicity', lines 11–12 (pp. 419, 424). For discussion of the debate about the relative desirability of brief personifications (relying upon the highly developed capacity of eighteenth-century readers for imaginative visual reconstruction), as against more fully developed and pictorialised visual representations, see Chapin, *Personification*, pp. 34–6, 59–60, 63; Wasserman, 'Inherent Values', pp. 437–8, 458, 459.

14 Samuel Johnson recounts in his 'Life of Collins' that the poet was in 1744 saved from the attentions of a bailiff by 'the booksellers, who, on the credit of a translation of Aristotle's Poetics, which he engaged to write with a large

commentary, advanced as much money as enabled him to escape into the country'; *Lives of the Most Eminent English Poets*, ed. Roger Lonsdale, 4 vols. (Oxford: Clarendon Press, 2006), Vol. IV, p. 120.

15 For a significant corrective see Richard Wendorf, '"Poor Collins" Reconsidered', *Huntington Library Quarterly* 42 (1979), 91–116.

16 Edmund Spenser, *The Faerie Queene*, IV.v.3, 1–5; V.iii.27–8; IV.v.1–20.

17 As Earl R. Wasserman points out ('Collins' "Ode on the Poetical Character"', *ELH* 34 (1967), 92–115 (pp. 103–4)), Collins' myth is not made anew 'out of whole cloth'. Wasserman argues for an elaborate Platonic construction, including, for instance, identification of the neo-Platonic heavenly Venus, conceived as Mind (*nous*), as proprietor of the girdle (but Collins does not mention Venus in the relevant parts of the poem). It is more likely that Collins' sources for his idea are English and literary, Spenserian and Miltonic, and biblical (particularly the scriptural figure of Wisdom from Proverbs), than unmediatedly Platonic.

18 Langhorne, Barbauld, Woodhouse, and Lonsdale are surely correct in reading the 'rich-haired youth of morn' as a personification of the sun, not of the poet himself. As Lonsdale puts it, Collins is describing 'the imaginative act of creation by which God, through the embodiment of his "Fancy", himself became the supreme type of the Poet' (Gray, Collins, and Goldsmith, *Poems*, p. 432).

19 For detailed discussions of these lines and their background, see A. S. P. Woodhouse, 'The Poetry of Collins Reconsidered', in *From Sensibility to Romanticism: Essays Presented to Frederick A. Pottle*, ed. Frederick W. Hilles and Harold Bloom (London: Oxford University Press, 1965), pp. 93–138; Wasserman, 'Inherent Values'; and Lonsdale's headnote and notes to the poem in Gray, Collins, and Goldsmith, *Poems*.

20 In William Collins, *The Poetical Works of Mr. William Collins* (London, 1797), pp. xxiii–xxiv.

21 The reference is no doubt to *Il Penseroso*, lines 59–60.

22 Spenser, *The Faerie Queene*, II.xii.83.

23 Amongst other closely contemporary parallels, see Gray, 'The Progress of Poesy', lines 111–13.

24 S. Musgrove, 'The Theme of Collins's Odes', *Notes and Queries* 185 (1943), 214–17, 253–5 (p. 215).

25 Letter of 9 March 1755. Thomas Gray, *Correspondence of Thomas Gray*, ed. Paget Toynbee and Leonard Whibley, rev. H. W. Starr, 3 vols. (Oxford: Clarendon Press, 1971), pp. 420–1. Cf. Johnson's comment on Gray's own odes: 'His stanzas are too long, especially his epodes; the ode is finished before the ear has learned its measures' (*Lives*, Vol. IV, p. 183).

26 Barbauld reasonably doubts whether Collins' odes in general have a 'claim to the epithet *descriptive*; by which we generally understand a delineation of some portion of real nature', and prefers *figurative*.

27 Cf. 'Ode to Fear': 'Be mine to read the visions old, / Which thy awakening bards have told' (lines 54–5).

28 Wasserman persuasively argues that personification died, not as a result of Wordsworthian distaste, but as a result of 'the metaphysics that Coleridge ushered in ... It performed its poetic function so long as man assumed that all human knowledge is empirical and that abstractions are fabricated by mind to unify human experience' ('Inherent Values', p. 437).

29 Edmund Burke, *A Philosophical Enquiry into the Origin of Our Ideas of the Sublime and Beautiful*, ed. James T. Boulton, rev. edn (Oxford: Blackwell, 1987), pp. 170, 174–5.

30 Joseph Warton, *An Essay on the Genius and Writings of Pope*, 2 vols. (London, 1782), Vol. II, pp. 222–3.

31 Home, *Elements of Criticism*, Vol. III, pp. 116, 119–20, 124.

32 In Collins, *Poetical Works*, pp. iv–v.

33 For Johnson's comment on the 'disgusting' (that is, distasteful) fictions of *Lycidas*, see *Lives*, Vol. I, p. 279.

34 Here Barbauld, surely deliberately, puts to approving use an expression that Johnson had used critically of Thomas Gray's linguistic peculiarity: 'finding in Dryden *honey redolent of Spring*, an expression that reaches the utmost limits of our language, Gray drove it a little more beyond common apprehension by making *gales* to be *redolent of joy and youth*' (*ibid.*, p. 181).

35 Gray, *Correspondence*, p. 797. Gray uses Pindar's phrase, in the original Greek, as an epigraph on the title-page of his *Odes* (1757).

36 Christopher Smart, 'On the Sudden Death of a Clergyman', *Student* 2 (1751), 393–4.

37 Christopher Smart, 'On an Eagle confined to a College Court', *Student* 2 (1751), 356–7; 'Ode to Lord Barnard', *Gentleman's Magazine* (1754), 575); 'To Admiral Sir George Pocock', in *Poems by Mr. Smart* (London, 1763), pp. 9–13; 'To General Draper', in *Poems by Mr. Smart*, pp. 14–18.

38 Christopher Smart, *Poetical Works of Christopher Smart*, ed. Marcus Walsh and Karina Williamson, 5 vols. (Oxford University Press, 1980–96), Vol. v, ed. Karina Williamson (1996), p. 158. All references to Smart's *Works of Horace Translated into Verse* are to this edition, and are provided within my text.

39 Smart uses it in his translation of the first ode of Horace's Book I, 'To Maecenas' (*Midwife* 2 (1751), 165–7); his translation of Psalm 42 in the *Universal Visiter* (1756); 'Ode to the Earl of Northumberland' (1764); *Hymns and Spiritual Songs* ('The Crucifixion' and 'St Mark'); *Hymns for the Amusement of Children* ('Learning' and 'Generosity'); verse translation of Horace (I.vi, xxiii; II.v; III. xvi; IV.v); and regularly in his *Translation of the Psalms* (1765).

40 All references to *A Song to David* are to my edition in Smart, *Poetical Works*, Vol. II (1983).

41 For example at I.xxiii.12, where Horace's 'Et corde et genibus tremit' is translated 'She trembles heart and knees'.

42 *Jubilate agno*, B130, B195, B219, B648; Smart, *Poetical Works*, Vol. I, ed. Karina Williamson (1980), pp. 49, 44, 84.

43 Karina Williamson, 'Smart's *Principia*: Science and Anti-Science in *Jubilate agno*', *Review of English Studies*, n.s. 30 (1979), 409–22; Albert J. Kuhn, 'Christopher Smart: The Poet as Patriot of the Lord', *ELH* 30 (1963), 121–36.

44 James Hervey, 'Reflections on a Flower Garden', *Meditations and Contemplations*, 2 vols. (London, 1749), Vol. I, pp. 185–6.

45 Umberto Eco, *The Infinity of Lists* (London: Maclehose, 2009), p. 49.

46 T. S. Eliot, *Selected Prose*, ed. John Hayward (Harmondsworth: Penguin, 1963), p. 155.

CHAPTER SEVEN

The retuning of the sky
Romanticism and lyric

David Duff

Lecturing on 'Various Classes of Poetry' at the Royal Institution in 1830–1, the poet James Montgomery remarked that 'It would be impossible to define the limits, or lay down the laws, of what passes in our own country under the title of Lyric Poetry', a classification now so broad as to be utterly 'nondescript'.[1] He offers no evidence but his point is illustrated by a recently published book, Robert Malcolm's *Lyrical Gems: A Selection of Moral, Sentimental, and Descriptive Poetry, From the Works of the Most Popular Modern Writers, Interspersed with Originals* (Glasgow, 1825). Where forty years earlier a critical authority such as Hugh Blair could restrict the term 'Lyric Poetry' to just four types of ode,[2] Malcolm's anthology encompasses a bewildering variety of poetic forms, including 'odes', 'ballads', 'songs', 'sonnets', 'hymns', 'pastoral stanzas', 'fragments', an 'anthem', an 'ancient gaelic melody', a 'hebrew melody', and a 'poetic sketch'. Alongside these named forms are many short poems without generic labels, as well as extracts from longer works such as Thomas Moore's *Lalla Rookh* and Byron's *Childe Harold's Pilgrimage* and *Don Juan*. The common denominator of these heterogeneous compositions is not at all obvious, and the editor provides no explanation of his principles of selection other than to refer to the poems as 'genuine effusions of the muse' (p. iv), a description that brings to mind Wordsworth's 'spontaneous overflow of powerful feelings' – as good a definition as any of the nebulous term 'effusion', though not intended as such.[3]

The volume is typical of the anthologies, keepsakes, and annuals that dominated the British poetry market in the 1820s. As the word 'popular' in the subtitle indicates, this is an anthology explicitly attuned to contemporary taste, and the type of poetry calculated to satisfy that taste is called 'lyrical'. A term once reserved, in formal literary criticism, for a complex, elevated type of poetry derived from Classical and biblical models was now being applied to any kind of short poem expressing intense personal emotion, as well as to extractable passages from longer, narrative works displaying, in short bursts, that same effusive quality (the 'lyrical gem' thereby replacing what an earlier generation of anthologists had called the 'elegant extract', suggesting a further specialisation of reading habits towards pursuit of this specific poetic effect). It is a small step from Malcolm's lyric connoisseurship to the full-blown canonisation programme of Francis Palgrave's *Golden Treasury* (1861), the most famous of all nineteenth-century anthologies, whose selection of 'The Best Songs and Lyrical Poems in the English Language' made a similar notion of lyric – melodious, highly polished verse that turns 'on some single thought, feeling, or situation' – a touchstone for poetry for all periods.[4]

In this chapter, I want to explore the genesis of the 'lyrical gem' as an index of supreme artistic value, and the process of colonisation whereby the category of lyric expanded to include large parts of the genre-spectrum, and ultimately the notion of poetry itself. Both processes – the crystallisation of an idea of lyric as exquisite, song-like expression of personal feelings, and the subsuming of other poetic forms – have been seen as part of an inexorable rise of lyric that began in the Romantic period and continued more or less unabated until the end of the nineteenth century. Closer inspection, however, reveals that the 'rise' was by no means straightforward; that 'lyric' was a contested term in the Romantic period with many meanings, not all of them compatible; and that the colonisation process began earlier, involving both inclusion and exclusion. Crucially, traditional accounts of Romantic lyric conflate two developments that need to be viewed separately to be properly understood. The first is the emergence of an introspective conception of lyric, involving not simply self-expression but also self-analysis, emotion observed by the 'self-watching subtilizing mind' (Coleridge's phrase).[5] The second is the emergence of a musical idea of lyric, one that re-establishes the ancient link between poetry and music but does so on different terms and in ways that vary greatly between different cultural spheres. In what follows I will examine these developments, offering examples of each and suggesting how different notions of lyricism compete and sometimes combine in the period.

A first point to note is that many of the developments that shape Romantic lyric have their roots in earlier poetic theory and practice. The idea of lyric as the 'most poetical' kind of poetry, a Romantic and Victorian commonplace, first emerges over a century earlier with critics such as Joseph Trapp and Edward Young, who claim for lyric poetry – the Pindaric ode in particular – unique stylistic, formal, and cognitive properties.[6] Despite its 'wild' and seemingly 'immethodical' manner, lyric poetry, argues Young, possesses an emotional 'logic' of its own, and its artistic appeal lies in the imaginative risks it takes, and the stylistic distance it maintains from ordinary prose (pp. 21–2). Later in the eighteenth century, this privileging of lyric as a genre that breaks the rules but upholds a higher artistic rationale crystallises in the doctrine of 'pure poetry', which, as Marcus Walsh showed in the previous chapter, claims for lyric the strongest features of the poetics of the sublime: emotional power, figurative inventiveness, mythopoeic creativity. The stylistic implications are spelt out in Thomas Gray's comments on 'the true Lyric style', which, 'with all its flights of fancy, ornaments & heightening of expression, & harmony of sound', is 'in its nature superior to every other style', though 'it could not be born in a work of great length'.[7] Primitivism, another influential strand in eighteenth-century criticism, adds further impetus to this revaluation of lyric, identifying it as the oldest and most primal form of poetic utterance, originating in what William Duff calls 'the effusion of a glowing fancy and an impassioned heart' and acknowledging no law 'excepting its own spontaneous impulse, which it obeys without control'.[8] On this view, lyric is at once the most grounded and the most elevated of genres, the most 'natural' form of poetic expression yet also the most artistic.

The Romantics adopt and develop this theory of lyric and the cultural mythologies that underpin it, and terms such as intensity, spontaneity, imagination, and self-expression increasingly displace older critical concepts, making lyric ultimately the norm for all poetry. However, as M. H. Abrams demonstrated in *The Mirror and the Lamp*, it is a later, post-Romantic development in critical theory – represented most influentially by John Stuart Mill – that severs lyric from its audience and its social function, removing the 'expressive theory' from 'the network of qualifications' in which Wordsworth and others had placed it.[9] The paradigm of Romantic lyric, for Abrams, is not the improvisatory, autotelic 'effusion' but the intricately crafted, intellectually complex genre he calls the 'greater Romantic lyric'.[10] This is a type of writing, he argues, that emerged in the 1790s, displaced what neoclassical critics had called the 'greater ode', and involved the expression not of single thoughts, feelings, or situations, as in Palgrave's definition of lyric, but, rather, of shifting mental states: what Wordsworth calls 'the fluxes and refluxes of the mind'.[11] This type of lyric is 'sentimental' rather than 'naive', in Schiller's distinction: its provenance lies in highly developed cultural forms such as the sonnet, the Pindaric ode, the inscription, the loco-descriptive poem, and the seventeenth-century poem of meditation. In an act of generic transformation and synthesis itself characteristic of Romanticism, Coleridge and Wordsworth, and others after them, fuse together these disparate forms and create a new type of lyric that is able to register, in an unprecedented way, 'the free flow of consciousness, the interweaving of thought, feeling, and perceptual detail, and the easy naturalness of the speaking voice' (pp. 211–12).

As I have suggested elsewhere,[12] Abrams' account of the evolution of Romantic lyric is open to question in so far as it implies a straightforward movement away from established forms like the ode and sonnet towards new, hybrid genres such as the one he describes. The mixing of previously distinct forms is certainly characteristic of this period, but what is striking in the work of the Romantics is the way new lyric forms are created without the old ones being destroyed. Writers such as Coleridge and Wordsworth are as assiduous in their cultivation of existing forms as they are in their invention of new ones, and some of the key formal developments of the period involve not innovation but the reactivation of older forms, or a type of innovation in which traditional properties are adapted rather than abandoned. An example is the sonnet, a form that had dropped out of the repertoire in the mid seventeenth century and that neoclassical critics ignored, but which was revived in the 1780s to become a vital part of the Romantic lyric spectrum.[13] Sonnets undergo every kind of formal manipulation in the Romantic period, including absorption into the new kind of complex lyric Abrams describes, but the form is also used in its traditional configurations, and the most consequential innovation wrought upon it is not metrical or linear alteration but rather a functional shift, a deepening of the self-reflexive tendencies already inherent in it, to make it an autobiographical, or confessional, form. Coleridge provides a rationale for this new deployment when he talks of the sonnet as a type of poem 'in which some lonely feeling is developed'. The structural properties of sonnet form (intricate rhyme scheme, the *volta*, and the fixed number of lines) enable the author to 'methodize' his thought through a progressive transformation of the emotional state that originally gave rise to the poem.[14] It is the ability of the sonnet to chart and analyse these mental trajectories that recommended it to the Romantics, and led them to use it as a model for other types of introspective lyric.

Another key feature of this new lyric mode, whether in sonnets or in larger, more complex forms, is its mimesis of the spoken voice. The importance of this element has not always been recognised. According to Cecil Day Lewis, who updated Palgrave's *Golden Treasury* in 1954, 'a true lyric … will always manifest itself as such by a certain tone and a certain kind of rhythm. The lyrical impulse makes words sing.'[15] Of 'singing' lyric I shall have more to say, but the opposite quality to which Abrams draws attention is fidelity to the 'speaking' voice, and it is no coincidence that the earliest examples he gives of the greater Romantic lyric are Coleridge's 'conversation poems', a label (applied by Coleridge only to 'The Nightingale' but now extended to other poems) that directly signals their vocal and dialogic character. Though introspective ('self-watching'), the poems are addressed to imagined interlocutors, and are crucially shaped by their sense of an audience. Coleridge's later term for the group, 'Meditative Poems in Blank Verse',[16] highlights two other features that distance them still further from Day Lewis's conception of lyric, which regards the 'singing tone' as diametrically opposed to 'that of the voice reasoning, arguing, describing' (as in meditative poetry), and which specifically excludes as incompatible with lyric rhythm (except in rare instances) a 'heavy' metre such as iambic pentameter (pp. 17–18). Even so rhythmically dextrous a poem as Wordsworth's 'Tintern Abbey', another blank-verse meditation whose expressive power partly rests in its ability to move between 'speaking' and 'singing' tones, and to accelerate or decelerate rhythmically as feelings intensify and philosophic climax approaches, finds no place in Palgrave's anthology, though it is now regarded as a supreme example of Romantic lyric.

The conversational turn that produces this new variety of lyric does not mean a total renunciation of the oratorical voice found in earlier modes of lyric, nor does the domestic focus of conversational lyric imply a retreat from public engagement, as in the narratives of 'internalisation' through which the careers of the Romantic poets were once interpreted.[17] The co-presence of different rhetorical modes, each responsive to shifting historical conditions, is illustrated by Coleridge's *Fears in Solitude* pamphlet of 1798, which sets side by side 'France: An Ode', an oratorical ode in the grand Pindaric manner; 'Fears in Solitude', a blank-verse lyric that intersperses conversational self-reflection with odic apostrophes in a much higher register; and his fully conversationalised meditative lyric, 'Frost at Midnight'.[18] Oratorical and conversational registers coexist, and the public realm is progressively reimagined within the private, the three poems exemplifying different aspects of the paradox Adorno defines as constitutive of lyric, 'a subjectivity that turns into objectivity'.[19]

Though this paradox is never fully articulated in Romanticism's own theories of lyric, Coleridge's friend George Dyer comes close to it in his essays on 'Lyric Poetry' and 'Representative Poetry' in his *Poems* (1802), where he tries to conceptualise what Anne Janowitz terms the 'communitarian' strand in lyric.[20] Writing possibly in response to Wordsworth's subjective definition of poetry in the preface to *Lyrical Ballads*, Dyer links the imaginative freedom of lyric to social and political freedom, and describes poetic composition not as an act of self-centring, as in Wordsworth's 'emotion recollected in tranquillity',[21] but as a way for the writer to resign his individuality and acquire 'new eyes, new ears, new feelings', 'lifting himself above his ordinary material self' to become the spiritual 'representative' of a larger community.[22] A similarly anti-subjective definition is offered by another important associate of Coleridge and Wordsworth, John Thelwall, who, in a long and original discussion of lyric poetry in the journal *The Champion*, grounds his account of the different varieties of lyric in an analysis of their different modes of recitation.[23] As Judith Thompson has shown, Thelwall offers an instrumentalist rather than an expressive account of lyric, one that draws on his experience as an orator and makes prosody ('rhythmus') the crux of all vocal performance.[24] As well as putting theory into practice in his own poetry (like Dyer, he specialised in odes, though experimented with many other forms), he also applied the same principle in his later profession as a speech therapist, using the recitation of lyric poetry as a therapeutic tool for speech disorders.

As these examples suggest, the rise of the personal lyric was a more complex and contradictory phenomenon than standard literary histories imply. Introspective lyricism led not (or not only) to amorphous effusion but to rigorous experimentation with the formal and linguistic resources of lyric, as well as to the development of counter-models that were professedly anti-subjective. I want to turn now, though, to another dimension of lyric that is equally important for Romanticism and that takes us back to the root meaning of lyric: poetry connected with music. One of the explanations often given for the rising status of lyric poetry is the revaluation of music, and the emergence, particularly in German Romantic aesthetics, of the idea of music as the quintessentially expressive medium to which all other art forms aspire (an idea later developed and popularised in England by Walter Pater).[25] Lyric, as the type of poetry most attentive to its own acoustic properties, was the genre best able to embrace this ideal. Accordingly, it is rightly said that lyric poetry of this period displayed an increased emphasis on what Ezra Pound called the 'melopoeic' aspect of verse;[26] or, to use Boris Eikhenbaum's more theoretical formulation, that it manifested a new 'orientation' to music, this being the 'extra-literary series' that exerted the dominant influence on its linguistic and formal patterning, in contrast to the orientation to oratory in lyric poetry of the neoclassical period.[27] From a broader historical perspective, this could be seen as a return, on different terms, to the Renaissance idea of lyric explored by David Lindley in an earlier chapter of this book – a partial reversal of the epochal separation between poetry and music that John Hollander referred to figuratively as 'the untuning of the sky'.[28]

The rapprochement of the two art forms is reflected in contemporary use of the word 'lyric' itself. The most famous usage is in *Lyrical Ballads* (1798), a title Wordsworth thought distinctive enough to consider changing when Mary Robinson published a volume of poems entitled *Lyrical Tales* two years later. Critics have used Wordsworth's 1800 preface to interpret the modifier 'lyrical' as signalling the importance of feeling over action in the poems, a reversal of the traditional priorities of the ballad, which can be seen as indicative of the authors' investment in an expressive, psychological conception of lyric.[29] However, in his later discussion of poetic terminology in the preface to his *Poems* (1815), Wordsworth defines 'Lyrical' to mean poems for which, 'for the production of their *full* effect, an accompaniment of music is indispensable', listing as subsets of lyrical poetry 'the Hymn, the Ode, the Elegy, the Song, and the Ballad'.[30] By this classification, 'lyrical ballad' is a tautology, and also a contradiction of his own practice, since there is no evidence that his or Coleridge's poems were ever intended for musical accompaniment. By contrast, this was precisely what was meant when the same phrase was used in another publication of 1800. *Positive John; or, Nothing Can Cure Him: A New Lyric Ballad* is a 'serio-comic song', published in Dublin, satirising supporters of the Act of Union ('Positive John' is John Bull, 'Immerged in Wars / Tattowed with Scars' from the struggle with revolutionary France, and determined to 'fleece / The Irish Geese' in an attempt to make himself feel better). This spirited broadside qualifies as a 'ballad' by virtue of the fact that it has some narrative content and is written in verse (though not in quatrains and without other traditional balladic features), but it is also a 'lyric' in the sense that it is set to music and intended for singing, the name of the tune ('Norah n' Kheestagh') appearing beneath the title.

This unlikely comparison alerts us to another, forgotten world of lyric that surrounds the lyric poetry of Romanticism: the world of popular urban song. When *The British Lyre; or, Muses' Repository, for the Year 1793* (London, 1793) promises on its title-page to be offering the public a selection of 'the Works of the Most Celebrated Lyric Geniuses of the Age', it is referring not to canonical Romantic poets but to popular songwriters and performers who had made a name for themselves in the theatres and pleasure gardens of the metropolis. There were many such collections with similar titles, among them *Parsley's Lyric Repository* (1788–90), *The New Lyric Repository* (1792–5), and *Kemmish's Annual-Harmonist; or, The*

British Apollo, being a Complete Lyric Repository and Banquet of Amusement (1792–?1795).[31] Published annually, these typically contained a mixture of the season's favourite new songs together with older songs, songs written specially for the publication itself, and a selection of 'toasts and sentiments'. Use of the term 'lyric' in anthologies of this kind serves as a legitimation device linking popular songs to Classical poetry and implicitly asserting the literary value of song-texts that were being sold, in most cases, without their accompanying music.

The tactic is particularly visible in *The Lyric Repository* of 1787, the first and most impressive collection to appear under this much imitated title. Subtitled 'A Selection of Original, Ancient, and Modern, Songs, Duets, Catches, Glees, and Cantatas, Distinguished for Poetical and Literary Merit', this differs from later 'lyric repositories' in interspersing theatre songs (by Charles Dibdin, John O'Keefe, and others) with lyric poems by prominent contemporary poets like Charlotte Smith, Anna Barbauld, and Peter Pindar, and works by earlier writers such as Shakespeare, Milton, and Dryden. Here the different worlds of lyric truly come together, elegiac sonnets (Smith's 'To a Nightingale', 'To the South-Downs', 'Supposed to be Written by Werther') appearing alongside songs from comic operas (*Love in a Village, Summer Amusement, The Double Disguise*), and famous songs, sonnets, and other lyrics by great authors from the past. Despite its literary aspirations, there is, nonetheless, an air of playfulness about the collection, as is confirmed by the frontispiece, a satirical engraving by Thomas Rowlandson depicting not a Classical lyre or Romantic harp – the usual icons of lyric poetry – but a group of drunken men singing around a table at a gathering of a 'convivial society' or some other gentlemen's club.

A more routine product of this publishing trend is *The Pocket Lyric Magazine; or, Convivial and Entertaining Vocal Miscellany* (single issue, ?1795–1800) – another 'Complete Repository of Lyric Poetry', which retains the playful air but drops the literary pretensions, the only type of poetry now on offer being songs (and other vocal compositions) 'Produced at the Different Public Places of Entertainment For the Past Twenty Years'. Such unashamedly ephemeral collections typify the 'modish insipidity' of which John Aikin had complained in his *Essays on Song-Writing* (1772), an annotated anthology that contained the first extended critical discussion of song.[32] Aikin sought to raise the status of the genre through a rigorous discrimination of its varieties, a declared aim of the anthology being 'to form a barrier' against the type of song found in comic operas, 'that vile mongrel of the drama, where the most enchanting tunes are suited with the most flat and wretched combinations of words' (p. iv). In practice, his intervention had little effect and the type of theatrical song he deplored went on to even greater success in the melodramas that dominated the Romantic stage. But his point about the mismatch between words and music was one of which many in the entertainment world were keenly aware. Charles Dibdin, the most prolific singer-songwriter of the time (and a key figure in the history of popular entertainment), often made the point – echoed many times before and since – that the best words for singing were not necessarily the best poems.[33] However good a marketing strategy, the attempt by late-eighteenth-century publishers to equate the two worlds of 'lyric poetry' – literary lyric and popular song – by printing examples of them side by side risked exposing popular songs to textual comparisons they could not sustain. It may be no coincidence, therefore, that the term 'lyric', applied to popular music, eventually lost its literary resonance and came to mean simply the words of a song as distinct from the music, with no suggestion of poetical merit (the *Oxford English Dictionary* dates this usage from 1876, and the plural form, 'lyrics', from the 1930s).

The relationship between Romantic poetry and theatrical song is a largely unexplored topic, confirming the critical segregation, insisted on by Aikin and generally upheld since, of these two artistic spheres. By contrast, Romanticism's engagement with another kind of popular song – the traditional ballad – has been extensively researched, and is regarded not as a debasement of lyric but as a tremendous enrichment of it. One reason why the balladisation of lyric has met with critical approval, whereas the theatricalisation of it has not, is that it took place under the sign of primitivism, presenting itself as a return to an older, purer state of lyric in which human feelings could find stronger and more natural expression than in the mannered neoclassical forms then current. Antiquarian collections such as Thomas Percy's *Reliques of Ancient English Poetry* (London, 1765) had, Wordsworth claimed, 'redeemed' English poetry by reconnecting it with its earlier traditions.[34] His and Coleridge's poetry is part of that redemption, a self-conscious revival of literary techniques and poetic forms ('chiefly of the lyric kind', as Percy's title has it) that had previously been considered obsolete or marginal. Though these atavistic trends were not to everyone's taste, they were inescapably part of the spirit of the age, and the literary products of this 'retrograde industry' (as one sceptical observer called it)[35] carried both popular appeal and cultural authority.

Some recent scholars have detected a tension between Romantic 'minstrelsy' and lyric introspection, Erik Simpson calling these 'antithetical' modes of composition 'that developed in dialogic opposition'.[36] Maureen

McLane sees a more symbiotic relationship, interpreting minstrelsy as a way for Romantic poets 'to think about the internal workings of poetry as well as a way to meditate on its legitimating and contextualizing apparatus', hence the abundance of editorial subtitles, glosses, footnotes, and other paratextual features that surrounded poetry of this kind.[37] Minstrelsy was, nonetheless, a self-contradictory mode: an openly anachronistic form of writing that was 'always imminently obsolete', requiring 'endless revival and equally endless burying', as exemplified by the common Romantic motif of the 'last minstrel' (pp. 139, 131). An even more serious problem, argues Terence Hoagwood, was its deceptive relationship to music. Minstrelsy involves nostalgia not only for orality – for the poet as performer, with audible voice and live audience – but also for musicality, the ancient link between poetry and music. The desire to restore this link is manifest in many kinds of Romantic poetry but especially in song, the revival of which was as central to the movement as the revival of romance that gave Romanticism its name. Yet despite the rage for song-collecting; the large number of new works that labelled themselves 'song' (or some other musical term such as 'ballad', 'hymn', 'lay', or 'melody'); and the ubiquity in Romantic poetry of harps, lyres, dulcimers, and other musical instruments; what often appeared under this rubric were not actual songs but 'pseudo-songs', words divorced from their music or words that never had, or were intended to have, any connection with music. 'Modern simulacra', writes Hoagwood, took the place of traditional songs, and the aspiration to the condition of music often involved no more than the cultivation of its 'mirage'.[38]

Hoagwood's exposé of the Romantic pseudo-song is unsparing, his demythologisation of minstrelsy complete (he takes his tone from Harker's *Fakesong*, a comprehensive study of the illusions, deceptions, and frauds that make up the history of British folk song).[39] What this critique does not allow for, however, is the frequency with which Romantic lyrics analyse their own musical illusions or aspirations, or use the imagined presence – but actual absence – of music to foreground their own 'unheard melodies'. For Shelley, as for Keats, it is the 'memory of music fled' that is often the starting-point for poetic creation, and the point about the 'damsel with a dulcimer' in 'Kubla Khan' is that her half-remembered 'symphony and song' cannot be revived. The poems, in other words, explore the very predicament Hoagwood describes, all too aware that verbal melody, however powerful, is no substitute for musical melody. Such lyrics are best understood not as pseudo-songs but as poems that, as Hollander puts it, sing their own song, in emulation of the music they can never become.[40]

A second difficulty with Hoagwood's approach is that it invokes criteria of authenticity and originality derived from other areas of Romantic poetics, and does not take into account that in the sphere of song a very different code of practice was operative, with different measures of artistic value. 'National song', a type of song widely discussed in this period, brings out these differences particularly clearly. The term, introduced by Joseph Ritson in 1783, refers not to a nation's official ceremonial song (as in 'national anthem', a later coinage) but to the traditional songs of a nation considered in their entirety.[41] The currency of the term reflects growing interest in the cultural origins and affiliations of genres, and in national canons, but it also underlines the perception of song as a collective rather than an individual mode of creativity: an art form that originates in and belongs to a community and a tradition. National song eludes, in this sense, the notions of ownership and originality associated in Romantic poetics with other types of poetry. Modern concepts of intertextuality and influence also cease to be meaningful in this context, so pervasive are the practices of imitation, adaptation, and variation that constitute the history of song. The combination of musical and verbal variability amplifies the instability found in all oral literature, and the transfer from orality to print does little to reduce this, songs continuing to metamorphose both in their printed form and through performance.[42]

Nowhere is this variation better demonstrated than in 'Auld Lang Syne', the best known of all national songs. Its attribution to Robert Burns is part of the popular mythology that surrounds every aspect of this iconic song, and is likely to prove irremovable from the public imagination. Knowledge of its actual provenance, however, makes the case even more interesting, since this is a song Burns collected and transformed, exercising his lyric gifts not in an act of original creation but in an inspired reworking of an already much reworked traditional song. The earliest printed form of it is a broadside, 'An Excellent and proper New Ballad, Entituled, Old Long Syne', conjecturally dated 1701.[43] This differs markedly from Burns' version in being double the length; in two parts; written almost entirely in English, not Scots; and on the theme of emotional rejection. Two lovers, one named Clorinda (a name Burns would famously use in another context, though not in his version of this song), have been separated from one another and are living apart: both reflect despairingly on their absent lover, imagining they have been rejected and forgotten, but vowing eternal fidelity. The song hinges on the idea of remembering and forgetting, as each lover assumes that only he or she will ever reflect on their time together. Each of the twelve verses, seven in the male voice (Part I) and five in the female (Part II), presents a new stage in the lovers' confused emotions, and is followed by a chorus that is not, as later in Burns, about the sharing of memories, but, on the contrary, about a past happiness that each feels only he or she will remember – a recollection process that brings, at different moments, either great joy ('My Heart is ravisht with delight, / when thee I think upon') or, as here, acute sadness:

> Dear will ye give it back my Heart,
>   since I cannot have thine;
> For since with yours ye will not part,
>   no reason you have mine:
> But yet I think I'le let it ly,
>   within that breast of thine,
> Who hath a Thief in every Eye,
>   to make me live in pain.
> *For Old long syne my Jo,*
>   *for Old long syne,*
> *That thou canst never once reflect,*
>   *on Old long syne.*
>
>   (verse 7)

The male lover's turmoil is nicely illustrated by these contradictory feelings, a contradiction repeated by Clorinda in the second part and left unresolved at the end, where the lovers are still apart, reflecting separately on their plight. In light of what follows, the opening line of the song, 'Should Old Acquaintance be forgot', thus carries a meaning almost opposite to the one in Burns, since the point here is that an old friendship *has* been forgotten, or so the lovers fear; in fact, they are both remembered but never find this out. This tragic irony, and the parallelism of their lament, are what give poignancy to the song.

The 1701 broadside introduces the ballad as 'Newly corrected and amended, with a large and new Edition of several excellent Love Lines'. The extent of these amendments can be judged from an earlier manuscript version that has recently come to light in a nobleman's commonplace book from the 1660s: this contains several verses that are not found in printed versions, and a refrain of just two lines: variations on 'That thou can never think upon / kind old long syne', clearly the original hook lines.[44] Over the course of the eighteenth century the song underwent many further changes, some of which can be traced in surviving song collections. It first reappears, abridged and modified, in James Watson's *Choice Collection of Comic and Serious Scots Poems Both Ancient and Modern* (Edinburgh, 1706–11), where, confusingly, some of the female verses are transferred to the male, making it hard to distinguish the two voices (later collections sometimes clarify this feature by labelling the second part 'The Answer'). A few years later a more drastically transformed version is published by Allan Ramsay in his *Scots Songs* (Edinburgh, 1718). Ramsay, a pioneering figure in the Scottish song revival and an influential literary mediator of popular song,[45] completely inverts the original sentiments of the ballad by rewriting it as 'The Kind Reception', celebrating a hero's return from war into the arms of his faithful lover, in whose voice the whole song is delivered. The refrain is now reduced to a single phrase, 'lang syne', variously incorporated into the final line of each verse; and unlike the previous pair of lovers, Ramsay's not only share their memories but also re-enact them: 'We'll please our Selves with mutual Charms / as we did lang syne', and 'We'll make the Hours run smooth away, / And laugh at lang syne' (verses 3, 4). The song ends with the lovers going to the altar. Though written to the same tune and with the same opening line, it is debatable whether such a comprehensively altered version can still be called the same song – an extreme example of the evolutionary process common in the history of song.

In Burns' hands, the song undergoes further transformation, to acquire the form by which it is best known today. He published two versions of 'Auld Lang Syne', one in Volume V of John Johnson's *Scots Musical Museum* (Edinburgh, 1796), and another, slightly different, in George Thomson's *Select Collection of Original Scottish Airs* (third set, 1799), which appeared after his death (a third variant exists in manuscript). In a letter to Thomson, he claims the song had 'never been in print, nor even in manuscript, until I took it down from an old man's singing',[46] the first part of which is palpably false, since he would have been well aware of previous printings from his extensive knowledge of Scottish song collections (and indeed a transcription of the Ramsay version in his hand survives). His insistence that that the song derived from oral rather than written sources is typical of ballad- and song-collectors of the time, and Burns is part of a long tradition of folk song editors who were economical with the truth. His motives, though, were artistically complex: by concealing his creative input and presenting the song as wholly traditional when it had actually been partially rewritten by himself, Burns absorbs himself into that tradition, an achievement he appears to value more highly than that of being an original author (a powerful example of what Janowitz calls the 'communitarian' poetics).

In the absence of firm evidence about performed versions he may have heard, conclusions about the compositional process remain conjectural, but what seems clear is that Burns mixed elements from previous printed versions, abridging or deleting some sections, extending or replacing others, and making a series of artistic adjustments that greatly enhanced the quality of the song. He follows Ramsay in making it about reunion rather than separation, but a reunion now of old friends rather than lovers. Ramsay's 'kind reception' becomes in Burns a scene of exuberant male camaraderie, the love song metamorphosing into a drinking song that includes such memorable verses as this last one:

> And there's a hand, my trusty fiere!
> And gie's a hand o' thine!
> And we'll tak a right gude-willie-waught,
> For auld lang syne.
>
> (verse 5)[47]

Burns' transposition of the song into Scots represents a deepening of its 'national' qualities but also an enhancement of its expressive effects, as illustrated by the multiply alliterative phrase 'a right gude-willie-waught' (a hearty drink), which literalises the metaphorical 'cup o' kindness' of the reinstated chorus and brings to a colourful vernacular climax the drinking theme that has been building throughout.

Burns' ear for resonant Scots phrases extends, of course, to 'auld lang syne' itself (meaning 'old long ago', 'auld' acting as a tautological intensifier for the common Scots phrase 'lang syne'),[48] whose 'exceedingly expressive' quality Burns remarks on in another letter, noting of the original song – in essence, a lyric fantasia on this phrase – that 'There is more of the fire of native genius in it, than in half a dozen of modern English Bacchanalians'.[49] Burns uses his own 'native genius' to create a Scots bacchanalian, but he also retains the pathos of the original love song, converting the lovers' bitter-sweet reflections into a poignant nostalgia for childhood friendship that encompasses the sense both of lost time and lost place. In a few simple words, he evokes an entire shared world, rooted in a specific national landscape and remembered all the more fondly for the intervening years of separation (with echoes of the Highland clearances that so often underpin Scottish parting songs):

> We twa hae run about the braes,
> And pou'd the gowans fine;
> But we've wander'd mony a weary fitt,
> Sin auld lang syne.
> *For auld lang, &c.*
>
> We twa hae paidl'd in the burn,
> Frae morning sun till dine;
> But seas between us braid hae roar'd
> Sin auld lang syne.
> *For auld lang, &c.*
>
> (verses 3–4)

Like Wordsworth in his poetic recollections of a more solitary childhood, Burns is able to capture the past in precise, seemingly insignificant details (running over the hillsides, pulling wild daisies, paddling in the stream) that, focalised and amplified through verse, acquire huge emotional force. Read as poetry, Burns' rewriting of 'Auld Lang Syne' is a minor masterpiece of Romantic lyric, but it is a lyric ultimately inseparable from the music to which he set it,[50] whether it be the melancholy air of the original song (printed in Johnson) or the more jaunty tune of 'The Miller's Daughter' substituted in the Thomson edition, which better matches the mood of his version and is the tune to which it is usually sung and danced today.

Burns' unmatched achievements in the making and remaking of Scottish vernacular song represent one pinnacle of Romantic lyric, and his poetic career, the last ten years of which were almost exclusively devoted to song, is a compelling illustration of Tynianov's thesis about lyric poetry's reorientation to music. As a final example, I will turn to another Romantic poet who was attracted to music, and even wrote a number of 'popular songs' (though not, it seems, for musical accompaniment),[51] but whose greatest accomplishments were in more elevated, Classical forms of lyric. Shelley's 'Ode to the West Wind' shows how the grandest of all lyric forms – the Pindaric ode – could be remade so as to sing its own song while losing none of its oratorical power and at the same time yielding itself as a vehicle for impassioned self-expression and self-analysis. As such, it marks a synthesis of the different kinds of lyricism I have considered in this chapter, and the fulfilment of Shelley's search for 'a language in itself music and persuasion'.[52] Shelley applies this description to Dante but it also defines his own ideal of poetic communication, an ideal realised in the lyric eloquence of the 'Ode to the West Wind'. Implementing this through the medium of the Pindaric ode meant harnessing the ode's formal and linguistic conventions in a highly original way, and combining the ode with other lyric forms in an equally innovative act of genre-mixing.

As so often in Romantic poetry, though, innovation also involves a return to origins. Shelley restores the apostrophic, mythopoeic, metaphoric essence of the Pindaric ode. He removes the neoclassical accretions – the prefabricated grandeur and bombastic formulas of many eighteenth-century odes – and attains genuine sublimity and audacity, taking the ode form to daring new heights. Like Gray and Collins before him, he regularises the Pindaric, but does so in a new way that both enhances its expressive power and strengthens the emotional and imaginative 'logic' described by Young. Of the poem's apostrophic qualities there can be no doubt. The whole poem is an extended address to the wind. Each of the five sections renews the apostrophe, the exclamatory 'O' appearing no fewer than eight times. 'Thou' appears eleven times, and there are many other 'thee's and 'thine's, this accumulation of vocatives enacting the summoning that is the essence of the figure of apostrophe. This is performative language in its strongest form: lyric as 'amplified exclamation in verse' (Arthur K. Moore's apt definition)[53] but also as exhortation. The poem begins as an appeal, a summons, and ends as a prayer.

The high turnover of metaphor, a much discussed feature of Shelley's style, is one of the factors that impart imaginative momentum to the poem. But the dynamism is generated too by its form. This is a Pindaric ode, but of a highly unusual kind. It has the thematic transitions we would expect of a Pindaric, and the corresponding emotional transitions, but structurally the five sections are identical: the poem is regular and mono-strophic. However, it is regularised in a very special way because each section consist of a fourteen-line sonnet, a formal innovation unique to this poem. Moreover, the sonnet form itself has undergone crucial modification: the *volta* has been removed and the Italian octave/sestet or English quatrains have been converted into four groups of *terza rima* followed by a final rhyming couplet (creating another five-part structure mirroring the five sections of the poem). The conjunction of ode form and sonnet form, and of sonnet form and *terza rima*, creates some interesting effects. The sonnet is a self-contained form with its own poetic logic, which depends on rapid exposition, drastic compression, and neat closure (its 'methodizing' qualities, in Coleridge's term). Shelley harnesses this sonnet logic: each section is a discrete exposition of one aspect of his theme, one manifestation of the wind's power; and each moves to the partial closure of the final couplet. But it is only a partial closure, because the first three sections all end on a note of anticipation, with the words 'O hear!'. These have a cumulative anticipatory effect – we listen and wait, ever more urgently – and indeed metaphors of accumulation abound in the poem. The 'congregated might' – or 'vault' – of line 26 is a perfect emblem of the poem's own formal architecture and compressed power.

The *terza rima*, meanwhile, contributes its own dynamic energy, the point about this verse form being that the rhyme always carries forward. It is thus a perfect formal vehicle for describing motion or journeys (as in Dante's *Divine Comedy*), and by the same token it is a perfect way of suggesting the onward, driving force of the wind. The substitution of quatrain for *terza rima* accelerates the sonnet form, and the sonnet form – the sonnet *sequence* – in turn increases the momentum of the ode. No other poem captures so effectively the sensation of speed, of raw elemental force. Yet at the same time the elaborate formal architecture contains that force, amplifying but also controlling and directing it.

The question of control becomes explicit in the final two sections, where for the first time in the poem Shelley uses the first person singular. This is the lyrical 'I' to the apostrophised 'Thou'. It is here that we get to 'hear' the poet's deferred message. At this point, however, the rhetorical confidence of the earlier sections wavers. Syntactically, we move from the imperative to the conditional, with an anaphoric sequence of 'if' clauses, one of many instances of grammatical parallelism in the poem. The three 'if' clauses recapitulate the leaf, cloud, and wave analogies of the earlier sections, as Shelley imagines *himself* subject to the wind's influence and able to partake of its strength. Only in line 51 is the conditional construction completed, as Shelley admits that he is not part of the natural cycle and therefore must, in his 'sore need', resort to 'prayer'. But the prayer fails, and there is a sudden, near-total collapse: 'I fall upon the thorns of life! I bleed!'. This should not be read literally: it is the conventionalised cry of despair of the poet-prophet, as in the Book of Psalms, another of his odic models along with Pindar. But it is a collapse nonetheless, and the section ends at an emotional low-point:

> A heavy weight of hours has chained and bowed
>   One too like thee: tameless, and swift, and proud.

Even as he voices his despair, however, the poet regains his lyrical strength, and, in another spectacular odic transition, the last section returns to the apostrophic, imperative mode: 'Make me thy lyre, even as the forest is'. In a final, bold reversal, Shelley turns the tables on the wind and achieves the identification deemed impossible moments earlier. Instead of 'I' – Shelley – being like 'you' – the Wind – 'Be thou, Spirit fierce, / My spirit! Be thou me, impetuous one!' Shelley is now both wind and winged seed; transmitted and transmitter; his own apocalyptic clarion, blowing the 'trumpet of a prophecy'; and his own fire source, whose words are like 'ashes and sparks' from an 'unextinguished hearth', to rekindle revolutionary hope.

Shelley's poem, then, is an act both of persuasion and of self-examination, an oratorical lyric and a confessional one. Like the introspective, 'self-watching' lyrics described earlier, it charts an emotional and imaginative trajectory, using the structural devices of the ode and sonnet to take us through a complex meditative sequence at astonishing speed. Its expressive mode, however, is declamatory rather than conversational, involving not the linguistic modulations found in Coleridge's blank-verse conversation poems or 'Tintern Abbey', but a sustained rhetorical performance in the highest poetic register. To call this language 'melodious' is to give little idea of either its sonic properties or its signifying power: however carefully orchestrated, this is poetic language in which no element of meaning has been sacrificed to pure sound, and in which the grammatical and logical structure is as tight as the metrical architecture and rhyme scheme. Yet the sound patterns of the poem have their own expressive function, and the 'incantation' referred to in line 65 is an accurate description of the rhythmic and melodic effects of the verse, with its elaborate syntactic and phonetic parallelism and insistent forward motion.[54] In a quite literal sense, this is a poem that demands to be heard, not merely read on the page. In this respect, Shelley's ode is an example of musicalised lyric too, more than earning its symbol of the lyre in line 57, even if the music produced in this retuned sky is irreducibly verbal and message-laden.

Notes

1 James Montgomery, *Lectures on Poetry and General Literature* (London, 1833), p. 195.

2 Hugh Blair, *Lectures on Rhetoric and Belles Lettres*, 2 vols. (London, 1783), Vol. II, p. 355.

3 William Wordsworth and Samuel Taylor Coleridge, *Lyrical Ballads 1805*, ed. Derek Roper, 2nd edn (Plymouth: Macdonald and Evans, 1976), preface p. 22.

4 Original preface to Francis Turner Palgrave, ed., *The Golden Treasury of the Best Songs and Lyrical Poems in the English Language: With an Introduction and Additional Poems Selected and Arranged by C. Day Lewis* (London: Collins, 1954), p. 21.

5 'Frost at Midnight' (first printed version, line 26), in Samuel Taylor Coleridge, *Fears in Solitude: Written in 1798, during the Alarm of an Invasion. To which are added, France, an Ode; and Frost at Midnight* (London, 1798), p. 20.

6 Joseph Trapp, 'Of Lyric Poetry', in *Lectures on Poetry … Translated from the Latin* (London, 1742), pp. 202–9 (p. 203); Edward Young, 'On Lyrick Poetry', appended to *Ocean: An Ode* (London, 1728), pp. 14–30.

7 Letter to Mason, January 1759, quoted by Penelope Wilson, '"High Pindaricks upon Stilts": A Case Study in the Eighteenth-Century Classical Tradition', in *Rediscovering Hellenism: The Hellenic Inheritance and the English Imagination*, ed. G. W. Clarke (Cambridge University Press, 1989), pp. 23–41 (p. 26).

8 William Duff, *An Essay on Original Genius* (London, 1767), pp. 270, 282–4.

9 M. H. Abrams, *The Mirror and the Lamp: Romantic Theory and the Critical Tradition* (New York: Oxford University Press, 1953), p. 23.

10 M. H. Abrams, 'Structure and Style in the Greater Romantic Lyric' (1965), in *Romanticism and Consciousness: Essays in Criticism*, ed. Harold Bloom (New York: Norton, 1970), pp. 210–29.

11 Preface to Wordsworth and Coleridge, *Lyrical Ballads*, p. 23.

12 David Duff, *Romanticism and the Uses of Genre* (Oxford University Press, 2009), p. 204.

13 See Stuart Curran, *Poetic Form and British Romanticism* (New York: Oxford University Press, 1986), pp. 29–55.

14 Samuel Taylor Coleridge, 'Introduction to the Sonnets', in *Poems, by S. T. Coleridge, Second Edition. To which are now Added Poems by Charles Lamb, and Charles Lloyd* (Bristol, 1797), pp. 71–4.

15 C. Day Lewis, in Palgrave, *The Golden Treasury*, p. 17.

16 In his collected poems, *Sibylline Leaves* (London, 1817).

17 For a lucid critique of such approaches, see Sarah M. Zimmerman, *Romanticism, Lyricism, and History* (Albany: State University of New York Press, 1999), pp. 1–37.

18 The link between form and history in the 1798 pamphlet is explored by David Fairer, *Organising Poetry: The Coleridge Circle, 1790–1798* (Oxford University Press, 2009), pp. 285–308.

19 Theodor Adorno, 'On Lyric Poetry and Society' (1957), in *Poetry in Theory: An Anthology 1900–2000* ed. Jon Cook (Oxford: Blackwell, 2004), pp. 343–9 (p. 347).

20 Anne Janowitz, *Lyric and Labour in the Romantic Tradition* (Cambridge University Press, 1998), pp. 52–6.

21 Preface to Wordsworth and Coleridge, *Lyrical Ballads*, p. 42.

22 George Dyer, 'Essay on Representative Poetry', in *Poems*, 2 vols. (London, 1802), Vol. II, pp. 4–5. For Dyer's implicit dialogue with Wordsworth, see Janowitz, *Lyric and Labour*, pp. 52–3.

23 John Thelwall, 'On Lyrical Poetry', in *The Poetical Recreations of The Champion* (London, 1822).

24 Judith Thompson, *John Thelwall in the Wordsworth Circle: The Silenced Partner* (New York: Palgrave Macmillan, 2012), pp. 235–53.

25 Abrams, *Mirror and the Lamp*, pp. 50–1, 91–4; Walter Pater, *The Renaissance: Studies in Art and Poetry. The 1893 Text* (Berkeley: University of California Press, 1980), p. 109. For other examples, see Peter Le Huray and James Day, eds., *Music and Aesthetics in the Eighteenth and Early Nineteenth Centuries* (Cambridge University Press, 1981).

26 Ezra Pound, 'How to Read' (1927–8), in his *Literary Essays*, ed. T. S. Eliot (London: Faber and Faber, 1954), p. 25.

27 Boris Eikhenbaum, *The Melodics of Verse* (1922), cited by Victor Erlich, *Russian Formalism: History-Doctrine*, 3rd edn (New Haven: Yale University Press, 1981), pp. 222–3. See also Yuri Tynianov, 'The Ode as an Oratorical Genre' (1927), trans. Ann Shukman, *New Literary History* 34.3 (2003), 565–96 (p. 566).

28 John Hollander, *The Untuning of the Sky: Ideas of Music in English Poetry 1500–1700* (Princeton University Press, 1961). See David Lindley, '"Words for music, perhaps": early modern songs and lyric', above, pp. 10–29.

29 See e.g. Zachary Leader, '*Lyrical Ballads*: The Title Revisited', in *1800: The New 'Lyrical Ballads'*, ed. Nicola Trott and Seamus Perry (Basingstoke: Palgrave, 2001), pp. 23–43.

30 William Wordsworth, *Shorter Poems, 1807–1820*, ed. Carl H. Ketcham (Ithaca, NY: Cornell University Press, 1989), p. 633.

31 Place of publication in each case is London.

32 John Aikin, preface to *Essays on Song-Writing: With a Collection of Such English Songs as Are Most Eminent for Poetical Merit* (London, 1772), p. iv.

33 Cited by Jon A. Gillaspie in the entry for Dibdin (*c*. 1745–1814) in the *Oxford Dictionary of National Biography*. For his place in the history of theatrical song, see Roger Fiske, *English Theatre Music in the Eighteenth Century* (Oxford University Press, 1973), pp. 348–59.

34 Wordsworth, 'Essay, Supplementary to the Preface' (1815), in *Shorter Poems*, p. 653.

35 *Imperial Review* (November 1804), quoted by John Jordan, *Why the Lyrical Ballads? The Background, Writing, and Character of Wordsworth's 1798 "Lyrical Ballads"* (Berkeley: University of California Press, 1976), pp. 71–2.

36 Erik Simpson, *Literary Minstrelsy, 1770–1830: Minstrels and Improvisers in British, Irish, and American Literature* (New York: Palgrave Macmillan, 2008), p. 1.

37 Maureen N. McLane, *Balladeering, Minstrelsy, and the Making of British Romantic Poetry* (Cambridge University Press, 2008), p. 144.

38 Terence Allan Hoagwood, *From Song to Print: Romantic Pseudo-Songs* (New York: Palgrave Macmillan, 2010), pp. xi, xiv.

39 Dave Harker, *Fakesong: The Manufacturing of British 'Folksong' 1700 to the Present Day* (Milton Keynes: Open University Press, 1985).

40 John Hollander, 'Romantic Verse Form and the Metrical Contract' (1965), in Bloom, *Romanticism and Consciousness*, pp. 181–200 (p. 182).

41 'A Historical Essay on the Origin and Progress of National Song', in *A Select Collection of English Songs*, [ed. Joseph Ritson], 3 vols. (London, 1783), Vol. I, pp. i–lxxii.

42 See Kirsteen McCue, '"An individual flowering on a common stem": Melody, Performance and National Song', in *Romanticism and Popular Culture in Britain*, ed. Philip Connell and Nigel Leask (Cambridge University Press, 2009), pp. 89–106.

43 Quotations below are from the copy in the National Library of Scotland, available in digital facsimile at http://digital.nls.uk/broadsides/broadside.cfm/id/14548/criteria/old long syne (last accessed 1 June 2013).

44 Manuscript commonplace book of James Crichton, second Viscount Frendraught, exhibited at The Morgan Library and Museum, New York, December 2011–February 2012, partially available in digital facsimile at www.themorgan.org/exhibitions/online/AuldLangSyne/ (last accessed 1 June 2013).

45 See Thomas Crawford, *Society and the Lyric: A Study of the Song Culture of Eighteenth-Century Scotland* (Edinburgh: Scottish Academic Press, 1979); and Steve Newman, *Ballad Collection, Lyric, and the Canon: The Call of the Popular from the Restoration to the New Criticism* (Philadelphia: University of Pennsylvania Press, 2007), pp. 44–96.

46 Early September 1793: Robert Burns, *The Letters of Robert Burns*, 2 vols. (Oxford: Clarendon Press, 1985), ed. G. Ross Roy and J. DeLancey Ferguson, Vol. II, p. 246. Thomson quotes this remark in a later edition of the *Select Collection*, remarking that Burns probably said it 'merely in a playful humour', since the song 'affords evidence of our Bard himself being the author'. In Johnson's *Scots Musical Museum*, Burns modifies his position, signing the poem 'Z', a code denoting 'old verses, with corrections or additions'. For a review of the debate about authorship, see introduction to *The Songs of Robert Burns*, ed. Donald A. Low (London: Routledge, 1993), pp. 25–7, which concludes contradictorily that Burns' disclaimer to Thomson 'ought to be believed' but that the song 'seems to bear his stamp' (p. 27).

47 The text used here is the Johnson version, as given in Low's edition of the *Songs*, *ibid.*,

48 My thanks to J. Derrick McLure for advice on the linguistic history of this phrase.

49 To Mrs Dunlop, 7 December 1788, in Burns, *Letters*, Vol. I, p. 345.

50 For an exemplary analysis of Burnsian song as 'text-tune complex', see Catarina Ericson-Roos, *The Songs of Robert Burns: A Study of the Unity of Poetry and Music* (University of Uppsala, 1977).

51 See Jessica K. Quillin, *Shelley and the Musico-Poetics of Romanticism* (Farnham: Ashgate, 2012); and Susan J. Wolfson, 'Popular Songs and Ballads: Writing the "Unwritten Story" in 1819', in *The Oxford Handbook of Percy Bysshe Shelley*, ed. Michael O'Neill and Anthony Howe (Oxford University Press, 2012), pp. 341–58.

52 'A Defence of Poetry' (1821), in Percy Bysshe Shelley, *Shelley's Poetry and Prose* (New York: Norton, 1977), p. 499. All quotations below are from this edition.

53 Arthur K. Moore, *The Secular Lyric in Middle English* (Lexington: University of Kentucky Press, 1951), p. 6.

54 For these features of the poem as agents of 'lyric transport', see my 'Melodies of Mind: Poetic Forms as Cognitive Structures', in *Cognition, Literature, and History*, ed. Mark Bruhn and Donald Wehrs (New York: Routledge, forthcoming, 2013).

CHAPTER EIGHT

Victorian lyric pathology and phenomenology

Marion Thain

In 1889, John Addington Symonds declared the significance of the lyric genre within poetry of the nineteenth century: 'No literature and no age has been more fertile of lyric poetry than English literature in the age of Victoria.'[1] Even when we discover that Symonds is loose enough in his designation of 'Victorian poetry' to include much of the Romantic poets' work, this might still come as a surprise when our established critical narrative characterises nineteenth-century literature through the growing importance of the novel and of narrative and dramatic poetic forms. Critics have long written of a 'crisis' in lyric poetry in the nineteenth century caused by the dominance of the novel in the literary marketplace. For example, Carol Christ wrote at length about 'The Victorians' concern with what they feel are the dangers of Romantic subjectivity' and lyric poetry's preoccupation with the self. Christ finds continuities between Victorian and modernist poetics in the search for more 'objective' poetic forms of expression to engage better with the modern world and a novel-reading public.[2] Herbert Tucker, in what is still one of the most engaging essays written on dramatic monologue, also argues that Browning's *Dramatic Lyrics*, or what Arthur Hallam described as Tennyson's 'graft of the lyric on the dramatic', 'began as a response to lyric isolationism'.[3] It is this conjunction of the apparent pre-eminence of lyric and the threat of its irrelevance due to its introspective nature that marks the particular interest of this period in lyric history.

These can be seen, through closer examination of Symonds' essay, to be two sides of the same coin. The essay is ostensibly, as it proclaims through its own title, 'A Comparison of Elizabethan with Victorian Poetry', and this long piece is an extended analysis, from the end of the era, of the nature of Victorian lyric poetry. As such it provides a substantial, illuminating, and thus far critically overlooked piece of evidence on how the concept of 'lyric' poetry was conceived at this time. In the essay, Symonds argues for the significance of lyric among the poetic genres on the basis that the novel has come to occupy the space that used to be taken by other forms of poetry: 'just as the novel has absorbed our forces for the drama, so has it satisfied our thirst for epical narration'. What is left to poetry, in Symonds' taxonomy is classified under two headings: the 'idyll' and the 'lyric'. The idyll includes 'all narrative and descriptive poetry', while lyric encompasses all that poetry which is subjective and introspective: 'The genius of our century, debarred from epic, debarred from drama, falls back upon idyllic and lyrical expression. In the idyll it satisfies its objective craving after art. In the lyric it pours fourth personality.'[4] Symonds' essay suggests that the growing importance of the lyric genre within poetry is a result of the same erosion of the importance of poetry within the literary marketplace as a whole. The more poetry was defined in relation to and in opposition with the novel, the more it was equated with lyric as its quintessential form. A key marker of the rise of lyric within the decline of poetry is the 1861 publication of Palgrave's *Golden Treasury*. While the general readership for poetry dwindled, Palgrave's *Golden Treasury*, a book aimed at the mass, middle-class, reading public, was thriving. Marjorie Perloff has noted how the publication marks an important moment in 'the codification of Romantic theory, with its gradual privileging of the lyric above the other literary modes'.[5] The volume both reflects and is a formative moment in the Victorian conception of lyric as a short poetic form (that which can be extracted and printed within the *Treasury*) and one associated with introspective subjectivity. To quote the introduction: 'Lyrical has been here held essentially to imply that each Poem shall turn on some single thought, feeling, or situation. In accordance with this, narrative, descriptive, and didactic poems – unless accompanied by rapidity of movement, brevity, and the colouring of human passion – have been excluded.'[6]

Yet, in a continuation of the process David Duff describes at the start of the century (see above, pp. 136–40), 'lyric' was simultaneously becoming an ever more capacious category, and Symonds meditates on the multiplicity of forms lyric can take:

> But what a complex thing is this Victorian lyric! It includes Wordsworth's sonnets and Rossetti's ballads, Coleridge's 'Ancient Mariner' and Keats' odes, Clough's 'Easter Day' and Tennyson's 'Maud', Swinburne's 'Songs before Sunrise' and Browning's 'Dramatic Personae', Thomson's 'City of Dreadful Night' and Mary Robinson's 'Handful of Honeysuckles', Andrew Lang's Ballades and Sharp's 'Weird of Michael Scot', Dobson's dealings with the eighteenth century and Noel's 'Child's Garland', Barnes's Dorsetshire Poems and Buchanan's London Lyrics, the songs from Empedocles on

Etna and Ebenezer Jones's 'Pagan's Drinking Chaunt', Shelley's Ode
to the West Wind and Mrs Browning's 'Pan is Dead', Newman's hymns
and Gosse's Chaunt Royal. The Kaleidoscope presented by this lyric is so
inexhaustible…[7]

Lyric, as Symonds notes, was by the end of the nineteenth century not
a particular song form of poetry, but was gradually encompassing a variety of forms and modes. What is interesting about Symonds' list is that
'song' appears within it as something of a dead metaphor for lyric of many
different formal hues, from the ballads and the odes to the chaunts and
hymns.

John Stuart Mill's earlier and much better known essay – 'Thoughts on
Poetry and Its Varieties' – helps to establish this case from the other end
of the period. Originally published as two separate pieces in *The Monthly
Repository* (1833), in it Mill writes that 'Lyric poetry, as it was the earliest
kind, is also, if the view we are now taking of poetry be correct, more
eminently and peculiarly poetry than any other.'[8] Mill may have been
criticised by his contemporaries and by recent scholars for characterising all poetry as lyric, but in doing so he was identifying an ongoing
trajectory to lyric's poetic pre-eminence. Significantly, both Mill and
Symonds emphasise the role of print in defining Victorian lyric. For Mill
it is a 'soliloquy' staged for the reader on 'hot-pressed paper': a print performance 'overheard' not aurally but through the pages and between the
covers.[9] Symonds elaborates much more on this essential quality of the
modern lyric, meditating on the separation of the printed lyric poem
from any actual song tradition. He devotes considerable space in this
essay to elaborating the idea that while Elizabethan lyric poems 'are the
right verbal counterpart to vocal and instrumental melody', 'We discover
but little of this quality in the lyrics of the Victorian age.' 'It is noticeable', he goes on, 'that those poets upon whom we are apt to set the least
store now, as Byron, Scott, Hood, Campbell, Moore, Barry Cornwall,
Mrs. Hemans, possessed it in greater perfection than their more illus-
trious contemporaries.' In a marked change from the Wordsworthian
description of 'lyrical' poems quoted by David Duff in the previous chapter ('for the production of their *full* effect, an accompaniment of music
is indispensable', p. 141), for Symonds it is a mark of the better poetry of
the age that it exploits its textual medium so it can exist complete without added music: 'the best lyrics of the Victorian age are not made to
be sung'. Symonds recognises that the lyric poem has become a textual
genre that, while it may be set to music, exists on its own terms, finding its melody within itself rather than in an accompanying strain. 'The

Victorian lyric', he concludes, is less spontaneous and song-like than the Elizabethan, but 'superior in its range, suggestiveness, variety and richness'; it 'corresponds to the highly-strung and panharmonic instrument of the poet's spirit which produced it, and to the manifold sympathies of the reader's mind for which it was intended'.[10] While it is possible to trace an ongoing song tradition over the Victorian period that would tie neatly to a preconceived definition of lyric, I want to focus here on how far lyric has travelled from an identification with song. This chapter is about what 'lyric' poetry becomes when it can no longer so easily find its core identity in song and when even the figure of oral transaction with an audience has become a site of anxiety.

To compare Mill's analysis with Symonds' is to book-end the Victorian period, and it is striking how both present Victorian poetry as characterised by what we might call, to borrow a term from Matthew Rowlinson, the 'totalization' of lyric in print: 'only in the nineteenth century does print become for lyric the hegemonic medium'. This is a process that gained momentum over the course of the century, and by 1889 Symonds theorises it more fully than Mill. As Rowlinson notes: 'by the 1860s British lyric poetry displays a new sense of confronting the prior history of lyric as a totality, a sense which I have argued results from confronting it in print'. Moreover, the Victorian lyric became itself an archive of its own imagined lyric heritage: 'print-lyric was able to incorporate the totality of its own antecedents, becoming the medium for a coherent summing up of its own history. Such an appearance can only be sustained by innumerable omissions and forgettings, as we can see by the prominence of fragments in the lyric canon'.[11] I think Symonds refers to something similar when he writes that 'Victorian poetry is in large measure the criticism of all existing literatures.'[12]

Lyric had become a poetic genre in which the aural (and the manuscript) incarnation was now combined with and mediated through print as the mode of transmission that subsumed all others – although it is important to note that this is not a claim for print providing textual stability. Edward FitzGerald's *Rubáiyát of Omar Khayyám*, first published in 1859, went through five different editions up to 1889 (a posthumous edition, after FitzGerald's death in 1883), each edition presenting a rather different text: expanded, revised, and changed in various, sometimes quite radical, ways. Christopher Decker has documented the impossibility of identifying one 'definitive' text for this work.[13] The text itself is a selection of verses taken from manuscript sources in the Bodleian and in Calcutta, 'mashed' and 'tessellated'

together, as FitzGerald himself described his method. This involved
not only rearranging the order of the quatrains but 'creating completely new ones by conflating lines and images from more than one
of the originals'.[14] Add to this FitzGerald's linguistic misunderstandings
of his sources and his attempt to Hellenise and orientalise them,[15] and
one sees how the text is an important example of how a rich aural and
manuscript history of lyric was contained within, combined with, and
superseded by a print rendition of it that largely fabricated its own pre-
Romantic generic origins.

When Symonds writes of lyric as a form now written to be read rather
than heard he is identifying an anxiety newly prominent in the age of
mass print,[16] which echoes Mill's earlier formulation of poetry as a private, interiorised mode whose isolation on the page renders it 'overheard',
rather than heard, by the reader.[17] The accepted critical narrative tells a
history of lyric that sees it as progressively more and more isolated from
its addressee – a process that we can see as culminating in the 'lyric crisis' of the nineteenth century.[18] Jonathan Culler recently summarised this
narrative with reference to work by W. R. Johnson in the following way:
'the Greek lyric is direct, addressed to its real audience, while the modern
lyric is no longer addressed and is therefore solipsistic'.[19] Typically, Culler
asserts, 'the classical is held up as a norm to suggest the individualistic,
alienated character of the modern'.[20] The modern lyric (roughly 1780 to
the present), then, is characterised in this narrative by a failure to connect
with 'you'. In fact, this is a narrative written by nineteenth-century commentators, from Mill to J. A. Symonds; and late-nineteenth-century poets,
certainly, often show awareness of their own practice as underpinned by
a sense of the lost lyric address.[21] There are many possible lines to follow
through the set of concerns traced above, but in the rest of this chapter I
will explore just two responses. The first, which I introduce only briefly,
is what has been seen as an emblematic 'turn' to the dramatic monologue
by some Victorian poets in the first half of the period as an escape from
lyric introspection, and the latter a much less well recognised reconsideration of lyric that came along with the influence of Decadence and aestheticism in the second half. This emphasis builds on well-established
discussions of a mid-Victorian problematisation of lyric in order to draw
attention to a connected but much less discussed part of Victorian lyric
history. Accounts of lyric history tend to skip from Browning, Arnold,
and Tennyson straight to high modernism, with the strict-form poems of
Decadence and aestheticism often ignored or omitted.[22] Yet this poetry
represents a major feature within the period (and is more representative

than the work of poets such as G. M. Hopkins who are more easily assimilated to our current lyric canon), and is one I deal with in the second half of this chapter.

Robert Browning's complex struggle with the concept of lyric poetry, specifically, is a prominent feature of the mid-Victorian critique that interests me here. His writing on Shelley presents a dichotomy central to a consideration of the nineteenth-century lyric: that between the subjective and objective poet. The subjective poet writes a transcendent poetry, spiritually motivated rather than directed towards the earthly realm. 'He' does not craft but rather exudes, and 'That effluence cannot be easily considered in abstraction from his personality, – being indeed the very radiance and aroma of his personality, projected from it but not separated.' The 'objective poet' 'chooses to deal with the doings of men (the result of which dealing, in its pure form, when even description, as suggesting a describer is dispensed with, is what we call dramatic poetry)'. The 'subjective poet', on the other hand, 'prefers to dwell upon those external scenic appearances which strike out most abundantly and uninterruptedly his inner light and power, selects the silence of the earth and sea in which he can best hear the beating of his individual heart'. Browning makes it clear that these different modes of poetry are commonly found intermingled, yet it is also clear that the subjective poet is associated here with the Romantics, and the objective with the dramatic, with Shakespeare, and by implication with Browning himself.[23] Crucially, Browning was alienated by what he took to be a Romantic introspection, without wanting to abandon lyric altogether. The 'dramatic lyric' hybrid form is the best recognised result of his desire to make poetry more socially relevant (although Britta Martens argues convincingly that even when he doesn't use a dramatic persona, the tussle is still evident).[24] It is not surprising to see that the continuing rise of lyric over the nineteenth century went hand in hand with poets' desire to find forms newly alternative to the dominant lyric model – even if lyric's capacity to absorb those forms back into itself is also quite astonishing.[25] When Browning was using the dramatic lyric it was part of a self-conscious effort to write something that both was and was not lyric, as Britta Martens has documented. This ambivalence is well expressed in a letter to John Kenyon of 1855:

> In your remarks on the little or no pleasure you derive from dramatic – in comparison with lyric – poetry … I partake your feeling to a great degree: lyric is the oldest, most natural, most *poetical* of poetry, and I would always get it if I could: but I find in these latter days that one has a great deal to say, and try and get attended to, which is out of the lyrical element and

> capability – and I am forced to take the nearest way to it: and then it is undeniable that the common reader is susceptible to plot, story, and the simplest form of putting a matter 'Said I', 'Said He' & so on.[26]

Again, lyric is revered while simultaneously in danger of becoming irrelevant.

Indeed, Browning seems more interested in dramatising a commentary on lyric than in writing it. This is true not just of poems such as 'Transcendentalism', in which, as critics have noted, the injunction to 'sing' rather than 'speak' is not borne out in the poem's own register.[27] In 'The Bishop Orders His Tomb at Saint Praxed's Church' we see, to be sure, a humorous satire of the excesses of the clergy, which has been linked to various historical sources, but we also surely see a dramatisation of the lyric subject who insists on fashioning his own immortal monument in stanzaic form.[28] Written in 1845, it was composed before D. G. Rossetti proclaimed in print the sonnet as a 'moment's monument' – 'memorial from the soul's eternity', carved in ebony or ivory – yet it is nonetheless resonant with the idea of lyric Rossetti reflects.[29] The charge of 'Vanity… vanity!' might be Browning's charge to the personal lyric poet as much as to the luxuriant bishop, and the bishop's lavish tomb might be equated with Rossetti's embellished sonnet. Indeed, Browning's poem consists almost entirely of the bishop's instructions to his interlocutors for the construction of his monument, every detail of which he specifies in a manner similar to the formal crafting of the lyric poet: the spatial and decorative construction set up an echo between the elaborate room of the lyric stanza and the tomb of 'peach-blossom marble' with its curlicues of lapis lazuli and jasper. A poem in key part in blank verse and running to 125 lines, this is no sonnet but a poem that perhaps refuses the memorialising of the lyric stanza in order to satirise the voice that might seek to command it.

To read Browning's interest in the psychology of pathological poetic subjects as commentary on lyric might be to recognise not only the gendered and social politics of his dramatic monologues, but also a pathologisation of what the lyric transaction has come to appear in a totalised print poetics. In 'My Last Duchess', in the 1842 *Dramatic Lyrics* collection, the duke's need for complete control over his environment – 'Oh sir, she smiled, no doubt, / Whene'er I passed her; but who passed without / Much the same smile? This grew; I gave commands; / Then the smiles stopped together' – might be that of the solipsistic lyric subject, separated from meaningful interaction with the lyric 'you' and confined to a damaging introspection that yields only delusion.[30] The lyric stalker of 'Christina' (also in *Dramatic Lyrics*) also highlights the dangers of living too much in one's own mind:

'She should never have looked at me / If she meant I should not love her!' His declared possession of her, from just one glance, and his conviction that he has found the secret to some transcendent experience is presented here as the sickness of the love lyric.[31] Most compellingly as a meditation on lyric pathology is 'Porphyria's Lover' (again from *Dramatic Lyrics*), where the subject's response to his final certainty that Porphyria 'worships' him is to strangle her with her own hair. This he does to preserve the moment at which 'she was mine, mine, fair, / Perfectly pure and good', and to fend off the reality that outside this perfect moment she was 'too weak' to sever herself from 'vainer ties' and 'give herself to me for ever'.[32] A parody of the lyric subject's immortalisation of the beloved lyric addressee in literary form, the woman is preserved as a love object – idolised, silenced, and eternally beautiful. Browning again denounces the solipsism of the lyric 'I', who appears pathologically disconnected from society and from the living reality of any other individual. Originally paired with 'Johannes Agricola in Meditation', neither this poem nor its companion appeared with an individual title, both going under the heading 'Madhouse Cells'. The inspiration for 'Porphyria's Lover' is perhaps the news item from *Blackwood's Magazine* described in the *Complete Poems*, but the title also enables echoes of J. S. Mill's 1833 description of lyric as 'like the lament of a prisoner in a solitary cell, ourselves listening, unseen in the next'.[33] Browning's heading suggests the lyric stanza itself might be the 'madhouse cell' in which his deranged subjects can be found. Mill's intriguing analogy was erased when he republished the essay 'What Is Poetry?', but it was certainly available as an intertext for Browning.

While, later in the century, Swinburne's 'The Leper' might be seen as a continuation and intensification of the experiments of Browning's 'Porphyria's Lover', it is, crucially, a continuation that reclaims and celebrates much of what was problematic for the earlier generation. Here the lyric subject – a clerk – takes in the lady he used to serve when she has been cast out of her family for carrying plague. While she once scorned him, she has no choice but to succumb to his sexual attentions as she lies dying in his 'care' – attentions that continue after her death. As with Browning's narrators, the clerk's position is questioned within the poem: in part through his own nagging feeling that he perhaps hasn't quite handled things appropriately. Yet aestheticism's legacy in the final third of the nineteenth century was precisely to endorse the aesthetics, in spite of the morals, of the clerk's position: to unhinge aesthetic appreciation from moral imperatives, and to be able to find beauty in decay. The textual erotics of the poem enable a reclamation of lyric even within this scenario, the repetition of 'well' throughout the first stanza setting up an aesthetic in which 'ill' can become 'well'. This inversion is worked through the poem, as the description of the lady in passionate embrace with her old true love is textually mirrored by the clerk's interaction with her. The knight 'held her by the hair' while the clerk plaits her hair; the knight 'with kissing lips blinded her eyes' while it is implied that the clerk has 'worn off' her eyelids after her death (her eyes now really blind) with his kisses; her tears and cries at the knights embrace are mirrored by the lips that 'turn to cry' when she asks the clerk to be left in peace; the 'body broken up with love' becomes the body broken by plague. The mirrorings and linguistic patterns in the poem set up an erotic logic to the clerk's acts that has its own aesthetic momentum.[34] While lyric may have been unwittingly, and perhaps regretfully, pathologised by Mill, and deliberately so by Browning, Decadence was able to reclaim the genre through its own deep affinity with the very terms of that pathology.[35]

Of course many poets in the early part of this period did not question lyric in the way that Browning, Tennyson, and Arnold did, and, equally, many dramatic poems continued to be written at the *fin de siècle*, but the publication of Palgrave's *Golden Treasury* (1861) together with the appearance of volumes such as Swinburne's *Poems and Ballads* in 1866 marked something of a new phase in the formation of the genre. I devote the rest of this chapter to thinking about an engagement with lyric subjectivity in the final third of the century. Not only did the *Treasury* begin to cement a particular definition of lyric and a story of its history, but Swinburne's volume was credited by some influential commentators with opening the door for a new phase of lyric publications.[36] Herbert Tucker has written of 'The fin-de-siècle purism of Wilde, Yeats, Arthur Symons, [and] others' in the later part of the century, who 'wanted Mill's pure lyricism but wanted it even purer'. For Tucker, this part of the Victorian period represents a 'nostalgia for lyric … that never was on page or lip': 'It was, rather, a generic back-formation, a textual constituent they isolated from the dramatic monologue and related nineteenth-century forms; and the featureless poems the fin-de-siècle purists produced by factoring out the historical impurities that had ballasted these forms are now fittingly, with rare exceptions, works of little more than historical interest.' For Tucker, as for many others, this is a blip in the story of poetry before modernism returned again to 'the historically responsive and dialogical mode that Browning, Tennyson and others had brought forward from the Romantics'.[37] Decadent poets appear to regress to the lyric solipsism that Browning satirised in his sick subjects. Browning's lyric pathology was not disputed by the aesthetes but embraced as they sought the logic of degeneration at the end of the century. At a linguistic level this has been seen to result in a petrification of language: the intricate fashionings of the Parnassians – and a language of craft and bejewelling – directing attention to the surface materiality of language. Typically seen as the antithesis of social discourse, Decadent language is often cited critically as an aesthetic dead end: one that, most importantly for lyric, created a cynical deadlock between self and other.[38]

Yet, in what follows, I will argue that when embraced by British aesthetes the lyric pathology of the mid-century resulted in a focus on the body that had the potential to provide a route out of that deadlock. Walter Pater memorably described experience as 'ringed round for each one of us by that thick wall of personality', 'each mind keeping as a solitary prisoner its own dream of a world'. That 'solitary prisoner' resonates again with the lyric prison cells of Mill and Browning. Pater's solution is to heighten our receptivity to the pulsations the body receives from without: such moments of strange intensity, Pater thinks, can shock one out of one's own internal landscape; and it is art's job to help provide these.[39] This introduces the kind of opportunities I suggest one might see for lyric within poetry of the late nineteenth century. The lyric subject as a sensitised and overstimulated body is still a pathological one, but one whose pathology is its route to a physical connection with the world. 'Perverse' sexual and erotic encounter may have been seen as the Decadent disease (beautiful or degenerate, depending on the perspective), but it also had the potential within aestheticist and Decadent poetry to be a route to reinstating a type of contact or transaction with the world within a mode more essentially 'lyric' rather than dramatic. Poetry of the later nineteenth century is full of a language of intimate physical connection. Smell, taste, and touch characterise much of the most characteristically decadent literature, in addition to those better-recognised visual impressionist techniques. This might, I suggest, highlight a mode of transaction and connection with the world that is more somatic than vocal. While the typical choices of lyric 'others' in a poetry that teems with dancers, the insane, the dead, eroticised women, and animals might highlight the absence of shared discourse or meaningful vocal address, they are also figures with whom the poet can foreground a sensory encounter.

In the work of Arthur Symons, for example, the dancer poems stress a mutually experienced beat that enables a connection between the subject and bodies that frequently don't share his language (as in 'Javanese Dancers') or whose performance is a bodily mode of expression rather than a linguistic one (as in 'Nora on the Pavement').[40] In 'Morbidezza' smell acts as a synaesthetic expression of tactile desires, as the final exclamation about the 'alluring scent of lilies' cannot avoid referring back to the equation of the woman's flesh with the lilies made in the first line: 'your flesh is lilies'.[41] Smell, like touch, is a sense that rests on an experience of physical intimacy. Symons' translation of 'Le chat' depicts the interaction between the animal and the pathologically overstimulated body of the writer in an inhabitation of the kind of lyric subject Browning satirises. Here the 'sensual harmonies' of the diabolical cat's call become the perfect lyric, yet the transaction between the subject and the animal is ultimately rooted not just in pure sound but in the phenomenology of the perfume of his soft fur that 'embalm[s] in his delight'.[42]

Recognition of the importance of haptic experience to twentieth-century literature has been growing for some years now,[43] but (with the word 'haptic' used, in this sense, for the first time in discourses of the late nineteenth century)[44] it might be worth considering how that kind of interaction with the world could be relevant to literature of the previous generation. Here I do this through appeal to a phenomenological methodology, which draws on a German tradition of thought also rooted in the late nineteenth century, and which responds to some of the same questions that were pertinent for lyric. This potential for somatic lyric connection, rather than direct invocation of 'you', in a poetry of physical contiguity suggests that the lyric other might be rediscovered not as a separate character, as in the dramatic monologue, but as a necessary part of the poetic 'I': something felt as an extension of the self. To recognise the importance to poetry of the period of something like the intentionality of consciousness is to bring to the fore a potentiality of the lyric genre that although not newly available to later nineteenth-century poetry does appear to hold a particular significance for it. This response to the increasing threat of solipsism is apparent in poetry before 1860 (as poems such as Keats' 'This Living Hand' demonstrate), yet in the late nineteenth century, such gestures acquire an increasing significance and urgency as the body, and its senses, become a more central problematic for the lyric genre and for aestheticism more generally. They also, as I will suggest, acquire a particular phenomenological resonance in relation to a poetics of degeneration.

So while a poem such as Arthur Symons' 'Hands' may appear a piece of Decadent fetishisation, it might also demonstrate something of that phenomenological rediscovery of the other through the body of the lyric subject:

> The little hands too soft and white
>   To have known more laborious hours
> Than those which die upon a night
>   Of kindling wine and fading flowers;
>
> The little hands that I have kissed,
>   Finger by finger, to the tips,
> And delicately about each wrist
>   Have set a bracelet with my lips;
>
> Dear soft white little morbid hands.
>   Mine all one night, with what delight
> Shall I recall in other lands,
>   Dear hands, that you were mine one night![45]

The meeting of lips and hands here creates a point of physical contact between two body parts that have maximum tactile sensitivity, and
through the eroticism of this touch we see something of what a twentieth-
century phenomenologist such as Maurice Merleau-Ponty describes as a
bodily knowledge of the other: 'it is precisely my body which perceives
the body of another person, and discovers in that other body a miracu-
lous prolongation of my own intentions, a familiar way of dealing with
the world'.[46] The encompassing of the fingers in the kiss and the wrist in
the mouth via the 'bracelet' of lips suggests a literal physical incorporation
of the object into the subject that resonates with Merleau-Ponty's sense of
knowing the world through tactile contiguity:

> Visible and mobile, my body is a thing among things; it is caught in the
> fabric of the world, and its cohesion is that of a thing. But because it moves
> itself and sees, it holds things in a circle around itself. Things are an annex
> or prolongation of itself; they are incrusted into its flesh, they are part of its
> full definition …[47]

Read in this way, the eroticism of Symons' poem might actually represent a
phenomenological reinstatement of the lyric as a transaction with another.
Read as a response to Browning's and Mill's criticisms of lyric isolation,
that very pathology is transmuted into a form of lyric encounter.

   To read in this way is to revalue the Decadent lyric's association with
degeneration: regression to a sensual somatic lyric encounter has the
potential to capture an immediate (pre-reflective and pre-linguistic) and
intimate connection with the world that provides something of a response
to the threat of solipsism. Crucially, reading what Tucker calls the 'pur-
ist' lyric of the *fin de siècle* as a kind of phenomenological 'reduction' (a
method that ensures we focus simply on what we experience, free from
the prejudice of interpretation)[48] shows how the Decadent focus on the

materiality of language might ultimately be used to turn attention away
from language and towards an experience of being that exists outside it.
Indeed, the insistent linguistic reality of Browning's dramatic forms is a
conscious rejection of an aspiration towards spiritual transcendence he
saw as intrinsic to the Romantic characterisation of lyric. Yet I suggest
Decadent lyric phenomenology offers an alternative that nonetheless preserves the genre's connection with the extra-linguistic. By embracing the
mid-Victorian pathologisation of the lyric subject, the Decadent poetry I
have explored here finds a location for lyric's discursive 'excess' in the pre-
linguistic rhythms of the body rather than the ethereal communications of
the spirit. We do see this earlier in the period: perhaps encountered most
potently through *In Memoriam*'s search for an alternative to, and more
physical manifestation of, a spiritual communion with the dead. This is
one of the ways in which Tennyson's pathologised response to a specific
occasion of grief becomes a more general statement about the nature of
lyric in the nineteenth century. This is also why, I think, the grief-stricken
poems of 1912 emblematise something central to Thomas Hardy's poetic
oeuvre as a whole (as Marjorie Levinson wrote recently, 'One might even
say that their explicit mourning gives the atmosphere of all the poems a
rational form or brings them under a concept').[49]

While my focus so far on the erotics of poets such as Swinburne and
Symons in the second half of the period might suggest this is a strategy
with a particular gender dynamic, 'Glamour of Gold' by Olive Custance
helps show how we might see such concerns also reflected in women's
poetry. Custance was both the wife of Lord Alfred Douglas and the lover
of Natalie Barney, and it is significant that the immediate somatic transaction is imagined between two women in contrast to that sexualised male–
female encounter central to Symons' work:

> The white hands of my lady's maid
> Move deftly through the shining hair!
> How my heart falters half afraid
> Lest they should hurt a thing so fair
>   As my sweet lady's head!
> And how I wish that I stood there
>   Twisting the strands instead!
>
> Fortunate fingers those, that hold
> The handles of the steels that fret
> And dent each heavy tress of gold …
> Till all the golden mass is set
>   With waves bewildering,

Where fire and dusk together met
   Rival day's sunsetting!

Or so at least it seems to me
While gazing on my lady's face!
And when with leaping heart I see
Her soft shy breathing 'neath the lace
   That falls even to her feet …
The curves of her slim body trace –
   See her supremely sweet –

Ah! then love swoons too satisfied
Too passionate for words of praise
With but one prayer, to abide
Safely at her sweet side always!
   Even as that maiden there
That staid and silent still delays
   Winding the long gold hair! …[50]

The subject here sees the possibility of a reconnection with the lyric 'you' through touch, through a sense of physical contiguity. The figure of the maid dressing her lady's hair acts as an image of the kind of lyric connection that might be found outside language: her silence taking poetry not towards a spiritual connection that transcends language but to a physical connection that precedes it. While the subject of this lyric witnesses rather than experiences this her- or (more likely in the lyric economy when the subject invokes 'my lady') himself, it is interesting how the actions of dressing hair and writing lyric converge in this poem in the language of metal working. Andrew Lang's meditation on 'Arnold's jewel-work' and Browning's 'iron style' smiting 'gold on his rude anvil' lays out a language of poetic composition that identified it as craft.[51] It is no accident that the working with the hair is described by Custance as a process in which the steel implements 'fret / and dent each heavy tress of gold … / Till all the golden mass is set'. The hair is sculpted and worked like a metal in the same way that lyric lines are honed, for the aesthetes, out of solid materials.

Of course, in this poem the lyric subject is in the role of the voyeur. So, the relationship that I am suggesting provides a new model of lyric transaction is one only observed. Yet, when one looks again at the poem, this observed encounter does in fact appear to be enacted formally within the poem. Just as the hair here is twisted and wound, so too the stanza form she uses plaits in on itself. Using Spenser's variation on Chaucerian rhyme-royal, Custance uses a seven-line form (*ababcbc*) in which the middle line is both structurally the last line of an *abab* quatrain while also being the first line of a second *bcbc* quatrain. This form emphasises contiguity and mutuality: the point at which the maid and the lady meet in physical intimacy, but also the concept of the body as both touched and touching – both part of the external world and part of our internal and individual selves. The middle line of each stanza, like the body, simultaneously faces both ways – playing a role in both the first and second 'quatrain', and showing that while they can be seen as distinct they are inseparable. Formally, the poem enacts this sense that to feel through the body is necessarily to be of the world and in contiguity with others, even while acknowledging one's own individual subjectivity. In this way the poem points towards the intriguing possibility that the form of the print-lyric on the page may itself have a haptic presence and capability, providing a point of contact and mediation between the lyric subject and their audience.

Whether considering the phenomenology of form in aestheticist writing, or the actual physical availability of the beloved in Decadent poetry, late-nineteenth-century poetry offers a fresh emphasis on how lyric might figure a somatic transaction between the subject and the world at a time when the poet was less securely invested in even a metaphorical sense of his or her direct vocal address. In 'Glamour of Gold', literary form, the body, and silence give a powerful indication of the type of connection that might be sought through a genre that at times recognised itself to be inherently spatial rather than sung and carried on the airwaves. The growing sense of lyric as a haptic rather than ethereal experience must be seen in tandem, I suggest, with its sense of itself as having acquired not just a print medium but, for many publishing poets, a print character. Yet, of course, this recognition also generated opposing moves to return poetry to the voice. Celtic writers are particularly important to this impulse throughout the century. Maureen McLane has documented the significance of Scotland to Romantic minstrelsy at the start of the period.[52] At the other end, we might look for their importance through Oscar Wilde's declaration that 'We must return to the voice. That must be our test.'[53] The linguistic crisis at the heart of Decadence recognises the petrification of language in print and desires to return to the spoken voice.[54] The Rhymers' Club, with their strong, self-defined, Celtic roots tested their poetry by reading aloud to one another at their gatherings in the Cheshire Cheese pub.[55] W. B. Yeats provides a point of reflection on these issues when, in 1893, he claims that while England is in a lyric period of its development, in which literature takes in inspiration from the internal, he identifies the Irish as a younger nation still in an 'epic or ballad period' more associated with external action and shared voice.[56] For publishing poets, finding an association with song in a Celtic tradition acquired a particular significance, I suggest, in relation to the growing recognition that, at least for a core of English poetry, print has become formative for the very conceptualisation of lyric.

I suggest that the much maligned fashion for Parnassian forms of the later part of the period presents a recognition of and exploitation of the tangibility of the print-lyric form. Swinburne's late, and little studied, collection 'A Century of Roundels' (1883) offers a commentary on this shift to a tactile lyric through its very Parnassian forms:

> A roundel is wrought as a ring or a starbright sphere,
>   With craft of delight and with cunning of sound unsought,
> That the heart of the hearer may smile if to pleasure his ear
>   A roundel is wrought.
>
> Its jewel of music is carven of all or of aught –
>   Love, laughter, or mourning – remembrance of rapture or fear –
> That fancy may fashion to hang in the ear of thought.
>
> As a bird's quick song runs round, and the hearts in us hear
>   Pause answer to pause, and again the same strain caught,
> So moves the device whence, round as a pearl or tear,
>   A roundel is wrought.[57]

The roundel form holds a central role in Swinburne's invocation of lyric community (another response to the threat of lyric isolation), as I discuss elsewhere,[58] but it is also a physically 'wrought' form: a solid 'ring' or 'sphere', and a carved 'jewel'. The solid form is twice in the poem offered incongruously to the 'ear': invoking bird song as the archetypal figure for lyric song, Swinburne ends the poem by distilling the ethereal strains into the solid form 'round as a pearl or tear' of the roundel. Song and shape oscillate in this poem in a strange synaesthesia where song is felt as a tangible form. Reminiscent of a metaphysical aesthetic, and perhaps the circle that, as tear, coin, globe, and moon transmutes throughout Donne's 'A Valediction of Weeping', the poem nonetheless imagines the circle of the roundel as more tangible and objectified than Donne's expansive planetary moons and globes. The song of the roundel becomes a sculptural form rather than disembodied music or the vast universals of the metaphysicals.

In an 1879 review of the poetry of Dante Gabriel Rossetti, Thomas Henry Hall Caine acknowledges the importance of 'the music of sound, not of sight' to lyric, but goes on to comment on the importance to song of capturing 'the undulating swell of a sensation': something felt rather than merely heard. Writing of the aestheticist sonnet he says it 'should be solid, not spectral, concrete, not ideal in theme'. He continues: 'Mr. Rossetti's sonnets are solid rather than spectral, but of a solidity nearer akin to that of Michaelangelo [*sic*] than to that of Wordsworth. His is the reality of vision, not the solidity of fact. His sonnets embody at once the spirit of the sensuous and the sensuousness of spirit.'[59] This comparison is primarily with Michelangelo's sonnets, not his sculpture, but he invokes the physical presence of a sculptural text in the work of both artists. John Addington Symonds had, the previous year, published the first rhymed English translations of Michelangelo's sonnets, and his introduction also prefers tactile and physical, rather than aural, descriptors, saying there is 'no sweetness of melodic cadence' in this 'rough' and 'violent' 'masculine art of poetry'.[60] For poets in the late nineteenth century, lyric was sometimes ethereal music but they also discovered a somatic lyric transaction that was perhaps more relevant to the genre's negotiation with its formation on the page. It is in this way that we might consider the late-nine-teenth-century engagement with lyric not necessarily as a nostalgic flight from the problems of lyric solipsism, as a wallowing in the decay of a genre corrupted by print and the cheap thrills of illicit physical encounter, or as a regrettable interlude in the steady progress of Victorian poetry towards a more outward-looking dramatic accommodation to modernity. While Browning's lyric pathology (and Mill's somewhat inadvertent pathologisation of the lyric subject) seemed to mark insuperable problems for the relationship between the print lyric and modernity, that very pathology led, at least at times, back to the body and to the phenomenological potentiality of lyric form.

To think about poetry of the late nineteenth century as a part of the story of lyric might be, then, to complicate the idea of a shift between a nineteenth-century concept of lyric as song and a modernist lyric of the visual impression. To recognise the importance of tactility to lyric of the period, in addition to the undoubted significance of aurality and the visual, is perhaps also to recognise a potential in lyric that the particular resources of aestheticism and decadence were able to capitalise on in a distinctive way. Jonathan Crary's influential account of the dissociation of touch from sight during this period has resulted in a particular emphasis on modernity and visuality.[61] Yet, much as new technologies of vision and image-reproduction may have driven apart the body of the viewer and the object viewed, there was simultaneously an important late-nineteenth-century move to value a return to more 'empathetic' experiences of perception that drew the two together. Drawing on earlier German aesthetic theory particularly, Pater, Bernhard Berenson, and Vernon Lee articulated something much more phenomenological – as Lee's writing on 'empathy', and her experiments with somatic art criticism, demonstrate.[62] The somatic potential I recognise may not have provided any final resolution to the problems of reconciling the concept of lyric with the conditions of cultural modernity; literary modernism for the most part defined itself against the poetics of bodily pathology and the erotics of the *fin de siècle*. Yet what did remain was that uneasy sense, formulated across the period, of lyric's centrality to poetry combined with its potential incompatibility with modernity. As the following chapters demonstrate, this became something to be reckoned with in many different ways throughout the twentieth century.

Notes

1 John Addington Symonds, 'A Comparison of Elizabethan with Victorian Poetry', *Fortnightly Review* 45.265 (January 1889), 55–79 (p. 55).
2 Carol T. Christ, *Victorian and Modern Poetics* (Chicago and London: University of Chicago Press, 1984), p. 6, and *passim*.
3 Herbert F. Tucker, 'Dramatic Monologue and the Overhearing of Lyric', in *Lyric Poetry: Beyond New Criticism*, ed. Chaviva Hošek and Patricia Parker (Ithaca, NY and London: Cornell University Press, 1985), pp. 226–43 (pp. 236, 243).
4 Symonds, 'A Comparison', pp. 62, 64.
5 Marjorie Perloff, *The Dance of the Intellect: Studies in the Poetry of the Pound Tradition* (New York: Cambridge University Press, 1985), pp. 177–8.
6 Francis Turner Palgrave, *The Golden Treasury of the Best Songs and Lyrical Poems in the English Language* (Oxford University Press, 1964), p. ix.
7 Symonds, 'A Comparison', pp. 63–4.
8 John Stuart Mill ('Atiquus'), 'The Two Kinds of Poetry', *Monthly Repository* 7.80 (August 1833), 714–24 (p. 719).
9 John Stuart Mill ('Atiquus'), 'What Is Poetry?', *Monthly Repository* 7.73 (January 1833), 60–70 (p. 65).
10 Symonds, 'A Comparison', pp. 67–9.
11 Matthew Rowlinson, 'Lyric', in *A Companion to Victorian Poetry*, ed. Richard Cronin, Alison Chapman, and Antony H. Harrison (Oxford: Blackwell, 2002), pp. 59, 70, 77.
12 Symonds, 'A Comparison', p. 65.
13 In Edward FitzGerald, *Rubáiyát of Omar Khayyám*, ed. Christopher Decker (Charlottesville: University of Virginia Press, 1997), p. xli.
14 Josephine Guy and Ian Small, *The Textual Condition of Nineteenth-Century Literature* (London: Routledge, 2012), p. 75.

15 *Ibid.*, p. 74.
16 Symonds, 'A Comparison', p. 69; see also p. 62: 'The public of the present time is a public of readers rather than of hearers.'
17 Mill, 'What Is Poetry?', pp. 64–5.
18 See David Lindley on Renaissance lyric as a halfway point in this process, where we see a 'direct performance' that still addressed a certain person with a certain purpose; David Lindley, *Lyric* (London and New York: Methuen, 1985), pp. 63–4. See also John Henriksen, who writes of apostrophe in Romantic poetry as 'somewhere between address and non-address: Romantic apostrophe affirms the convention of poetic speaking-to-someone-else, even as it empties that same convention'; John Henriksen, 'Poem as Song: The Role of the Lyric Audience', *Alif: Journal of Comparative Poetics* 21 (2001), 77–100 (p. 80).
19   Jonathan Culler, 'Why Lyric?', *PMLA* 123.1 (2008), 201–6 (p. 204). See also W. R. Johnson, *The Idea of Lyric: Lyric Modes in Ancient and Modern Poetry* (Berkeley and Los Angeles: University of California Press, 1982), p. 3.
20 Culler, 'Why Lyric?', p. 204.
21 See, for example, Alice Meynell, 'The Lady of the Lyrics', in *Prose and Poetry*, ed. F. P., V. M., O. S., and F. M. (London: Jonathan Cape, 1947), pp. 49–51.
22 See, for example, Scott Brewster's recent *Lyric* (London and New York: Routledge, 2009), p. 92, which turns from Romantic and mid-Victorian poetry to high modernism.
23 Robert Browning, *Essay on Shelley: Being His Introduction to the Spurious Shelley Letters*, ed. Richard Garnett (London: Alexander Moring, 1903), pp. 38–40.
24 Britta Martens, *Browning, Victorian Poetics and the Romantic Legacy* (Farnham: Ashgate, 2011), pp. 13–20.
25 See David Duff, above, p. 138.
26 Martens, *Browning*, p. 150: autograph file A.L.s. to John Kenyon, London, 1 October 1855, Houghton Library, Harvard University.
27 Robert Browning, *The Poetical Works of Robert Browning*, 15 vols., Vol. V, ed. Ian Jack and Robert Inglesfield (Oxford: Clarendon Press, 1995), pp. 470–2; Joseph Bristow, *Robert Browning* (Brighton: Harvester, 1991), p. 17.
28 Browning, *Poetical Works*, Vol. IV, ed. Ian Jack, Rowena Fowler, and Margaret Smith (1991), pp. 69–75.
29 D. G. Rossetti, 'A Sonnet', in *Ballads and Sonnets* (London: Ellis and White, 1881), p. 161.
30 Browning, *Poetical Works*, Vol. III, ed. Ian Jack and Rowena Fowler (1988), pp. 186–8.
31 *Ibid.*, pp. 241–3.
32 *Ibid.*, pp. 250–2.
33 *Ibid.*, p. 249; Mill, 'What Is Poetry?', p. 66.
34 A. C. Swinburne, *Major Poems*, ed. Jerome McGann and Charles L. Sligh (New Haven: Yale University Press, 2004), pp. 113–17.

35 Arthur Symons termed Decadence 'a new and beautiful and interesting disease'; Arthur Symons, 'The Decadent Movement in Literature', *Harper's New Monthly Magazine* 87 (June/November 1893), 858–68 (p. 859).

36 See, for example, Edmund Gosse, 'Mr Hardy's Lyrical Poems', *Edinburgh Review* 227.464 (April 1918), 272–93 (p. 274).

37 Tucker, 'Dramatic Monologue and the Overhearing of Lyric', pp. 237–9.

38 Peter Nicholls, *Modernism*, 2nd edn (London: Palgrave Macmillan, 2009), p. 65.

39 Walter Pater, *The Renaissance*, in *Three Major Texts*, ed. William E. Buckler (New York University Press, 1986), p. 218.

40 Arthur Symons, *London Nights*, 2nd edn (London: Leonard Smithers, 1897), pp. 5, 7–8.

41 Arthur Symons, *Silhouettes*, 2nd edn (London: Leonard Smithers, 1896), p. 13.

42 Arthur Symons, *Decadent Poetry*, ed. Lisa Rodensky (London: Penguin, 2006), pp. 52–4.

43 Resulting in books such as Abbie Garrington's *Haptic Modernism: Touch and the Tactile in Modernist Writing* (Edinburgh University Press, 2013).

44 Abbie Garrington, 'Touching Texts: The Haptic Sense in Modernist Literature', *Literature Compass* 7.9 (2010), 810–23 (p. 811).

45 Symons, *London Nights*, p. 47.

46 Maurice Merleau-Ponty, 'The Body, Motility and Spatiality', in *Phenomenology and Existentialism*, ed. Robert C. Solomon (Lanham, MD; Boulder, CO; New York; and Oxford: Rowman & Littlefield, 1972), p. 354.

47 Maurice Merleau-Ponty, 'Eye and Mind,' trans. Carleton Dallery, in *Phenomenology, Language and Sociology: Selected Essays of Maurice Merleau-Ponty*, ed. John O'Neill (London: Heinemann, 1974), p. 284.

48 Maurice Merleau-Ponty, *Phenomenology of Perception*, trans. Colin Smith (London: Routledge and Kegan Paul, 1962), p. ix.

49 Marjorie Levinson, 'Object-Loss and Object-Bondage: Economies of Representation in Hardy's Poetry', *ELH* 73 (2006), 548–80 (p. 557).

50 Olive Custance, *Opals* (London: John Lane, 1897), pp. 13–14.

51 Andrew Lang, 'Ballade for the Laureate', in *Ballads and Rondeaus, Chants Royal, Sestinas, Villanelles, &c*, ed. and intro. Gleeson White (London and Felling-on-Tyne: Walter Scott Publishing, 1887), p. 30.

52 See Maureen McLane on the importance of Scotland to Romantic minstrelsy: *Balladeering, Minstrelsy, and the Making of British Romantic Poetry* (Cambridge University Press, 2008), Chapter 3.

53 Oscar Wilde, *The Artist as Critic: The Critical Writings of Oscar Wilde*, ed. Richard Ellmann (University of Chicago Press, 1969), p. 351.

54 Linda Dowling, *Language and Decadence* (Princeton University Press, 1986), p. 202.

55 George Mills Harper and Karl Beckson, 'Victor Plarr on "The Rhymers' Club": An Unpublished Lecture', *English Literature in Transition* 2002.4 (2002), 379–85 (379–80).

56 W. B. Yeats, *Uncollected Prose*, ed. John P. Frayne and Colton Johnson (London: Macmillan, 1970–6), Vol. I: *First Reviews and Articles, 1886–1896* (1970), p. 273.

57 A. C. Swinburne, *Collected Poetical Works*, 6 vols. (London: Chatto and Windus, 1904), Vol. v, p. 161.

58 Marion Thain, 'Desire Lines: Swinburne and Lyric Crisis', in *Algernon Charles Swinburne: Unofficial Laureate*, ed. Catherine Maxwell and Stefano Evangelista (Manchester University Press, 2013), pp. 138–54.

59 T. H. Hall Caine, 'The Poetry of Dante Gabriel Rossetti', *New Monthly Magazine* 116 (July 1879), 800–12 (pp. 804, 806, 809).

60 Michelangelo Buonarroti and Tommaso Campanella, *The Sonnets of Michael Angelo Buonarroti and Tommaso Campanella*, trans. John Addington Symonds (London: Smith, Elder, & Co., 1878), p. 14.

61 Jonathan Crary, *Techniques of the Observer* (Cambridge, MA: MIT Press, 2001 [1990]), p. 19.

62 Carolyn Burdett has explored this aesthetic in '"The Subjective Inside Us Can Turn into the Objective Outside": Vernon Lee's Psychological Aesthetics', *19: Interdisciplinary Studies in the Long Nineteenth Century* 12 (2011), 1–31.

CHAPTER NINE

Modernism and the limits of lyric

Peter Nicholls

The priority lyric has acquired among modern poetic forms has provoked much comment in recent years. Virginia Jackson, for example, observes in the new edition of the *Princeton Encyclopedia of Poetry and Poetics* that in the second half of the nineteenth century '*lyric* and *poetry* began to be synonymous terms'.[1] This modern lyric, says Scott Brewster, 'is characterized by brevity, deploys a first-person speaker or persona, involves performance, and is an outlet for personal emotion'.[2] Helen Vendler rather similarly defines the lyric poem as 'the representation of a single voice, alone, recording and analyzing and formulating and changing its mind'.[3] It is this form of lyric that has in the modern period become, according to Mark Jeffreys, 'the dominant force of poetry'.[4] I want to propose here a qualification of this view, one based on the notion that modernist poems are designedly hybrid things and that while literary critics have given the genre a high profile, many modern and contemporary poets have followed the Victorians in their awareness of the limits of lyric, seeking to *frame* it with varying degrees of scepticism and irony.[5] The insufficiency of lyric (to borrow a phrase from Donald Davie) lies, we might say, precisely in traditional assumptions of its self-sufficiency, of its capacity to constitute an autonomous, seductively suspended world. Yet, as poet John Wilkinson observes, 'If it is the fate of lyric poetry to feign the intimacy of the trustworthy speech-act and invariably to break trust, at every point exploiting the potential of language for at-least-duplicity, does not poetry actively bring about the erosion of the intimacy on which it presumes?'[6] In the poems I shall discuss here, this 'erosion' of a presumed intimacy is produced in part by insistent gyrations of tone and register that in a variety of ways 'break trust' with the assumed proximities of the lyric voice.

I begin with Ezra Pound because it is he who proposes for modernism a model of lyricism that in prizing musicality above interiority tacitly resists the growing tendency to assimilate all poetic modes to that of lyric expressivism. 'Music begins to atrophy when it departs too far from the dance', Pound declares, and 'poetry begins to atrophy when it gets too far from music; but this must not be taken as implying that all good music is dance music or all poetry lyric'.[7] I shall return to the caveat with which this comment ends, but the conjunction of musicality and verbal precision would remain a prominent feature of Pound's poetics, underlying his famous definition of 'melopoeia' as 'a sort of poetry where music, sheer melody, seems as if it were just bursting into speech'.[8] This poetic 'music', which 'has long been called lyric', seems, however, to halt at the threshold of speech; it is, we might say, a lyricism that doesn't at all project itself as Vendler's 'solitary speech' but is embodied in 'Sounds that stop the flow, and durations either of syllables, or implied between them, "forced onto the voice" of the reader by nature of the "verse"'.[9] The sounds of the poem, then, may work against emergent contours of normal verbal expression, and this explains the importance Pound attached to his early study of the troubadours, since their polyphonic lyricism, frequently mimicking birdsong, as in Arnaut Daniel's 'Doutz brais e critz', produces a kind of song that, in the words of critic Robert Stark, 'becomes dense and opaque; its musical and rhythmical properties exert their priority and make the sense more difficult to fathom immediately or directly'.[10] This effect of 'nascent communication', as Stark aptly terms it, is central to Pound's understanding of the function of sound in poetry. Lyric, from this point of view, is strikingly remote from the forms of dramatic monologue by which, as Jonathan Culler has argued, it has so frequently been subsumed in modern criticism.[11] Instead, it either borders upon 'speech' or supplements it, as in the account of 'melopoeia' where Pound argues that 'the words are charged, over and above their plain meaning, with some musical property, which directs the bearing or trend of that meaning'.[12] Pound's translations of Daniel have often been considered mere technical exercises, mainly because of their fascination with the elaborate phonic patternings that 'set in cluster / Lines where no word pulls wry, no rhyme breaks gauges'.[13] Yet Pound's intensive reading of these songs revealed something more than mere virtuosity, directing him to what he called 'an aesthetic of sound': 'of clear sounds and opaque sounds, such as in *Sols sui*, an opaque sound like Swinburne at his best; and in *Doutz brais* and in *L'aura amara*, a clear sound with staccato; and of heavy beats and of running and light beats, as very heavy in *Can chai la feuilla*'.[14] Elsewhere he emphasised that Arnaut 'made the birds sing IN HIS WORDS; I don't mean that he merely referred to the birds singing … he kept them at it, repeating the tune, and finding five rhymes for each of seventeen rhyme sounds in the same order'.[15]

Several things are notable about this adumbration of 'an aesthetic of sound', not least its emphasis on repetition and echo. The Provençal song is tightly bound by an intricate rhyme scheme – in that sense it is a form of lyric 'moment' but one that does not so much suspend time as reveal its contour. The aim, though, is less meditative intensity than, in Pound's phrase, 'to cut a shape in time'.[16] When we are told, then, that 'the art of En Ar. Daniel is not literature but the art of fitting words well with music',[17] the distinction is meant to divert emphasis away from content and self-expression and towards an extreme stylisation that Pound associates with 'sheer melody'. In his statement on 'Vorticism', this lyricism is also distinguished from the epic and didactic modes, Pound noting at the same time, however, that we can find passages of lyric in drama and in long poems. As Elizabeth Helsinger for one has observed, Victorian poets frequently embedded lyrics in their long poems – Tennyson and Swinburne are her principal examples – and this interruption by song evokes 'its own space and time, differently shaped than that of the surrounding text. Old songs re-sung create connections with distant, temporally discontinuous occasions: the song text remembers and invites other performances past and future, and in so doing constructs communities with singers at other times.'[18] It is the temporal reach of lyric thus considered that we must then place over against what Pound defines as '[t]he other sort of poetry [that] is as old as the lyric and as honourable, but, until recently no one had named it'; this is the 'Image'.[19] So much has been said of Pound's discovery of the image and of the turn from the auditory to the visual that is generally taken to characterise the evolution of modernism that we are likely to forget his continuing emphasis on the 'fitting words well with music': a practice he, somewhat unexpectedly perhaps, associates here with 'an opaque sound like Swinburne at his best'.

On the face of it, of course, Pound's early career, from the Pre-Raphaelite tonalities of his first collections through to the imagist poems of *Lustra*, might seem a clear enactment of that shift from ear to eye that Roman Jakobson finds at the origins of modernism.[20] Pound's thinking on these matters was shaped in part by Wyndham Lewis's arguments for what Lewis called his 'philosophy of the EYE' and the related 'external method' of satire.[21] Certainly, Pound's own attempt to work free of the Browningesque dramatic monologue resonated with Lewis's contempt for the forms of inwardness he associated partly with Freud, and especially with Henri Bergson.[22] As Martin Jay observes in *Downcast Eyes*, his monumental study of 'occularcentrism' in the western tradition, it was not until Bergson that 'the rights of the body were explicitly set against the tyranny of the eye'.[23]

For Lewis, that turn to the body and to the dark 'stream' of the inner life epitomised the 'empiric of sensational chaos' that he saw as the distinctive feature of contemporary culture. Bergson, he said, 'is indeed the arch enemy of every impulse having its seat in the apparatus of vision, and requiring a concrete world'.[24] By way of contrast, the 'tyrannical' eye of the painter looks out upon an intelligible world, where the clear separation of subject from object allows the operation of intelligence rather than mere sensation. The main elements in Lewis's critique of Bergson would also appear in Pound's poetics, especially in the latter's emphatic commitment to the 'distinct and geometric' and in his related attachment to light and clarity. Indeed, the first version of Canto I announces the visual emphasis in a quite program-matic way: 'Mantegna a sterner line, and the new world about us: / Barred lights, great flares, new form, Picasso or Lewis. / If for a year man write to paint, and not to music'[25] The conjunction of Mantegna, Picasso, and Lewis registers Pound's preference for an art of clarity and formal precision – an art, too, of a certain austerity, purging sentimentality and substituting the 'stern' line for the more curvaceous attractions of corporeal form and what he later called in *The Cantos* 'the brown meat of Rembrandt'.[26]

Yet while Pound was keen to assert his modernist commitment to a painterly aesthetic, he also recognised in particular prosodic and musical forms a set of devices by which to readmit the ear as an organising device of what was to be his long poem. In this aspect of his thinking and prac-tice, Pound again found himself at the junction between two competing aesthetics: one prizing a traditional prosody rich in affective and mythic meanings (we might think parenthetically of Yeats' suspicion of free verse as lacking in memory), the other a more clearly modernist one in which the perceived constraints of metre were yielding to the intoxications of free verse.[27] Pound, like Eliot, was, of course, strongly aware of this con-junction and of his ambivalent relation to it.[28] Metrical features could certainly survive into free verse, but as something partly hidden, as the ghost 'behind the arras', as Eliot famously put it.[29] This ghost, however, was a far from silent one, and the accumulated knowledge of metre and rhythm that Pound set himself to master was one that attributed a power-fully expressive, even thematic function to aspects of poetic form that very soon younger generations of poets would regard as *non-semantic* defences against any reduction of the poem to propositional content. On this mat-ter, however, as on so many others, Pound was for his part unequivocal: 'Rhythm MUST have meaning', he told Harriet Monroe.[30]

Here we should recall Pound's identification of his 'aesthetic of sound' with 'Swinburne at his best', a comparison that begins to make sense when we see how the earlier poet's sophisticated command of metre and rhythm invested his work with allusive meanings that far exceeded conventional lyric expectations of interior monologue and a suspended temporality. Of course, we know that both Pound and Eliot criticised Swinburne's writing for its failure of 'objectivity'; Swinburnian excess had to be purged if we were to have modernism, so the familiar story runs. Pound did indeed observe of Swinburne's poem *Dolores* that its sound 'is in places like that of horses' hooves being pulled out of mud', but, more importantly, he also praised the poet's 'surging and leaping dactylics' and the genius of his 'rhythm-building faculty'.[31] Swinburne is partly forgotten now and little read, but for Pound, as he moved towards free verse, the older poet's metrical expertise was something to cleave to in the face of modernity's 'accelerated grimace'. Indeed, for anyone familiar with Pound's earlier Cantos the partially concealed imprint of Swinburne's *Poems and Ballads* and *Atalanta in Calydon* is fairly easy to discern, though here it provides the model not for the narcotic swathes of rhythm the modernists condemned, but for precise rhythmic phrasing, sound echo, and innovative placing of caesurae. Examples are legion, but compare, from Swinburne's *Atalanta* (36), 'Sun, and clear light among green hills, and day / Late risen and long sought after';[32] and, from Pound's Canto III, 'Light: and the first light, before ever dew was fallen'.[33] And again, from *Atalanta*: 'There in cold remote recesses / That nor alien eyes assail, Feet, nor imminence of wings, / Nor a wind nor any tune'; and, from Pound's Canto XVII : 'Nor bird-cry, nor any noise of wave moving, / Nor splash of porpoise, nor any noise of wave moving'.[34] Many of Pound's rhythmic signatures are announced in Swinburne's once familiar poems: the trochaic rather than the iambic opening, for example, along with the use of the spondaic double stress, the suppression of pronouns and connectives, and the fondness for the hendecasyllabic line. These amount to more than 'breaking the pentameter' (the 'first heave' of modernism, as Pound remembered it at Pisa),[35] for rhythmic items with strong metrical associations could also have an allusive, *signifying* function. This is what Swinburne had in mind when he contended that 'There is a science of verse as surely as there is a science of mathematics: there is an art of expression by metre as certainly as there is an art of representation by painting.'[36] This 'science', which is based, says Swinburne, on 'metre, rhythm, cadence not merely appreciable but definable and reducible to rule and measurement', yields a conception of 'form' or 'trace' that is at once vestigial and yet also somehow impersonal, 'beyond intention and conscious control'.[37]

There is, then, a certain kind of lyric *abstraction* in Swinburne's verse that, 'at its best', resonates with the 'sheer melody' Pound discerned in Arnaut's songs and that similarly exceeds the notion of a single speaking voice. Indeed, as Jerome McGann has noted, the famous 'monotony' of Swinburne's verse is founded in a view he shared with Stéphane Mallarmé that the ideal poetry is 'impersonal, toneless, even (in a sense) without meaning'.[38] We can add to this that the two poets shared a commitment to poetic theatre, and that, in Swinburne's *Atalanta in Calydon* and *Erechtheus*, Mallarmé discerned something already approximating to his own ideal alternative to what he called an 'everyday and national theatre'.[39] In his review of *Erechtheus*, Mallarmé discerned a 'sublime music' that lingered in the mind 'long after its cessation', a rhythm of 'pure motifs moving against a background of the most subtle and noble emotion'.[40] This was, crucially, a kind of inner music, a 'singing within oneself', as Mallarmé put it, the presage of a theatre of which, he said, 'one is a spectator only within oneself, with a book open or one's eyes closed'. Elsewhere, Mallarmé would call it 'a theatre inherent in the mind'.[41]

Mallarmé also makes it clear that the music of poetry has no mimetic relation to music or voice as such (and, implicitly, to the music of Wagner).[42] In fact, it is music reconceived as writing that is the principal issue, or poetry read silently, rather than recited.[43] Yet while Mallarmé never ceases to emphasise the idea of *clarity* when he speaks of 'music' – and it is this that he discerns pre-eminently in the work of Swinburne – Pound and Eliot are both troubled by what they perceive as an exactly opposite tendency in Swinburne's verse, to vagueness and loss of focus. As Eliot puts it in a famous passage: 'Language in a healthy state presents the object, is so close to the object that the two are identified. They are identified in the verse of Swinburne solely because the object has ceased to exist, because language, uprooted, has adapted itself to an independent life of atmospheric nourishment.'[44] Here we may read not only one modernist verdict on both Swinburne *and* Mallarmé, but also the germ of what would soon become an authoritative version of that modernist 'turn' from music to vision. Swinburne thus remains, somewhat paradoxically, a figure to be reckoned with for both Pound and Eliot precisely because it is he who so fully and so deliberately seems to deny the power of the 'sharp visual image' that, for Eliot, should complement 'verse intended to be sung'; Swinburne's emotion, remarks Eliot, 'is never particular, never in direct line of vision, never focused'. If 'you take to pieces any verse of Swinburne', says Eliot, 'you find always that the object was not there – only the word'.[45] Swinburne, he suggests, is guilty of taking his eye off the object at the crucial moment, allowing it to evaporate in a mere froth of alliteration. It's a sort of wilful or self-indulgent blindness, in short, that the modernist project is designed at all points to correct. Yet the characteristic absoluteness of Eliot's terms doesn't acknowledge that there *is* a type of lyricism that operates, like Mallarmé's poetic theatre, with 'eyes closed' – that is, we might say, premised on a moment of non-visuality. This is the kind of lyricism we might find in a poet like Rilke, whose blind people, as Jacques Derrida puts it in his book *Memoirs of the Blind*, 'sing of the poetic condition, namely of lyricism itself insofar as it opens beyond the visible.'[46] Derrida goes on to quote the first lines of Rilke's poem 'Gong': 'We must close our eyes and renounce our mouths, / remain mute, blind, dazzled: / Vibrating space, as it reaches us / demands from our being only the ear.'[47]

Derrida is concerned here with the art of drawing, an art that commonsense tells us is generally mimetic. But what actually happens in the act of drawing? '[I]t is as if', says Derrida, 'just as I was about to draw, I no longer *saw* the thing'; and 'how can one claim to look at both a model and the lines [*traits*], that one jealously dedicates with one's hand to the thing itself. Doesn't one have to be blind to one or the other? Doesn't one always have to be content with the memory of the other?'[48] As the eye moves from object to figured space, it is memory that suddenly comes into play. 'What happens when one writes without seeing?', asks Derrida – his answer is that the groping hand finds itself 'trusting in the memory of signs and supplementing sight'.[49] To write without seeing – isn't this precisely the modernist charge against Swinburne and Mallarmé? If so, this 'memory of signs' that makes the act of construction possible is perhaps nothing less than that 'musicality' of which I spoke earlier, an inner music of echo and silence, of 'strophe and antistrophe', as Mallarmé finds it in Swinburne's *Erechtheus*.[50] This emphasis on formal values entails, in these terms, a *necessary* blindness, just as metrical form, with its preordained feet and turns, creates (in the words of Rilke's poem) a 'Vibrating space, [which] as it reaches us / demands from our being only the ear'. Once again, Mallarmé's words might come to mind: 'To create is to conceive an object in its fleeting moment, in its absence … We conjure up a scene of lovely, evanescent, intersecting forms.'[51] And while Mallarmé, in marked contrast to Swinburne, is keen to stress that 'the great literary rhythms … are being broken up and scattered in a series of distinct and almost orchestrated shiverings',[52] his notion of 'musicality' does coincide closely with Swinburne's sense of what the latter calls 'the mystic metre' as a mnemonic and associative system.[53] As Yopie Prins puts it in her *Victorian Sappho*, 'the

automatism of Swinburne's writing can be understood as another version
of rhythmic transport, the conversion of "natural" rhythms into a metrical
sublime that was implicit, all along, in his Sapphic imitations'.[54] So for
all Swinburne's fascinated attention to the sounds of winds and waters,
the rhythms of nature are ultimately sublimated into the laws of metre, a
movement that once again parallels that shift between vision and figural
space that underpins Derrida's account of 'blindness'.

This is not, in Eliot's terms, 'bad' poetry, though it is poetry that
dwells almost exclusively within a world of words rather than of things.
'The world of Swinburne', he concludes, 'does not depend upon some
other world which it simulates; it has the necessary completeness and
self-sufficiency for justification and permanence. It is impersonal, and no
one else could have made it.'[55] The comment might seem paradoxical:
at least if 'no one else could have made' this poetic world, one might
assume that it bears almost too weighty an imprint of personality. But
by deeming it 'impersonal', Eliot signals that the Swinburnian repertoire of echo and variation creates merely 'the hallucination of meaning', refusing engagement with 'a world of objects' in favour of a hopeless
fascination with, in Derrida's phrase, 'lyricism itself insofar as it opens
beyond the visible'. This particular 'self-sufficiency' and its dependence
on auditory memory are finely exemplified in the 'mirroring' of rhyme
sequences in Swinburne's 'Anactoria' (lines 36–58). Here, as Elizabeth
Helsinger observes, 'Its mirroring, rhyming passages emerge only with
careful attention: two unmarked twelve-line "stanzas" in which not only
syllables but the key words within each set of lines repeat exactly in the
next set, but with shifted or reversed meanings – strophe and counter-
strophe, turn and counter-turn.'[56] Jerome McGann concludes of this
intricate modulation that:

> The repetition of six couplets with identical rhyme words defines a prosodic
> scheme where musical rather than linguistic structure governs the poetic
> transformations. The terminal rhyme words epitomize a scheme where ver-
> bal units – words, word phrases, and even sentential units – are handled
> primarily as prosodic rather than semantic elements, with grammar there-
> fore emerging as a formal rather than a logical structure.[57]

Pound, of course, does not aim at this high degree of formalism, though
his way of intermittently echoing Swinburnian cadences calls into play
a similar pattern of prosodic echoes and allusions. In fact, in *The Cantos*
lyrical language combines an imagistic directness with a subtle sense of
the experience as a remembered one. As Susan Stewart observes, 'lyric is

not music – it bears a history of a relation to music – and, as a practice of writing, it has no sound – that is, unless we are listening to a spontaneous composition of lyric, we are always *recalling* sound with only some regard to an originating auditory experience'.[58] Pound remarks rather similarly on 'the finer audition which one may have in imagining sound', and quotes Remy de Gourmont's proposal that 'one reads with the memory of speech'[59] – formulations that, like the 'sound: as of the nightingale too far off to be heard' in Canto XX, work to undermine the kind of presence and simultaneity associated with the visual model. This music is at once palpable and impalpable, heard and unheard; and while the images are crisply rendered – 'the stair of gray stone / the passage clean-squared in granite', 'The leaves cut on the air'[60] – the recurring elements of this visionary landscape have about them an elusive quality, something that uncannily escapes the order of clearly determined meaning that Pound has tended to associate with the visual analogy. For Pound, as for Swinburne, then, a certain momentary 'blindness' to the object permits a form of ecstatic perception that occurs in a dimension beyond the visual. This is how Pound puts it in a famous passage from his essay on Cavalcanti where he discovers 'the radiant world where one thought cuts through another with clean edge, a world of moving energies, [of] magnetisms that take form, that are seen or that *border the visible*, the matter of Dante's *paradiso*, the glass under water, the form that seems a form seen in a mirror, these realities perceptible to the sense, interacting'.[61]

It is the insubstantiality of lyric thus conceived – it 'border[s] the visible', just as melopoeia is 'poetry on the borders of music'[62] – that makes it, for Pound, just one among the 'sorts' of poetry, even if its passionate and visionary associations give it a special status.[63] In *The Cantos* it would have to make its way alongside the more demotic modes in which the matter of 'history' entered the poem. Lyric was to be 'earned', as it were, with any transcendence of the prosaic or 'bust thru from quotidien' won from a struggle to penetrate the less tractable opacities of economic and political reality.[64] This was a bold way to reconfigure lyric values but it was one that also raised questions about the special *privilege* accorded to the heightened stylistic register with which it was associated. *The Cantos* could hardly be tasked with what poet Charles Olson would later condemn as 'the lyrical interference of the individual as ego, of the "subject" and his soul',[65] but younger poets, partly in reaction to Pound's later political stance, would find the sense of lyric *occasion* in *The Cantos* increasingly difficult to accept as a model. George Oppen, for example, regarded Pound's 'sheer melody' as the expression of a lofty aestheticism. 'A hypnotic art', he called it, 'a dithyrambic art protected by its special vocabulary etc. – It produces such a destitute world, such a destroyed world when that music stops.'[66] For Oppen, the ascending, 'rhythm-building' set pieces of *The Cantos* may be beautiful, but they are so in a *negative* way, as a paean of praise to art rather than as an affirmation of being in the world. (We may recall Eliot's account of the damaging 'self-sufficiency' of '[t]he world of Swinburne'.[67])

Oppen's distrust of Poundian melopoeia is amply expressed in the gnarled and deliberately 'impoverished' forms of his own late poems, but it also reflects a larger anxiety about any too easy investment in what he calls 'the lyric valuables'.[68] Indeed, for many poets writing in the wake of *The Cantos*, Oppen's worry about the temptations of the 'dithyrambic' speaks for a scepticism about lyricism generally and about the 'comfortable occupancy' it allows the conventional poet.[69] Oppen's late work supplies just one example of an important formal and conceptual shift away from the *melodic* conception of the poem – the 'sheer melody' as we find that in the modernist verse of, say, Yeats and Pound, with their dependence on the rich resources of the auditory memory – to a more purely *rhythmic* one that brings non-semantic elements to the fore.[70] Oppen's habitual use of strong caesurae in these poems gestures mutely towards a severance from tradition, creating an empty moment in which any ascending melody is abruptly curtailed. Take, for example, the following lines from 'To the Poets: To Make Much of Life':

> … (the old men were dancing
>
> return
> the return of the sun)   no need to light
>
> lamps in daylight working year
> after
> year the poem
>
> discovered
>
> in the crystal
> center of the rock image
>
> and image …[71]

The syntax is regular – 'no need to light // lamps in daylight' – but the enjambing of the line is deliberately interrupted by the two-line space that intervenes between 'light' and 'lamps', while the forward movement is further checked by the break that occurs between 'daylight' and 'working'. The lines produce a kind of counter-rhythm to work against the more familiar contour of a sense-making rhythm.[72] Take as another example the opening lines of 'The Little Pin: Fragment':

> of this
> all things
> speak if they speak the estranged
>
> unfamiliar sphere thin as air
> of rescue   huge
>
> pin-point …[73]

Here it's as if one rhythm carries us forwards in the expectation of continuity, while another sends us back to revise what we have already read.
Is 'the estranged' the object of 'speak' – to 'speak the estranged' – or do we
retrospectively discover a caesura inscribed after 'speak'? If so the phrase
will run 'the estranged unfamiliar sphere'. In other words, we read these
lines belatedly, as it were, because a 'counter-rhythm' seems to be working
against the rhythm that would produce the familiar shape of a sentence.

Of course, not all poets writing after Pound have adopted Oppen's strin-
gently 'impoverished' style. Yet even those who, like Susan Howe, have
remained keenly responsive to rich phonic and rhythmic effects have also
made their work a register of the constraints and limits of the lyric mode.
Howe's poetry, in fact, under the pressure of a pervasive and often melancholy
irony, grasps the very matter of lyric – its sounds, cadences, and textures – as
an obstacle to the movements of desire and memory that are its primary concern. The 'articulation of sound forms in time' provides a shimmering mesh of
echoes and repetitions that for all its phonic intricacy can never quite ascend
to the kinds of pure lyric 'occasion' that Pound offers us in *The Cantos*.[74] The
suspended lyric moment is constantly broken open, revealed once more as
belated and displaced, its 'sound forms' and myriad voices exposed as 'mere'
text. Nowhere is this process clearer than in the volume *Pierce-Arrow*, and
especially in its coda, *Rückenfigur*, where the hierarchical impulse of lyric is
repeatedly dissolved in the seriality of writing. Swinburne is a presiding spirit
here, and his version of the legend of Tristram and Iseult is one of the key
strands in Howe's exploration of love and loss:

> He worked over *Tristram*
> in fits and starts
> Love refrain of wind and
> sea its intellectual
> purpose in spirit *Tristram*
> is ecstatic song if
> printed and confined
> Love's sail is black[75]

Swinburne's poem strives, like love itself, to be the pure expression of
'ecstatic song', but (again like love) it cannot escape a deadly 'confinement';

like Tristram espying the black sail that falsely announces Iseult's death, Swinburne's lyricism cannot rise above the black print in which its song takes shape. Lyric becomes instead a mode of looking back – the myth of Orpheus and Eurydice is central to the poem – but one that is always frustrated in its desire to repossess the past. As in the *Rückenfiguren* of Caspar David Friedrich's art, where figures enigmatically present their backs to us, thereby both partially blocking our view of the landscape and asserting their own priority, so the language of lyric is fragmented and of uncertain origin. This is not at all the speaking voice of conventional modern lyric, but one that seems to cancel or disperse itself in the very act of enunciation:

> I have loved come veiling
> Lyrist come veil come lure
> echo remnant sentence spar
> never never form wherefor
> Wait some recognition you
> Lyric over us love unclothe
> Never forever whose move
>   (p. 144)

This is, as one critic puts it, 'a lyric voice that is paradoxically predicated on the loss of voice';[76] it is a language whose 'lyric valuables', as Oppen calls them, have always already suffered the damage and (to use Howe's word) the 'hurt' of history's violence and its 'Iliadic heroism'.[77] The lyric might seem to offer shelter from the storm of epic, but for Howe it is constantly revealed as at once 'veil' and 'lure', drawing us on even though the object sought will never fully disclose itself to memory. As Maurice Blanchot suggests, 'Writing begins with Orpheus's gaze.'[78] 'He loses Eurydice because he desires her beyond the measured limits of the song, and he loses himself, but this desire, and Eurydice lost, and Orpheus dispersed are necessary to the work.'[79] And again: 'the work's demand is this: that Orpheus look back. That suddenly, desire should wreck everything'.[80] We are left, says Blanchot, with a relation that 'is not [one of] cognition, but of recognition, and this recognition ruins in me the power of knowing, the right to grasp'.[81] The lines from *Rückenfigur* quoted above characteristically 'Wait some recognition' that is figured in the space between 'echo' and 'remnant'. Phonic repetition may seem to offer continuity and formal coherence, as in the songs of Arnaut that Pound translated, but here echo is that of an 'other' voice marked now by emptiness and 'brokenness'. The birdsong that intimates this otherness is not, as in Pound's Arnaut, a sign of formal order; Howe's nightingale 'sings in / secret language the bird / is betrayed when her love / song is made public'. And the linnet, for all its 'mimic reputation', doesn't actually get to sing.[82] All of which is in line with Howe's underlying sense that the coherence to which lyricism aspires is always compromised by a contrary desire to expose its limits. 'This tradition that I hope I am part of', she writes, 'has involved a breaking of boundaries of all sorts. It involves a fracturing of discourse, a stammering even. Interruption and hesitation used as a force. A recognition that there is an other voice, an attempt to hear and speak it. It's this brokenness that interests me.'[83] Much is contained for Howe in that idea of hesitation – a word, as she notes, 'from the Latin meaning to stick. Stammer. To hold back in doubt, have difficulty in speaking'.[84] Like Pound, Howe writes with a keen sensitivity to the nineteenth-century prosody that shadows modernist poetry, but this 'stammering' effect, recalling perhaps Oppen's broken rhythms, denies the fluent mnemonics of Pound's 'sheer melody'. In Howe's 'wounded syntax' we read the traces of a deep desire for lyric vision – 'Not look back oh I would'[85] – but a desire that now is bounded, acknowledging its origin in the very 'hurt' of history that disfigures it.

Notes

1 Virginia Jackson, 'Lyric', in *Princeton Encyclopedia of Poetry and Poetics* (Princeton University Press, 2012), pp. 826–34 (p. 832).

2 Scott Brewster, *Lyric* (London and New York: Routledge, 2009), p. 1.

3 Helen Vendler, *Invisible Listeners: Lyric Intimacy in Herbert, Whitman, and Ashbery* (Princeton University Press, 2007), p. 2. Vendler offers a complication of this view that stresses the importance of an 'invisible addressee' in many lyric poems. Elsewhere she defines lyric as 'the genre that directs its *mimesis* toward the performance of the mind in solitary speech' (*The Art of Shakespeare's Sonnets* (1997), quoted in Jackson, 'Lyric', p. 833). For a critique of 'the fixed standpoint of the lyrically meditative "I"', see Donald Davie, *Czeslaw Milosz and the Insufficiency of Lyric* (Knoxville: University of Tennessee Press, 1986), p. 10.

4 Mark Jeffreys, 'Ideologies of Lyric: A Problem of Genre in Contemporary Anglophone Poetics,' *PMLA* 110.2 (March 1995), 196–205 (p. 200).

5 See Marion Thain's account of the perceived limits of lyric in the Victorian period in the previous chapter (pp. 160–3). We should add too that poststructuralism and the literary tendencies it has influenced (most notably Language poetry) have been hostile to lyric's 'reference to a single speaker ensconced in hermetically composed space' and its apparent dismissal of forms of 'otherness'; see Rachel Cole, 'Rethinking the Value of Lyric Closure: Giorgio Agamben, Wallace Stevens, and the Ethics of Satisfaction', *PMLA* 126.2 (2011), 383–97 (pp. 383–4). Note also the much earlier but caustic critique

of Georg Lukács, *Theory of the Novel*, trans. Anna Bostock (London: Merlin Press, 1978 [1916]), pp. 63, 65: 'only in lyric poetry is the subject, the vehicle of such experiences, transformed into the sole carrier of meaning, the only reality', and 'In its experience of nature, the subject, which alone is real, dissolves the whole outside world in mood, and itself becomes mood by virtue of the inexorable identity of essence between the contemplative subject and its object.'

6 John Wilkinson, *The Lyric Touch: Essays on the Poetry of Excess* (Cambridge: Salt, 2007), p. 8.

7 Ezra Pound, *ABC of Reading* (London: Faber and Faber, 1968 [1934]), p. 14. Cf. T. S. Eliot, 'The Three Voices of Poetry' (1953), in *On Poetry and Poets* (New York: Farrar, Straus, and Cudahy, 1957), pp. 96–112 (p. 105): 'The term "lyric" itself is unsatisfactory. We think first of verse intended to be sung … But we apply it also to poetry that was never intended for a musical setting, or which we dissociate from its music.'

8 Ezra Pound, 'Vorticism' (1914), repr. in *Gaudier-Brzeska: A Memoir* (Hessle: Marvell Press, 1960 [1916]), pp. 81–94 (p. 82).

9 Ezra Pound, *Selected Letters of Ezra Pound 1907–1941*, ed. D. D. Paige (London: Faber and Faber, 1971), p. 254. Pound's robust phrasing doesn't conceal the conventionality of this view; cf. Yopie Prins, 'Victorian Meters', in *The Cambridge Companion to Victorian Poetry*, ed. Joseph Bristow (Cambridge University Press, 2000), p. 91 on Victorian approaches to the 'metrical mediation of voice'. At the same time, though, as Jonathan Culler notes in 'Why Lyric?', *PMLA* 123.1 (2008), 201–6 (p. 202), the recent critical emphasis on lyric as dramatic monologue with its 'stress on the reconstruction of the dramatic situation deprives rhythm and sound patterning of any constitutive role (at best they reinforce or undercut meaning)'.

10 Robert Stark, 'Pound among the Nightingales: From the Troubadours to a Cantabile Modernism', *Journal of Modern Literature* 32.2 (Winter 2009), 1–19 (p. 9).

11 Culler, 'Why Lyric?'.

12 Ezra Pound, 'How to Read' (1937), repr. in *Polite Essays* (Plainview, NY: Books for Libraries Press, 1966), pp. 155–92 (p. 170).

13 From Pound's translation of 'Doutz brais e critz', in Ezra Pound, *The Translations of Ezra Pound*, intro. Hugh Kenner (London: Faber and Faber, 1970), pp. 172–5 (p. 173).

14 Ezra Pound, *Literary Essays*, ed. T. S. Eliot (London: Faber and Faber, 1968), p. 114.

15 Pound, *ABC of Reading*, pp. 53–4.

16 Pound, *Selected Letters*, p. 254. Again, the notion of 'sheer melody' has strong connections with the poetry of Swinburne and Tennyson. See Elizabeth Helsinger, 'Song's Fictions', *YES* 40.1–2 (2010), 141–59 (p. 145) on a tendency to create 'song as pure otherness to lyric self-expression' in some of Tennyson's more hypnotic poems. Pound's association of rhythm and space also has connections to the Victorian period 'when meter was being theorized as a principle of spacing that is mentally perceived or internally "felt" as an abstract form, rather than heard'; Prins, 'Victorian Meters', p. 107.

17 Pound, *Literary Essays*, p. 112.

18 Helsinger, 'Song's Fictions', p. 150.

19 Pound, 'Vorticism', p. 83.

20 For a definitive formulation of this 'turn', see Roman Jakobson, 'Marginal Notes on the Prose of the Poet Pasternak', in *Language and Literature*, ed. Krystyna Pomorska and Stephen Rudy (Cambridge, MA: Belknap Press, 1993), pp. 301–17 (pp. 302–3): 'The Romantic slogan of art gravitating toward music was adopted to a significant degree by Symbolism. The foundations of Symbolism first begin to be undermined in painting, and in the early days of Futurist art it is painting that holds the dominant position.' Even surrealism, with its fascinated attention to the occulted movements of the unconscious, saw the historical transition in much the same way, with the editors of the journal *Surréalisme* writing, for example, in 1924 that 'Until the beginning of the twentieth century, the *ear* had decided the quality of poetry: rhythm, sonority, cadence, alliteration, rhyme; everything for the ear. For the last twenty years, the *eye* has been taking its revenge. It is the century of the film.'

21 Wyndham Lewis, *Men without Art* (1934), ed. Seamus Cooney (Santa Rosa, CA: Black Sparrow Press, 1987), p. 99.

22 See *ibid.*, p. 97.

23 Martin Jay, *Downcast Eyes: The Denigration of Vision in Twentieth-Century French Thought* (Berkeley and Los Angeles: University of California Press, 1994), pp. 191–2.

24 Wyndham Lewis, *The Art of Being Ruled* (1926), ed. Reed Way Dasenbrock (Santa Rosa, CA: Black Sparrow Press, 1989), p. 104.

25 Ezra Pound, 'Canto I', in *Personae: The Shorter Poems*, ed.Lee Baechler and A. Walton Litz (New York: New Directions, 1990), p. 234.

26 Ezra Pound, *The Cantos of Ezra Pound* (New York: New Directions, 1996), p. 531.

27 On Yeats' association of free verse with the loss of tradition and memory, see Michael Golston, *Rhythm and Race in Modernist Poetry and Science* (New York: Columbia University Press, 2008), pp. 158–9.

28 See Annie Finch, *The Ghost of Meter: Culture and Prosody in American Free Verse* (Ann Arbor: University of Michigan Press, 1993), p. 128 for the argument that *The Waste Land*'s 'prosody was an attempt to establish a new metrical idiom for a generation jaded and disillusioned with free verse, and exhausted by the apparent lack of any viable prosodic alternative to it'.

29   T. S. Eliot, 'Reflections on "Vers Libre"', in *Selected Prose*, ed. John Hayward (Harmondsworth: Penguin, 1965), pp. 86–91 (p. 85): 'the ghost of some simple metre should lurk behind the arras in even the "freest" verse; to advance menacingly as we doze, and withdraw as we rouse'.

30 Pound, *Selected Letters*, p. 49.

31 Pound, *Literary Essays*, p. 293.

32 A. C. Swinburne, *Atalanta in Calydon: A Tragedy* (London: Chatto and Windus, 1896), p. 36.

33 Pound, *The Cantos*, p. 11.

34 Swinburne, *Atalanta*, p. 57; Pound, *The Cantos*, p. 76.

35 Pound, *The Cantos*, p. 538.

36 A. C. Swinburne, 'Whitmania' (1887), in *The Works of Algernon Charles Swinburne*, ed. Edmund Gosse and Thomas J. Wise, 20 vols. (New York: Russell and Russell, 1968 [1925]), Vol. XVI, pp. 307–18 (p. 310).

37 The last phrase of this sentence is quoted from Yopie Prins, *Victorian Sappho* (Princeton University Press, 1999), p. 173.

38 Jerome McGann, *Swinburne: An Experiment in Criticism* (Chicago University Press, 1972), p. 65.

39 Stéphane Mallarmé, '*Erechtheus*: Tragédie par Swinburne', in *Oeuvres complètes*, ed. Henri Mondor and G. Jean-Aubry (Paris: Gallimard, 1979), pp. 700–3 (p. 703).

40 *Ibid.*, p. 702.

41 Stéphane Mallarmé, *Crayonné au théâtre*, in *Oeuvres complètes*, p. 328.

42 On this set of distinctions, see Philippe Lacoue-Labarthe, *Musica ficta (Figures of Wagner)*, trans. Felicia McCarren (Stanford University Press, 1994), pp. 41–84; and Jacques Rancière, *Mallarmé: La politique de la sirène* (Paris: Hachette, 1996), pp. 67–78.

43 See Suzanne Bernard, *Mallarmé et la musique* (Paris: Nizet, 1959), p. 74.

44 T. S. Eliot, 'Swinburne as Poet', in *Selected Essays* (London: Faber and Faber, 1972), pp. 323–7 (p. 327).

45 *Ibid.*, pp. 324, 325.

46 Jacques Derrida, *Memoirs of the Blind: The Self-Portrait and Other Ruins*, trans. Pascale-Anne Brault and Michael Naas (University of Chicago Press, 1990), p. 39n42. The emphasis is also familiar from Charles Baudelaire's *The Painter of Modern Life*, in *Selected Writings on Art and Artists*, trans. P. E. Charvet (Harmondsworth: Penguin, 1972), pp. 390–436 (p. 407): 'all true draughtsmen draw from the image imprinted in their brain and not from nature'.

47 Derrida, *Memoirs of the Blind*, p. 40 n42. For the text, see Rainer Maria Rilke, *The Complete French Poems of Rainer Maria Rilke*, trans. A. Poulin, Jr (Saint Paul, MN: Graywolf Press, 1986), pp. 59–61.

48 *Ibid.*, p. 36 (his emphasis). Cf. Jacques Derrida, *Speech and Phenomenon and Other Essays on Husserl's Theory of Signs*, trans. David B. Allison (Evanston, IL: Northwestern University Press, 1973), p. 62: 'There is a duration to the blink, and it closes the eye.' See also Leonard Lawlor, *The Implications of Immanence: Toward a New Concept of Life* (New York: Fordham University Press, 2006), p. 32: 'Without this minuscule hiatus, one would *either* have the vision of the model *or* the vision of the paper, but *not* drawing on the paper.'

49 Derrida, *Memoirs of the Blind*, p. 3.

50 Mallarmé, '*Erechtheus*', p. 702.

51 Stéphane Mallarmé, *Mallarmé: Selected Prose Poems, Essays, and Letters*, trans. Bradford Cook (Baltimore, MD: Johns Hopkins University Press, 1956), p. 48.

52 *Ibid.*, p. 42.

53 A. C. Swinburne, 'Epicede', in *Swinburne's Collected Poetical Works*, 2 vols. (London: William Heinemann, 1924), Vol. I, p. 368.

54 Prins, *Victorian Sappho*, p. 172.

55 Eliot, 'Swinburne as Poet', p. 327. Cf. McGann, *Swinburne*, p. 73: 'the uniform tone persuades us that all systems of echo and correspondence are realities which stand beyond personality, immutably and eternally "real"'.

56 Helsinger, 'Song's Fictions', p. 152.

57 Jerome McGann, 'Wagner, Baudelaire, Swinburne: Poetry in the Condition of Music', *Victorian Poetry* 47.4 (2009), 619–32 (p. 627). Helsinger also discusses the expanded version of this 'mirroring' effect in *Tristram of Lyoness*, where two forty-four-line passages echo each other from the opening of the first canto to that of the final one ('Song's Fictions', p. 156).

58 Susan Stewart, *Poetry and the Fate of the Senses* (Chicago University Press, 2002), p. 68.

59 Ezra Pound, 'A Study in French Poets', *Little Review* 4.10 (February 1918), p. 27.

60 Pound, *Cantos*, pp. 69, 99.

61 Pound, *Literary Essays*, p. 154 (my italics).

62 Pound, 'How to Read', pp. 171–2.

63 Pound, 'Vorticism', p. 82.

64 Pound, *Selected Letters*, p. 210. For a detailed working through of this argument see my *Ezra Pound: Politics, Economics and Writing* (London: Macmillan, 1984).

65 Charles Olson, *Human Universe and Other Essays*, ed. Donald Allen (New York: Grove Press, 1967), p. 59. Even in the 1914 essay 'Vorticism', Pound is sceptical about the poem as revelation of some stable self: 'In the "search for oneself", in the search for "sincere self-expression", one gropes, one finds some seeming verity. One says "I am" this, that, or the other, and with the words scarcely uttered one ceases to be that thing' (p. 85).

66 George Oppen, *Selected Prose, Daybooks, and Papers*, ed. Stephen Cope (Los Angeles and Berkeley: University of California Press, 2008), p. 67.

67 See above, p. 184. Pound's conjuring with 'How many worlds we have!' in the first draft of Canto 1 shows a similar set of doubts about the autonomy of lyric: 'Oh, we have worlds enough, and brave *décors*, / And from these like we guess a soul for man / And build him full of aery populations' (Pound, *Personae*, p. 234).

68 George Oppen, *New Collected Poems*, ed. Michael Davidson (New York: New Directions, 2008), p. 50. For a discussion of 'impoverishment' and Oppen's late poetry, see my *George Oppen and the Fate of Modernism* (Oxford University Press, 2007), Chapters 6 and 7.

69 The phrase 'comfortable occupancy' is from J. H. Prynne, 'Mental Ears and Poetic Work', *Chicago Review* 55.1 (2010), 126–57 (p. 157 n56).

70 The distinction is employed in regard to Hölderlin's concept of the caesura in Philippe Lacoue-Labarthe, *Typography: Mimesis, Philosophy, Politics*, ed. Christopher Fynsk (Stanford University Press, 1998), p. 234.

71 Oppen, *New Collected Poems*, p. 260.

72 The term 'counter-rhythm' is used in a famous discussion of the caesura by Friedrich Hölderlin, *Essays and Letters on Theory*, trans. Thomas Pfau (Albany, NY: SUNY Press, 1988), p. 102.

73 Oppen, *New Collected Poems*, p. 254.

74 I refer to the title of Susan Howe, *Articulation of Sound Forms in Time* (Windsor, VT: Awede Press, 1987).

75 Susan Howe, *Pierce-Arrow* (New York: New Directions, 1999), p. 54. Cf. Swinburne, *Collected Poetical Works*, Vol. II, p. 147: 'And she that saw looked hardly toward him back, / Saying, "Ay, the ship comes surely; but her sail is black."'

76 Will Montgomery, *The Poetry of Susan Howe: History, Theology, Authority* (New York: Palgrave Macmillan, 2010), p. 151.

77 Susan Howe, *The Europe of Trusts* (Los Angeles, CA: Sun & Moon Classics, 1990), p. 26: 'Only / what never stops hurting remains // In memory …'. Compare Friedrich Nietzsche, *On the Genealogy of Morals and Other Writings*, trans. Carol Diethe (Cambridge University Press, 2006), p. 38: 'A thing must be burnt in so that it stays in the memory: only something that continues to *hurt* stays in the memory' (his italics). For 'Iliadic heroism', see Howe, *Pierce-Arrow*, p. 27.

78 Maurice Blanchot, *The Gaze of Orpheus and Other Literary Essays*, ed. P. Adams Sitney (New York: Station Hill, 1981), p. 176.

79 Maurice Blanchot, *The Space of Literature*, trans. Ann Smock (Lincoln: University of Nebraska Press, 1982), p. 173. Compare Susan Howe, 'Sorting Facts; or, Nineteen Ways of Looking at Marker', in *Beyond Document: Essays on Nonfiction Film*, ed. Charles Warren (Hanover, NH: Wesleyan University Press, 1996), pp. 295–344 (p. 332): 'A documentary work is an attempt to recapture someone something somewhere looking back. Looking back, Orpheus was the first known documentarist: Orpheus, or Lot's wife.'

80 Blanchot, *The Gaze of Orpheus*, p. 14.

81 *Ibid.*, p. 31.

82 Howe, *Pierce-Arrow*, pp. 101, 140, 139.

83 Susan Howe, 'Encloser', in *The Politics of Poetic Form: Poetry and Public Policy*, ed. Charles Bernstein (New York: Roof, 1990), pp. 175–89 (p. 192).

84 Susan Howe, *My Emily Dickinson* (Berkeley, CA: North Atlantic, 1985), p. 21. On the association of a 'rhetoric of obscuration' with prophecy in the biblical tradition, see Herbert Marks, 'On Prophetic Stammering', *Yale Journal of Criticism* 1 (1987), 1–19.

85 Howe, *Pierce-Arrow*, p. 35. The phrase 'wounded syntax' is from Montgomery, *The Poetry of Susan Howe*, p. 146.

CHAPTER TEN

The lyric 'I' in late-twentieth-century English poetry

Neil Roberts

Writing in 1995, Mark Jeffreys noted that 'The term *lyric* has all but disappeared from the title pages of anthologies, making it all but impossible to determine what the contemporary lyric canon – as opposed to a general poetic canon – might look like.'[1] One reason for this, he suggests, is that anthologists and critics 'conflate the terms *poetry* and *lyric*'.[2] In 2000, as if in confirmation of Jeffreys' argument, Edna Longley wrote in the preface to her *Bloodaxe Book of 20th Century Poetry*, 'This anthology is essentially an anthology of 20th century lyrics.' Longley refers back to Yeats' *Oxford Book of Modern Verse* (1936), quoting his Paterian definition of modern poetry as the expression of 'life at its intense moments, those moments that are brief because of their intensity', and appears to borrow his criterion: 'The common factor is concentration: language "at its intense moments".'[3] But she has made a surprisingly silent shift: in her definition, the intensity belongs to language, not to 'life'. In the examples of late-twentieth-century poetry that I shall be considering, I shall argue that the intensity is indeed one of language, though at least one of the poets would deny it.

Longley is also at pains to refute the solipsism that lyric has often been accused of in this period: 'The drama of lyric poetry begins where the merely personal ends.'[4] A parallel with both these contentions might be found in Mutlu Konuk Blasing's more theorised approach in *Lyric Poetry: The Pain and the Pleasure of Words*, though not quite in the way Longley intended. Blasing locates lyric on the borderline between sound, signification, and formal structure: 'Poetic rhythm … is a mentally audible movement of sounds that will not reduce to discursive meanings or formal effects.' It 'makes audible an intending "I"'.[5] This 'I', however, 'is not prior to its words, and its words have nothing to do with "self-expression"'.[6] It is, rather, 'a rhythmic pulse "between" music and figure; it is neither music nor figure and without it there is neither music nor figure'.[7] A critic of Longley's persuasion might protest that this is even more solipsistic than conventional definitions of lyric, but I will argue that in my chosen poets the lyric is defined by an escape from the ego or social self, and the discovery of another 'I' in the act of writing.

Philip Larkin and Ted Hughes are routinely regarded as opposite, even incompatible, poles of late-twentieth-century English poetry. Despite their very real differences, some of which will be clear in the course of my chapter, I wish to draw attention to parallels both in their situations as poets who strove for lyric utterance in this period, and in some of their strategies. Although, as the introduction to this book states, this is a period in which 'poetry has, in the minds of many, become synonymous with definitions of the lyric' (p. 3), most of its major practitioners (among whom one might include Geoffrey Hill as well as Hughes and Larkin) are haunted by voices questioning the lyric's integrity.

Larkin and Hughes were both, at the heart of their endeavours, lyric poets. Larkin published two novels, which he later claimed were really poems, and abandoned novel-writing in his early twenties. Thereafter, apart from a substantial body of lively journalism, he published only short poems. Many of his best poems have important narrative elements, but it is telling that his one attempt that might have developed into a lengthy narrative, 'The Dance', was left unfinished. Hughes is a more complex case. As well as several short stories he published one book-length narrative poem, *Gaudete*; wrote several verse plays for radio (mostly unpublished); translations of verse and prose drama; and a number of much more ambitious works of criticism than Larkin's, most notably *Shakespeare and the Goddess of Complete Being*. If we also consider his writing for children, his achievements in prose narrative and drama are even more numerous. Yet Hughes too, I will argue, is centrally a lyric poet. Nevertheless, the work of both poets was in different ways, as Peter Nicholls has argued for poets of the modernist period in the foregoing chapter, a 'hybrid' lyric.

Blasing's lyric 'I' is in language but is also profoundly somatic, negotiating between signification and our earliest experience of pre-verbal sound. Such an approach seems comically incongruous with Larkin's 'plain man' definition of poetry in his essay 'The Pleasure Principle':

> [The writing of a poem] consists of three stages: the first is when a man becomes obsessed with an emotional concept to such a degree that he is compelled to do something about it. What he does is the second stage, namely, construct a verbal device that will reproduce this emotional concept in anyone who cares to read it, anywhere, any time. The third stage is the recurrent situation of people in different times and places setting off the device and re-creating in themselves what the poet felt when he wrote it.[8]

Psychoanalytic approaches such as Blasing's were less common when Larkin wrote this in 1972, otherwise one might suspect a satirical intention in his lifting of a Freudian phrase for his title. This is Larkin the 'philistine', a role for which Barbara Everett praised him, setting him in a tradition that 'has for centuries refused to avail itself of the self-indulgent securities of "Art"'.[9] However, there is a revealing aporia at the centre of this bluff utterance, in Larkin's phrase 'emotional concept'. What 'the poet felt when he wrote' was surely not a 'concept', yet Larkin's repetition of this phrase indicates that it is not a careless slip. The main thrust of his essay is that poetry is nothing unless it communicates with an audience, and one can applaud this while maintaining that this communication is not the same as a person trying to explain his or her feelings to another. The odd, borderline phrase, 'emotional concept', might betray that Larkin has in mind something closer to Blasing's 'movement of sounds that will not reduce to discursive meanings or formal effects' than his manner implies. I shall hope to demonstrate that Larkin's genuine lyricism is stranger and less companionable than the 'philistine' would have us think.

In contrast to Larkin, Hughes from an early stage in his career espoused a conception of the lyric 'I' that was much more in line with Eliotic and New Critical orthodoxy. In 1973 he wrote: 'Whatever person I've projected, in the body of my poems, will have to bear whatever ideas people have about him. I've freed myself fairly successfully from too great a concern about his fate. What does disturb me, I'm afraid, is to see him identified with me – in the details of my life.'[10] His reference in this same letter to readers having 'scraps of [his] hair and nails' – a well-known motif of Sylvia Plath biography – betrays the obvious personal motives that support his espousal of impersonality. Much later in his career, however, when he published *Birthday Letters*, he vehemently renounced this stance: 'My high-minded principal [*sic*] was simply wrong – for my own psychological & physical health.'[11] Is not the 'I' of *Birthday Letters* 'prior to its words'? This is one case that I shall be investigating.

For both Larkin and Hughes, not surprisingly given the period of their literary formation, the most significant lyric precursor was Yeats, who, however, played differently into the poetic formation of each. Hughes' account of his early development has a home-made feel, and is very convincing. His first model was what he called the 'lockstep rhythms and resounding deadlock rhymes' of Kipling. He gives an example from an otherwise lost poem: 'And the curling lips of the five gouged rips in the bark of the pine were the mark of the bear'.[12] This is the style of the first two poems in *Collected Poems*, 'Wild West' and 'Too Bad for Hell'. Yet

over the page from the latter in *Collected Poems*, and first published in
the same issue of the Mexborough Grammar School magazine in Hughes'
eighteenth year, we find this:

> O lean dry man with your thin withered feet,
> Feet like old rain-worn weasels, like old roots
> Frost-warped and sunken on the cold sea beach,
> You have a sad world here:
> Only the bitter windy rain and bareness of wet rock glistening;
> Only the sand-choked marram, only their dead
> Throats whispering always in despair:
> Only the wild high phantom-drifting of the gulls …[13]

Hughes's second great poetic discovery had been *The Wanderings of Oisin*,
especially its third section, whose long lines struck him as a 'wilder and
more hauntingly varied' version of the Kipling metre. The influence is
obvious in this poem, 'The Recluse', which has its share of immature
Yeatsian pastiche, but also lines of a rhythmic subtlety to match the best
of his early poetry, such as the last one quoted, and imagery such as that
in the second line, which is redolent of Hughes' intimacy with the wildlife
of his locality.

Larkin's early formation was ostensibly more sophisticated, contemporary, and, for its time, mainstream. His first major influence was not Yeats
(and certainly not Kipling) but Auden, and he had an Auden-inspired
poem, 'Ultimatum', published in a national journal, *The Listener*, at the
age of eighteen. His infatuation with Yeats came later, and is pervasively
evident in his first collection, *The North Ship*, written between 1941 and
1944, when Larkin was between nineteen and twenty-three years old.
Hughes, by contrast, collected only one juvenile Yeats imitation, 'Song',
written in 1949 when he was nineteen, five years earlier than any other
poem in his first collection, *The Hawk in the Rain*. A comparison of 'Song'
with Larkin's 'I dreamed of an out-thrust arm of land', and of both these
poems with an early Yeats lyric such as 'A Poet to His Beloved' shows a
surprising similarity of inspiration:

> O lady, consider when I shall have lost you
> The moon's full hands, scattering waste,
> The sea's hands, dark from the world's breast,
> The world's decay where the wind's hands have passed,
> And my head, worn out with love, at rest
> In my hands, and my hands full of dust
>   O my lady.[14]
>
> I was sleeping, and you woke me
> To walk on the chilled shore …

Till your two hands withdrew
And I was empty of tears …[15]

I bring you with reverent hands
The books of my numberless dreams,
White woman that passion has worn
As the tide wears the dove-grey sands …[16]

Note that in both cases it is the early, *fin de siècle* Yeats that the young poets are drawn to: a version of lyricism already outmoded when they were writing. Their Yeats-inspired early verse is at the centre of contrasting, but equally suspect, narratives of poetic formation. Larkin's is well known. He started trying to write like Yeats 'out of infatuation with his music', but discovering Hardy brought 'the sense of relief that I didn't have to try and jack myself up to a concept of poetry that lay outside my own life … Hardy taught one to feel rather than to write.'[17] It is true that most of the poems of *The North Ship* are marked by an affected literariness that is not present in Larkin's mature work, but as B. J. Leggett has pointed out, this narrative of development really tells us nothing because it 'ignore[s] the status of the poems as written texts'.[18] Moreover, as Andrew Motion argued more than thirty years ago, 'Even in the poems that adopt primarily Hardyesque neutral tones, there are frequent flashes of rhetoric which recall Yeats's grander manner.'[19] The important issue, however, is not which earlier poets Larkin's work reminds us of, but a recognition that his mature work is no less lyrical than his juvenilia, and that the 'intensity' of this lyricism, as Longley implies, is a quality of the writing, rather than a Paterian pre-existent moment construed from the writing.

Hughes, as I have said, collected only one Yeats-inspired early poem, 'Song', but, far from disavowing it, he made the remarkable claim late in life that it was 'the one song I sang in Arcadia – that came to me literally out of the air … like Aphrodite blowing ashore', and hinted that it could be a model for what might have been if his development had not been thwarted by 'the critical exhalations and toxic smokestacks and power stations of Academe'.[20] Hughes did not collect any poetry written when he was reading English at Cambridge, and this characterisation of 'Song' serves a narrative in which academic study stifles creativity. Whereas Larkin's narrative is designed to obscure the continuing presence of Yeats and the essentially *written* character of his oeuvre, Hughes is eliding the literary character of 'Song' itself, which came, not 'literally out of the air', but largely from the pages of Yeats. Despite the contrast between the poets' valuations of this early work, there is a shared motive: a denial of the essentially literary character of lyric poetry. We can also see that these narratives reinforce their contrasting poetic personae: while Larkin grounds his in daily life, Hughes' references to Arcadia and Aphrodite signal the importance of myth and shamanism to his conception of the poet.

This lyricism inherited from early Yeats was not, however, adequate equipment for poets writing after the Second World War. Larkin and Hughes were both (unlike Yeats) admirers of Wilfred Owen, and therefore writing in the shadow of Owen's 'Above all I am not concerned with Poetry' as well as of Eliot's 'The poetry does not matter.'[21] It is unlikely that either poet read Theodor Adorno's influential essay 'Cultural Criticism and Society', but Hughes at least was aware of the famous rhetorical gesture with which that essay ends: 'To write poetry after Auschwitz is barbaric. And this corrodes even the knowledge of why it has become impossible to write poetry today.'[22] In his introduction to translations of the Hungarian poet János Pilinszky, Hughes quotes Pilinszky's statement, 'I would like to write as if I had remained silent', and comments, 'The silence of artistic integrity "after Auschwitz" is a real thing.'[23] However, both poets were aware that European culture had already been compromised by its own barbarism before their birth. Larkin's references to the First World War are less frequent and emphatic than Hughes', but his poem 'MCMXIV' concludes, 'Never such innocence again' – an innocence that includes such lyricism as that of the early Yeats.[24] Hughes' work is pervasively haunted by the post-traumatic stress of his infantryman father. His first collection includes a pastiche of Owen, 'Bayonet Charge', but more telling is the way imagery drawn from that conflict erupts in places that are ostensibly thematically remote from it: crabs emerging from the sea are 'staring inland / Like a packed trench of helmets'; his West Yorkshire birthplace is also a 'trench' under 'A sky like an empty helmet / With a hole in it'; a dying salmon is 'already a veteran, / Already a death-patched hero' clothed in 'clownish regimentals'.[25]

It is no surprise therefore to find that both poets self-consciously foreground, and perhaps parody, received ideas of the 'lyric'. 'Sad Steps' is one of several Larkin poems that belie his asserted dislike of 'casual allusions in poems to other poems or other poets',[26] quoting in its title Sidney's *Astrophil and Stella*, XXXI. As if in reaction to this, like the more famous 'This Be the Verse' (which takes its title from Stevenson's 'Requiem' and begins 'They fuck you up, your mum and dad')[27] its opening line is in Larkin's most 'philistine' register: 'Groping back to bed after a piss' (Sidney's poem begins, 'With how sad steps, O moon, thou climb'st the skies! / How silently, and with how wan a face!').[28]

Uniquely, however, the 'philistine' persona is dropped after a single line. The poem continues:

> I part thick curtains, and am startled by
> The rapid clouds, the moon's cleanliness.
>
> Four o'clock: wedge-shadowed gardens lie
> Under a cavernous, a wind-picked sky.[29]

There is little that is overtly poetic about these lines, but, despite the metonymic gestures of the thick curtains, the time of night, and the domestic gardens, their effect has little to do with referentiality: the referential
meaning is quite banal. The experience of parting the curtains and seeing the moon is raised to significance by the exceptional sensitivity of the
language, which lends itself to the speaker's vision of the scene. Internal
rhyme draws together the two clauses of the first line, emphasising the
contrast between the slight mimetic resistance of the first and the sudden
ease of the second. The moon's cleanliness is not in itself a particularly
original image, but the dropping of a metrical syllable and consequent
spondee-effect reinforces the consonance to make the phrase stand out
almost literally from the line (compare the weaker effect of the metrically regular 'moon's bright cleanliness'). The last line quoted is another
example of the poetry of contrasting sound-values: the open vowels of
'cavernous' against the densely consonantal 'wind-picked'. The phrase is
strictly contradictory: 'cavernous' ought logically to signify enclosure and
confinement but the combination with 'wind-picked' suggests rather a
vast, draughty space.

This is lyric poetry at its most refined, and the 'philistine' persona recoils
from it: 'There's something laughable about this.' Within a few lines he
bursts into what seems like a series of parodic exclamations:

> Lozenge of love! Medallion of art!
> O wolves of memory! Immensements!

'Wolves of memory' is reminiscent of Dylan Thomas, 'Medallions of art'
of the early Pound. 'Immensements' is a neologism – as far as I know
the only one in Larkin – its cumbersome grotesqueness perhaps a comment on neologism as a poetic device. There is however a French word,
immensément, and there may be a satirical allusion to modernist franco-
philia. 'Lozenge of love' is equally grotesque: a lozenge may be a heraldic
image, a pane of glass, or a facet of a precious stone, but in every case is
rhomboid, hardly a suitable metaphor for the moon. This outburst highlights the self-consciousness of the speaker, but emphasises by contrast the
unparodiable subtlety of the poem's genuinely lyrical passages.

Hughes described his fourth collection *Crow* as 'songs with no music
whatsoever', adding 'I throw out the eagles and choose the Crow.'[30] This

must be an allusion to the poem 'Crow and the Birds'. This poem is a single sentence of fifteen lines. Each of the first fourteen names a bird in a subordinate clause dependent on the main clause, which is deferred to the fifteenth line: 'Crow spraddled head-down in the beach-garbage, guzzling a dropped ice-cream.' Crow is thus privileged by his status in the sentence (and by being 'Crow' as if a proper name, rather than 'the crow'), casting an ironic shadow over the foregoing lines. There may also be an allusion to the sonnet form, and its usurpation by Crow. (This would be an abstruse link with 'Sad Steps', whose title alludes to a sonnet and whose form could be described as three Petrarchan sestets.)

The poem begins:

> When the eagle soared clear through a dawn distilling of emerald
> When the curlew trawled in seadusk through a chime of wineglasses
> When the swallow swooped through a woman's song in a cavern
> And the swift flicked through the breath of a violet[31]

Critics routinely describe these lines as parodic. Honesty demands that I cite myself as an example: 'The mode of the first stanza is parodic: each bird is engulfed in a gratuitous romantic idea.'[32] I now think the case is less simple. In each line the verb is precise, energetic, and carefully chosen. The language is certainly heightened in comparison with what I have called the refined lyricism of 'Sad Steps'. But 'distilling of emerald' is a far from hackneyed or cheaply glamorised metaphor for dawn; Hughes had used 'emerald' in a completely unironic context in one of his most admired nature poems, 'Pike': '[Pike] move, stunned by their own grandeur, / Over a bed of emerald'.[33] 'A chime of wineglasses' is a vivid and accurate representation of a curlew's song, and 'the breath of a violet' registers the precision of the swift's flight. Only the 'woman's song in a cavern' is self-evidently 'poetic' in a derogatory sense. This perhaps casts a shadow over the whole stanza, but the real shadow is cast by 'Crow spraddled head-down in the beach-garbage, guzzling a dropped ice-cream.'

We might think that this is Hughes' equivalent of 'Groping back to bed after a piss' or 'They fuck you up, your mum and dad', but Hughes' line differs from Larkin's in that, while Larkin shows consummate skill in incorporating these lines into works of great lyrical power, they are not intrinsically of great poetic interest. Hughes' line is. It is rhythmically extremely accomplished, stretching a rhythmic unit based on the alliterative line to the limit, nailing it together with actual alliteration, and with energetic diction ('spraddled', 'garbage', 'guzzling') that has a wide lexical reach (English dialect, American, English slang). If Hughes were taking the easy option of opposing parodied conventional poetry to the language of Crow, the poem's merit would shrink to its final line. He has actually achieved something more difficult and interesting: he has composed genuinely accomplished, though conventional, lyrical verse (allowing for the lapse of the 'woman's song in a cavern') and challenged it with a new, harsher, and more quotidian lyricism.

But a poet cannot just go on repeating this kind of gesture. In the rest of this chapter I will explore the strategies adopted by each poet, in the face of this self-consciousness and resistance, to approach something like Blasing's 'rhythmic pulse "between" music and figure' that 'makes audible an intending "I"'.

In an early (1977) and influential essay David Lodge argued that Larkin displaced poetry, 'an inherently metaphoric mode … towards the metonymic pole', which he characterised as 'an "experimental" literary gesture', because such poetry 'makes its impact by appearing daringly, even shockingly unpoetic'.[34] Lodge perhaps exaggerated the boldness of a gesture that had been made a generation earlier by William Carlos Williams, but Larkin's creation of the kind of 'philistine' persona whom we have seen emerge briefly in 'Sad Steps' has a special piquancy because it is usually framed by conventional, and very skilfully handled, metrical forms. Williams' startlingly anti-poetic gestures presuppose an avant-garde audience, whereas Larkin writes as if for a middlebrow readership. Lodge concludes his essay by observing that Larkin frequently 'surprises us, especially in the closing lines of his poems, by his ability to transcend – or turn ironically upon – the severe restraints he seems to have placed upon authentic expression of feeling in poetry'.[35] It is less a matter of 'authentic expression of feeling' than of language: the abandonment of the 'philistine' persona who implicitly or explicitly disavows 'art' ('Cleaned, or restored? Someone would know: I don't')[36] in favour of an 'intending "I"' that is wholly identified with the art of lyric poetry. Lodge was misled by the Jakobsonian framework of his book *The Modes of Modern Writing* to categorise poetry as 'inherently metaphoric'. As we have seen in 'Sad Steps' – 'I part thick curtains, and am startled by / The rapid clouds, the moon's cleanliness' – the achievement of a lyric style is not dependent on metaphor.

Larkin did, throughout his mature oeuvre, write more straightforwardly lyrical poems than is usually acknowledged – 'Going' and 'Absences' in *The Less Deceived*, 'Water' and 'First Sight' in *The Whitsun Weddings*, 'Solar' and 'Cut Grass' in *High Windows*. But mostly it isn't in these poems that we see his lyrical achievement. He made the point himself about 'Cut Grass', which ends:

> Lost lanes of Queen Anne's lace,
> And that high-builded cloud
> Moving at summer's pace.[37]

He wrote about this poem, 'Its trouble is that it's "music", i.e. pointless crap … About line 6 I hear a wonderful kind of Elgar river-music take over, for which the words are just an excuse.'[38] 'Music', the foregrounding of sound and rhythm, is of course essential to lyric poetry, but as his mention of Elgar suggests, this is an imitation of an already archaic music – the euphony of the first line quoted, his choice of the name 'Queen Anne's lace' rather than 'wild carrot', which is an alternative name for the same plant, and the archaism 'builded', with its echo of Blake's 'And did those feet'. Indeed, the effect is of a wholly indulgent and nationalistically tinged sense of pastness.

Larkin's distinctive lyrical achievement is more evident in a poem such as 'Vers de Société', which begins,

> *My wife and I have asked a crowd of craps*
> *To come and waste their time and ours: perhaps*
> *You'd care to join us?* In a pig's arse, friend.
> Day comes to an end.
> The gas fire breathes, the trees are darkly swayed.
> And so *Dear Warlock-Williams: I'm afraid* – [39]

'And so' in the final line quoted implies that the foregoing lines have somehow explained the speaker's refusal of the invitation, but logically they seem entirely tangential. 'In a pig's arse, friend' is a performance of the Larkin persona whom we have already met in 'Sad Steps'. Here its main function is to intensify the steep change of mood that follows. This is one of Larkin's most striking moves from Lodge's 'metonymic' to the lyrical, yet is achieved without the aid of metaphor. The line's simplicity, its elemental quality, its unexpected brevity and the rhyme emphasising the contrast combine to create the modulation from the 'performed' voice to something more resonant and pregnant, which continues into the next line. This effect isn't dependent on the shift from the social to the natural, since 'the gas fire breathes' wholly belongs in the new tone. There is in this phrase a touch of personification, the implied silence and stillness allowing the fire to be heard, and subliminally but perhaps most decisively an echo of the 'film, which fluttered on the grate' of Coleridge's 'Frost at Midnight', that canonical evocation of poetic solitude.[40] The period touch of the gas fire saves this from preciosity, but there's nothing parodic about it, and the feeling is preserved, allowing the more overtly lyrical gesture of 'the trees are darkly swayed', echoing from 'Frost at Midnight' the motif of the poet looking out of the window into the darkness.

'Vers de Société' is effectively a rewrite of a poem originally written twenty years earlier, and unpublished till after Larkin's death: 'Best Society'. The later poem is an improvement, in the liveliness of its comedy, the refinement of its lyricism, and its more complex feeling, recognising that solitude can bring 'Not peace, but other things'. But 'Best Society' makes explicit the production of the 'intending "I"' by the lyric:

> The gas fire breathes. The wind outside
> Ushers in evening rain. Once more
> Uncontradicting solitude
> Supports me on its giant palm;
> And like a sea-anemone
> Or simple snail, there cautiously
> Unfolds, emerges, what I am.[41]

There are a number of fine poetic effects here: as well as the gas fire that Larkin preserved in the later poem, there are the boldly polysyllabic 'Uncontradicting solitude' and the apparently modest substitution of the snail for the sea-anemone. These effects are more obviously worked-for, and therefore less distinctive, than in 'Vers de Société', but the emergence of 'what I am', not just from the solitude to which the poem refers, but from the lyrical language itself, makes explicit what is implicit in the later poem.

This solitude, almost a reduction of the subject to a finely perceiving sensibility, is at the heart of Larkin's lyricism. Lodge writes of many of his most characteristic poems ending 'with a kind of eclipse of meaning, speculation fading out in the face of the void'.[42] Such is the famous ending of 'High Windows':

> Rather than words comes the thought of high windows:
> The sun-comprehending glass,
> And beyond it, the deep blue air, that shows
> Nothing, and is nowhere, and is endless.[43]

'Rather than words' is of course a deceptive rhetorical device – these are words. The phrase 'high windows' startles by its complete unexpectedness and apparent randomness in a poem that has been about the delusiveness of freedom. 'Comprehending' fills the line mimetically, while suggesting a pun that can't quite be grasped. The cadence of the final line completes the feeling of entropy. This is as close as Larkin comes to Symbolist poetry. The social persona, even the persona who asserts his desire for solitude in amusing and therefore social terms, has dissolved into something that is nothing but the subject of these words.

The shift from the philistine or social persona (who starts 'High Windows' with 'When I see a couple of kids / And guess he's fucking her') to a poignant but strangely comfortless lyricism is the essential signature of Larkin's poetry. It is there in 'But if he stood and watched the frigid wind / Tousling the clouds' of 'Mr Bleaney', 'Man hands on misery to man. / It deepens like a coastal shelf' of 'This Be the Verse', the 'sense of falling, like an arrow-shower / Sent out of sight, somewhere becoming rain' of 'The Whitsun Weddings', and the evocation of 'money singing' in 'Money'.[44] These examples are thematically various, but a note of absence, what Lodge called 'the void', is recurrent. It is perhaps most intense in 'Here'. This is one of Larkin's most highly wrought poems, with long elaborate stanzas running into each other, and an opening sentence of twenty-four lines. There is no 'philistine' persona in this poem, though there are highly 'metonymic' lines such as 'Cheap suits, red kitchen-ware, sharp shoes, iced lollies'. The poem's lyrical accomplishment is by no means confined to its conclusion, but as usual it is the final stanza that is most distinctive:

> Here silence stands
> Like heat. Here leaves unnoticed thicken,
> Hidden weeds flower, neglected waters quicken,
> Luminously-peopled air ascends;
> And past the poppies bluish neutral distance
> Ends the land suddenly beyond a beach
> Of shapes and shingle. Here is unfenced existence:
> Facing the sun, untalkative, out of reach.[45]

The first half of this stanza is composed of variants of familiar lyrical motifs – Gray's *Elegy*, for example, is somewhere in the vicinity. The verbs 'thicken', 'flower', 'quicken', and 'ascend' combine in an affirmative chorus, which may be self-referential ('here' in this isolation is where this poet's creativity thrives) but somewhat resembles the 'Elgar river-music' that Larkin dismissed in 'Cut Grass'. Unlike that poem, however, 'Here' swerves (the dominant verb of its opening stanza) to something more disconcerting: the vagueness of 'bluish neutral distance', the abruptness of 'End the land suddenly', the renewed vagueness of 'shapes and shin-gle'. Like 'High Windows' the poem ends in a series of negatives. In place of the plenitude offered in the foregoing lines, 'Here' (in the most literal sense, the locus of the unstated 'I' of the poem?) is finally an absence.

In his essay on Coleridge, 'The Snake in the Oak', Hughes argues that the three 'visionary' poems, 'Kubla Khan', 'The Rime of the Ancient Mariner', and 'Christabel', 'together make a single myth, which is also, as a poet's myths always are, (among other things) a projected symbolic self-portrait of the poet's own deepest psychological make-up … It is the myth of what made him a poet. In that sense, it is specifically the 'creation myth' of his unique music'.[46] It takes no great insight to suspect that Hughes believed his own work to be informed by such a myth. I have written at length about what I construe as Hughes' 'single myth' elsewhere.[47] Here I just want to consider its role in the production of his 'unique music'.

One occasion on which Hughes partially revealed his own myth was in 1967, in a letter explaining the enigmatic note at the beginning of his collection *Wodwo*, instructing his readers that the poems, stories and play-script in the book are to be read as 'chapters of a single adventure'. A perceptive review by Daniel Hoffman[48] suggested that this adventure was shamanistic in character (Hughes enthusiastically reviewed Mircea Eliade's *Shamanism* a few years before *Wodwo* was published), but generally readers were baffled by this note until the publication of Hughes' *Letters* in 2007. This volume includes a letter to a friend explaining that 'The main event of the book – and of my life from 1961–2 onwards – is [the] invitation or importuning of a subjective world, which I refuse. I think I did refuse – or rather I deferred. And I paid for it quite heavily … I refused the invitation, & so was forcibly abducted.'[49] The dates tempt a correlation with the events leading up to Sylvia Plath's suicide, but I don't want to pin Hughes' myth down biographically. In fact the basic motifs of the myth are evident in work written long before this period. These motifs are visitation, usurpation, and abduction. I interpret this to signify a challenge to the ego-consciousness by another that Hughes regarded as a deeper, more authentic self, and that I name the 'intending "I"' of his poetry.

This myth is already at work in the iconic early poem 'The Thought-Fox', written in 1955, in which the consciousness of the speaker is visited and usurped by the fox that 'enters the dark hole of the head'.[50] The poem's status in 'the myth of what made him a poet' was reinforced when Hughes in 1994 published an autobiographical story about struggling to write an academic essay at university (which he considered hostile to his creativity) and dreaming of a burnt fox that placed a bloody hand-print on the essay and said, 'Stop this – you are destroying us.'[51] The myth is at work again in 'Pike', written a few years later. For most of its length this poem is a series of vivid anecdotes evoking the predatory ferocity of the pike in language of menacing harshness relieved by a hint of grim humour. In the final four stanzas, however, a musical change occurs, as the lines become slower, more resonant, echoing, and inward. The poem concludes by narrating a fearful fishing expedition of a younger self, whose imagination was possessed by tales of 'immense' pike that lurked in the depths of the pond he fished:

> The still splashes on the dark pond,
>
> Owls hushing the floating woods
> Frail on my ear against the dream
> Darkness beneath night's darkness had freed,
> That rose slowly towards me, watching.[52]

This is Hughes' equivalent of the 'refined lyricism', not dependent on metaphor or any very overt poetic devices, that I have identified in Larkin. It is there in the subtle touches of alliteration and assonance, in the shift from 'lighter' forward vowels to 'darker' backward vowels in the first line quoted, and the progression of 'dark' vowels in the next line (intensified if 'hushing' is spoken in the accent of Hughes' native Yorkshire, to assonate with 'woods'). This lyricism is evoked by the visitation of the fish, now unmistakably a psychic entity, and perhaps, as the poem ends on an uncompleted action, eventual usurpation.

The shift that occurs in this poem is not as drastic as that in Larkin poems such as 'High Windows' and 'Mr Bleaney', and Hughes never (except to a slight extent in *Birthday Letters*) constructs a clearly defined social persona, but there is a comparable trajectory. It is however characteristic that whereas the 'intending "I"' of Larkin approaches isolation, that of Hughes moves towards an encounter.

The lyricism of the ending of 'Pike', though authentically and unmistakably Hughesian, recognisably belongs to the western canon of lyric poetry. When, in the late 1960s, he wrote the poems that became *Crow*, he (uniquely, as it turned out) strove for a style that rejected that canon as completely as possible: 'As for the style – I simply tried to shed everything … My idea was to reduce my style to the simplest clear cell – then regrow a wholeness & richness organically from that point.'[53] Such an ambition is of course impossible literally to fulfil, but the aspiration has an important bearing on the style of *Crow*. Two overt influences on this style are what he called 'my tradition … the primitive literatures'[54] – most directly the Native American tales collected in Paul Radin's *The Trickster* and the work of some eastern European poets of a slightly earlier generation than his own, such as Pilinszky, whom he regarded as first-hand witnesses of the barbarism at the root of western civilisation. He claimed that his aim was to write 'the songs that a crow would sing … songs with no music whatso-ever, in a super-simple and a super-ugly language'.[55]

Note, however, that he still described the poems as 'songs', a word that he also used in the full title of the book: *From the Life and Songs of the Crow*. Marion Thain, in Chapter 8 of this book, remarks that for J. A. Symonds in the *fin de siècle*, 'song' has become 'something of a dead metaphor for lyric' that, however, was no longer 'a particular song form of poetry, but was gradually encompassing a variety of forms and modes' (p. 158). Hughes' description of his early Yeats-inspired poem as a 'song sung in Arcadia' is a comparatively inert remnant of this usage. The same word in the title of *Crow* signals a much more challenging exploration of different formal directions. That full title also indicates that the published book was a fragment of an abandoned project. Hughes' original intention had been to write what he called a 'saga' or 'epic folk-tale' into which the poems would be incorporated. Numerous prose drafts of this are preserved in archives. In an interview at the time he said, 'The story brought me to the poems' – in other words, he needed a prose scaffolding to construct his lyric utterance, even if that scaffolding proved redundant.[56] The most interesting part of the 'saga', and one of the few that Hughes revealed to his readers, connects *Crow* with Hughes' myth. The story begins immediately after the creation of the world, when God has a nightmare that mocks his creation. God challenges the nightmare to do better, and its response is to create Crow, who becomes a subversive partner in creation. For example, in the poem 'A Childish Prank' (which vividly illustrates the influence of Trickster mythology) God, unable to endow man and woman with souls, falls asleep. Crow responds by biting 'the Worm, God's only son, / Into two writhing halves' and stuffing the halves into the sleeping humans, thus awakening them by creating sex in the form of the Worm's attempts to join itself up.[57] This story grounds *Crow* in the key mythical motifs of visitation and usurpation: God, who for Hughes epitomises the ego-consciousness, is visited by the nightmare and usurped by Crow. Since Crow is not just a narrative persona but is identified with the style of the book ('songs that a crow would sing'), the style itself might be regarded as an expression of the myth: the canonical norms are usurped by Crow; or alternatively Hughes, in con-trast to the 'adventure' of *Wodwo*, accepts the invitation.

We have seen an explicit example of this usurpation in 'Crow and the Birds'. I will give one more example of the 'songs with no music', my main point being that this is, after all, a form of lyricism, that what emerges from the mythic struggle is an expression of the 'intending "I"'. The poem 'Lineage' is a parody of the biblical lineage form in which the elemental 'Scream' and 'Blood' lead to the Christian sequence 'Adam', 'Mary', and 'God'. The sequence concludes inevitably with Crow:

> Screaming for Blood
> Grubs, crusts
> Anything
>
> Trembling featherless elbows in the nest's filth[58]

As with all the other examples of the lyric that I have cited in this chapter, it is primarily a matter of language: of rhythm – the transition from the mimetic anapaestic opening to the compacted spondee of the line's end, of ingeniously handled alliteration – the condensation of the vowels of 'featherless' in 'filth', of the naked and comically human 'elbows' projecting in the middle of the line. The identification of Crow with the style of the poems, which occurs frequently in Hughes' comments on the book, is perfectly achieved here.

Although he wrote a great deal of discursive prose, Hughes claimed to hate this kind of writing, believing that it is 'essentially false' and even that it destroyed his immune system.[59] It epitomised the rational intellect that he considered the enemy of the 'animal/spiritual consciousness', represented in his myth by the fox.[60] A poetic style that combined metonymically the song a crow would sing with the influences of 'primitive' literature and the east European poets who bore witness to the barbarity of civilisation corresponds to this 'animal/spiritual consciousness', the 'intending "I"' of *Crow*. This explains why Hughes always looked back on the period of *Crow*'s composition as one in which he had a 'free energy' that he never recovered.[61]

Hughes gave the most overt creative expression to his myth in the narrative poem *Gaudete*. According to the terse 'Argument' of the first edition, 'An Anglican clergyman is abducted by spirits into the other world. The spirits create a duplicate of him to take his place in this world, during his absence, and to carry on his work.'[62] This summary gives little indication of the overwhelming and disturbing character of the narrative, which might well be Hughes' most controversial work if it were not so little read – a state of affairs perpetuated by its inexplicable omission from *Collected Poems*. The narrative lurches between horror and farce as the 'duplicate' seduces every woman in the parish in a single day and is hunted to death by the men. Hughes later said that he thought the 'underworld plot' (the experiences of the abducted clergyman) was 'the more interesting part of the story' but was diverted by his desire to write 'a headlong narrative'.[63] We get only fragmentary glimpses of the 'underworld plot', but after the death of the duplicate the original man returns with a manuscript of poems. These poems (which are in *Collected Poems*) form the 'Epilogue' of *Gaudete*. They are brief devotional lyrics, strongly influenced by the Dravidic *vacanas* that Hughes had read in A. K. Ramanujan's *Speaking of Siva*, but oriented to Hughes' own religious devotion to (in the title of his Shakespeare book) a Goddess of Complete Being. They are addressed to this Goddess, and permeated by a sense of remembered, dreamed, or imagined encounter, and of actual loss. They may therefore be said to stand in place of the unwritten narrative of Lumb's adventures in the other world: narrative has, as it were, been usurped by lyric. Unlike all the other examples I am considering in this chapter, it is very difficult to demonstrate the qualities of these lyrics by analysing their parts. Their effect is cumulative, and is one of stillness, absence, and absorption, as if the subject has been emptied by an encounter of overwhelming significance. For example:

> How will you correct
> The veteran of negatives
> And the survivor of cease?[64]

> But all it finds of me, when it picks me up

> Is what you have
> Already
> Emptied and rejected.[65]

> And for all the rumours of me read obituary.
> What there truly remains of me
> Is that very thing – my absence.

> So how will you gather me?[66]

Just as the fiction of Crow released an 'intending "I"' in the form of a stylistic signature, so has the fiction of Lumb. These signatures could not be more different – evidence for Blasing's case that this 'I' 'is not prior to its words'.

The narrative that enabled my final example of Hughesian lyric, however, is not a fiction – except in the sense that all reconstruction of the past is a fiction. When he finally published *Birthday Letters* in 1998 Hughes wrote defensively, describing them as 'so raw, so vulnerable, so unprocessed, so naïve, so self-exposing & unguarded, so without any of the niceties that any poetry workshop student could have helped me to'.[67] I would argue that the vulnerability of this collection is less a matter of exposed feeling than of often uninspired writing. Hughes' revisiting of his first marriage often takes the form of a leadenly metonymic narrative, which is particularly vulnerable when it invites comparison with Plath's own work, as in the case of 'The Rabbit-Catcher', much of which is a laborious reconstruction of the events that occasioned Plath's poem of the same title. The 'flat and literal' writing contributed to the 'affront' that a Plath devotee such as Linda Wagner-Martin felt at Hughes daring to write about his life with Plath.[68] Here is an example from the poem 'Visit':

> I was sitting
> Youth away in an office in Slough,
> Morning and evening between Slough and Holborn …
> Weekends I recidived
> Into Alma Mater. Girl-friend
> Shared a supervisor and weekly session
> With your American rival and you.
> She detested you.[69]

I shall be returning to this poem. Perhaps the best, certainly one of the most moving, of the poems that came from Hughes' communion with his dead wife is 'The Offers', which he inexplicably omitted from *Birthday Letters* and included instead in the expensive limited edition *Howls and Whispers*. In this poem Plath appears to him three times posthumously, implicitly in dreams. Each time she seems to be making him an offer that he twice fails to accept. The poem concludes with the third visitation:

> You came behind me
> (At my helpless moment, as I lowered
> A testing foot into the running bath)
> And spoke – peremptory, as a familiar voice
> Will startle out of a river's uproar, urgent,
> Close: 'This is the last. This one. This time
> Don't fail me.'[70]

Everything about this little scenario is beautifully judged, from the presence of the ghost 'behind' the consciousness of the speaker, his creaturely vulnerability in a posture every reader will have shared, the wonderful Wordsworthian note of 'as a familiar voice / Will startle out of a river's uproar', to the simply conveyed urgency of her voice, concluding with the half-line of ominous command. This is not only one of the most lyrically powerful of the poems, but the one that most explicitly represents itself as a drama of visitation – in this case, as menacing as that of 'Pike'.

To return to 'The Visit', which opens in such a prosaically metonymic fashion – the structure of this poem, and several others like it in *Birthday Letters*, seems almost like an imitation of the classic Larkin poem. Close to uniquely in these poems, Hughes constructs a self-disparaging, passive persona: 'As if a puppet were being tied on its strings, / Or a dead frog's legs touched by electrodes.' This poem concerns an incident immortalised in Plath's *Journals* when, after their first meeting, Hughes returned to Cambridge and with a friend drunkenly flung mud at what they mistakenly thought were the windows of her college room. Her journal records her anguish at knowing he was in Cambridge, and his failure to visit her – which in *Birthday Letters* is a foreshadowing of his later more serious failures. The dramatised occasion of the writing of the poem is Hughes reading the journal ten years after her death: 'Your actual words, as they floated / Out through your throat and tongue and onto your page'. The extraordinary physical immediacy of this account of reading, as if breaking through the mediation of the written words, is like a visitation, so that

> I look up – as if to meet your voice
> With all its urgent future
> That has burst in on me. Then look back
> At the book of printed words.
> You are ten years dead. It is only a story.
> Your story. My story.[71]

The language could not be more simple, and it has to be admitted that its lyrical power is dependent on a knowledge of the 'story'. The lyric effect comes from playing the energy of the visionary wish-fulfilment in 'urgent future' and 'burst in on me' against the deflating factuality of 'the book of printed words. / You are ten years dead.' There may be a disillusioned glance at the would-be triumphant final line of 'The Thought-Fox': 'The page is printed.'[72] But for a moment an extraordinary temporality is evoked, by which the 'urgent future' of the 23-year-old Plath, which is now factually the past, is still a future for them both. Such a temporality, in which the moment of writing is overwhelmed by the past, marks the conclusions of several *Birthday Letters* poems.

> And my life
> Forever trying to climb the steps now stone
> Towards the door now red
> Which you, in your own likeness, would open
> With still time to talk.[73]

> And the contemplative calm
> I drank from your concentrated quiet,
> In this contemplative calm
> Now I drink from your stillness that neither
> Of us can disturb or escape.[74]

> But then I sat, stilled,
> Unable to fathom what stilled you
> As I looked at you, as I am stilled
> Permanently now, permanently
> Bending so briefly at your open coffin.[75]

As these examples show, the experience is not necessarily one of illusion. The most lyrically accomplished moments of *Birthday Letters* are not (with a few exceptions) reconstructions of the past, but piercing revelations of the mourning – or more accurately melancholic – 'I' at the moment of writing. But the poems seem to need the 'flat and literal' reconstructions to arrive at this point.

Birthday Letters differs from the other poems I have considered in that it owes its very existence to the already known (or mis-known) life-history. It would be absurd to try to read these poems without reference to that history. Nevertheless, if the 'I' who, for example, was 'sitting / Youth away in an office in Slough' could hardly be said not to be 'prior to its words', the lyrical charge of the passages I have quoted is not dependent on reference. Like all the examples I have considered by both Hughes and Larkin they are the effect of breaking through to an intense, linguistically constructed subjectivity. Both poets combine a conservative-seeming attachment to the idea of lyric with a historically inevitable suspicion of its integrity. Lyric is hedged round and interrogated, in different ways, in both their oeuvres, but at their most distinctive and accomplished both achieve a style that honours the lyric impulse by its freedom from received ideas of the poetic.

Notes

1 Mark Jeffreys, 'Ideologies of Lyric', *PMLA* 110.2 (March 1995), 196–205 (p. 200).
2 *Ibid.*, p. 202.
3 Edna Longley, ed., *The Bloodaxe Book of 20th Century Poetry from Britain and Ireland* (Highgreen: Bloodaxe, 2000), pp. 15–16.
4 *Ibid.*, p. 22.
5 Mutlu Konuk Blasing, *Lyric Poetry: The Pain and the Pleasure of Words* (Princeton University Press, 2007), p. 55. As Ian Patterson points out in Chapter 11 of this book, citing Simon Jarvis, Blasing herself has been accused of conflating lyric with all poetry (p. 233 n. 3).
6 Blasing, *Lyric Poetry*, p. 31.
7 *Ibid.*, p. 86.
8 Philip Larkin, *Required Writing: Miscellaneous Pieces 1955–1982* (London and Boston, MA: Faber, 1983), p. 80.
9 Barbara Everett, 'Art and Larkin', in *Philip Larkin: The Man and His Work*, ed. Dale Salwak (Basingstoke and London: Macmillan, 1989), pp. 129–39.

10 Ted Hughes, *Letters of Ted Hughes*, ed. Christopher Reid (London: Faber, 2007), p. 337.

11 *Ibid.*, p. 720.

12 Ted Hughes, *Winter Pollen: Occasional Prose*, ed. William Scammell (London: Faber, 1994), p. 5.

13 Ted Hughes, *Collected Poems* (London: Faber, 2003), p. 6.

14 *Ibid.*, pp. 24–5.

15 Philip Larkin, *Collected Poems*, ed. Anthony Thwaite (London: Faber, 1988), p. 267.

16 W. B. Yeats, *Collected Poems* (London: Macmillan, 1963), p. 70.

17 Larkin, *Required Writing*, pp. 29, 175.

18 B. J. Leggett, *Larkin's Blues: Jazz, Popular Music and Poetry* (Baton Rouge: Louisiana State University Press, 1999), p. 122.

19 Andrew Motion, 'Philip Larkin and Symbolism', in *Philip Larkin*, ed. Stephen Regan (Basingstoke and London: Macmillan, 1997), pp. 32–54 (p. 52).

20 Hughes, *Letters*, p. 617.

21 Wilfred Owen, 'Preface' to *Collected Poems*, ed. C. Day Lewis (London: Chatto and Windus, 1963), p. 31; T. S. Eliot, 'East Coker', in *Collected Poems 1909–1962* (London: Faber, 1963), p. 198.

22 Theodor Adorno, *The Adorno Reader*, ed. Brian O'Connor (Oxford: Blackwell, 2000), p. 210.

23 Hughes, *Winter Pollen*, p. 232.

24 Larkin, *Collected Poems*, p. 127.

25 Hughes, 'Ghost Crabs', 'First, Mills', and 'October Salmon', in *Collected Poems*, pp. 149, 463, 667–8.

26 Larkin, *Required Writing*, p. 79.

27 Larkin, *Collected Poems*, p. 180.

28 Gerald Bullett, ed., *Silver Poets of the Sixteenth Century* (London: Dent, 1947), p. 184.

29 Larkin, *Collected Poems*, p. 169.

30 Ekbert Faas, *Ted Hughes: The Unaccommodated Universe* (Santa Barbara: Black Sparrow, 1980), p. 208.

31 Hughes, *Collected Poems*, p. 210.

32 Terry Gifford and Neil Roberts, *Ted Hughes: A Critical Study* (London: Faber, 1981), p. 109.

33 Hughes, *Collected Poems*, p. 84.

34 David Lodge, *The Modes of Modern Writing: Metaphor, Metonymy, and the Typology of Modern Literature* (London: Hodder and Stoughton, 1977), p. 214.

35 Lodge, *The Modes of Modern Writing*, pp. 218–19.

36 Larkin, 'Church Going', in *Collected Poems*, p. 97.

37 Larkin, *Collected Poems*, p. 183.

38 Philip Larkin, *Letters to Monica*, ed. Anthony Thwaite (London: Faber, 2010), p. 243.

39 Larkin, *Collected Poems*, p. 181.

40 Samuel Taylor Coleridge, *Poetical Works*, ed. Ernest Hartley Coleridge (Oxford University Press, 1967), p. 240.

41 Larkin, *Collected Poems*, p. 56.

42 Lodge, *The Modes of Modern Writing*, p. 219.

43 Larkin, *Collected Poems*, p. 165.

44 *Ibid.*, pp. 102, 180, 116, 198.

45 *Ibid.*, p. 136.

46 Hughes, *Winter Pollen*, p. 375.

47 Neil Roberts, 'Hughes's Myth and the Classics: *Gaudete* and *Cave Birds*', in *Ted Hughes and the Classics*, ed. Roger Rees (Oxford University Press, 2009), pp. 120–33.

48 Daniel Hoffman, 'Talking Beasts: The "Single Adventure" in the Poems of Ted Hughes', in *Critical Essays on Ted Hughes*, ed. Leonard M. Scigaj (New York: G. K. Hall, 1992), pp. 143–52; originally published in *Shenandoah* 19 (Summer 1968), 49–68.

49 Hughes, *Letters*, pp. 273–4.

50 Hughes, *Collected Poems*, p. 21.

51 Hughes, *Winter Pollen*, pp. 8–9.

52 Hughes, *Collected Poems*, pp. 84–6.

53 Keith Sagar, ed., *Poet and Critic: The Letters of Ted Hughes and Keith Sagar* (London: British Library, 2012), p. 29.

54 Hughes, *Letters*, p. 296.

55 Faas, *Ted Hughes: The Unaccommodated Universe*, p. 208.

56 *Ibid.*, p. 206.

57 Hughes, *Collected Poems*, pp. 215–16.

58 *Ibid.*, p. 218.

59 Ted Hughes, letters to Lucas Myers, Emory University, MARBL, MSS 865, Box 1, Folder 4; Hughes, *Letters*, p. 719.

60 Hughes, *Letters*, p. 581.

61 *Ibid.*, p. 720.

62 Hughes, *Collected Poems*, p. 1199.

63 Faas, *Ted Hughes: The Unaccommodated Universe*, p. 214.

64 Hughes, *Collected Poems*, p. 357.

65 *Ibid.*, p. 362.

66 *Ibid.*, p. 365.

67 Hughes, *Letters*, p. 720.

68 Linda Wagner-Martin, *Sylvia Plath: A Literary Life*, 2nd edn (Basingstoke: Palgrave Macmillan, 2003), p. 142.

69 Hughes, *Collected Poems*, p. 1047.

70 *Ibid.*, p. 1183.

71 *Ibid.*, p. 1049.

72 *Ibid.*, p. 21.

73 *Ibid.*, p. 1059.

74 *Ibid.*, p. 1071.

75 *Ibid.*, p. 1086.

CHAPTER ELEVEN

No man is an I
Recent developments in the lyric

Ian Patterson

The lyric performs the material ground of language.[1]

In 1985, when Jonathan Culler summed up the five changes that had reshaped the study of the lyric since New Criticism (they were 'attention to babble and doodle, exploration of intertextuality, interest in voice as figure, a new understanding of self-reflexivity, and the deconstruction of the hierarchical opposition of symbol and allegory'), he saw them as defining 'a new discursive space for criticism of the lyric'.[2] Some twenty years later, with a new wave of interest in the lyric, he laid his primary emphasis on lyric's 'foregrounding of language, in its material dimensions', and on lyric as 'memorable language': 'the power to embed bits of language in your mind, to invade and occupy it, is a salient feature of lyrics … The force of poetry is linked to its ability to get itself remembered, like those bits of song that stick in your mind, you don't know why.' While there is a residual sense of song underlying this, and although Culler sees lyric continuing to possess an apostrophic function – 'the poem as discourse addressed' – in much of the recent critical discussion of lyric the term has been broadened out from its generic specificity to mean something more like 'poetry'.[3] Culler hopes also to see a plurality of lyric typologies as a way of clarifying critical discourse about poetry, offering as one example the distinction between poems written in the lyric present and those written in the past tense.[4] Constructive and suggestive though this is, it is likely that lyric poetry will continue increasingly to overflow attempts at categorisation: the changes and developments in poetry and in thinking about poetry since modernism seem to require a less programmatic approach. Indeed, the term 'lyric' itself may be better considered as an aspect of poems – a mode – rather than as a hard and fast generic distinction. It is true, as Mark Jeffreys has argued, that a late-nineteenth-century paradigm dominated most accounts of poetry until not very long ago, as its cultural presence dwindled.[5] But that paradigm has been more than adequately challenged in recent years, and it is now time to recognise that poetry's remit is more extensive than the discussions of lyric sometimes allow.[6]

The problematic here can be framed in various ways. The current period has been at least as conscious of precedent as any other, and has probably been freer than others to experiment with relations between present and past. This self-consciousness has added an additional and occasionally ironic layer to the functioning and use of the self and the lyric 'I', sometimes resulting in the disavowal of ownership of a personal voice beyond the textures of the poem's language. Plenty of lyric poems have been written during the last fifty years, and they continue to be written, but often with a new awareness of an irony implicit in the genre, or of a structural complicity in capitalist oppression, or of a complication of the sense of self or subjecthood, or of a need to renew the formal procedures of their composition. The relation between poetry and politics has changed, and occasional verse tirades in the *Guardian* newspaper by Harold Pinter and Tony Harrison, laudable though their sentiments may have been, are very different from the complex responses to political imperatives in poems by Douglas Oliver, Denise Riley, or Keston Sutherland. Even the most graceful love lyrics, like some of Frank O'Hara's, foreground contingency and accident so as to force the reader to think about what state of being the poem is celebrating.[7]

English poetry has probably been as divided during the last fifty years or so as at any time in the past. An influential mainstream of anti-modernist lyric writing strives, with powerful support from the nationally determined school syllabus, to sustain a populist tradition of casually accessible lyric writing: Andrea Brady has characterised its products as 'poems which are appropriate to a famished definition of poetry … which exhibits obvious "technique" in its use of regular metres, meek in its politics, pithy, witty, accommodating'.[8] Its adherents are to be found reviewed or featured in the press, are likely to be sponsored by the British Council and to receive literary prizes and other accolades; they constitute, on the whole, the official, conventional face of English poetry. Away from this mainstream, the accomplished and various work of many other poets, working in what might loosely be called a late modernist tradition, demonstrates a more challenging resourcefulness and ranges across all poetic forms. Some of these poets are routinely dismissed as 'difficult' or 'marginal' or 'incomprehensible' by readers too wedded to premodernist models of poetry to enjoy the intellectual effort of exploring their work. But much of what is alive, linguistically inventive, alert to the politics – in the broadest sense – of living in the modern world, and genuinely exploratory in the poetry of the last few decades, is to be found in this writing, which traces its most conspicuous ancestry back to the loose group of poets who participated in the small-circulation worksheet, *The English Intelligencer*, in the late 1960s.[9] Diverse in their practices and interests as they are, it would not be possible to present a just overview of their work here, nor is that my intention; but however sketchy it is, some initial contextualisation is desirable.

The retrenchment of poetic ambition that characterised much British poetry in the decades after the Second World War – represented by 'The Movement' and a distrust of politics, literary experiment, dream, surrealism, and ungoverned imagination – hegemonic though it became, was never total: Hugh MacDiarmid, W. S. Graham, David Gascoyne, Gael Turnbull, Christopher Logue, Rosemary Tonks, Charles Tomlinson, Roy Fisher, Christopher Middleton, Brian Coffey, Basil Bunting, and others continued to explore the legacy of modernism, developing their poetics in the process. If one were to look for lineages and filiations for the writers I shall be discussing, it is among these, and their international connections, particularly in the USA, that one should start. Early in the 1960s, the liberating influence of the Beat poets had been complicated by a range of (mostly male) American writing from Black Mountain, New York, and elsewhere – notably Charles Olson and Frank O'Hara, but also George Oppen, Robert Creeley, Ed Dorn, Robert Duncan, John Ashbery, Leroi Jones (Amiri Baraka), Ted Berrigan, and Barbara Guest – bringing with it an openness to a greater range of thought and lived experience, and 'an awareness of language-as-material' (the phrase is Anselm Hollo's).[10] The transatlantic connections made by Gael Turnbull and Tom Raworth, Andrew Crozier and J. H. Prynne, along with Donald Allen's anthology *The New American Poetry 1946–1960* and a growing presence in England of an American counter-culture, all had a role to play in the new poetry of the late 1960s. The sense of connection was intensified by the Vietnam War, the political upheavals of May 1968, the resurgence of Marxism, the revolution in music, the rise of feminism, and the explosion of theoretical writing that accompanied or followed these events; they provided instances of the contingent too pressing for poetry to ignore. The 'melancholy of isolation' in which poetry of the mid-century seemed still encased was not adequate to the need to respond to the 'palpable outside world'.[11] Lyric poetry needed to escape the elegiac and find new rhetorics equal to the social and political questions that seemed so urgent. Similarly, the recent resurgence of interest in theorising the lyric responds to the twenty-first-century crises in economics and banking, global warming, religious fundamentalism, imperialism, and war in the Middle East. As Michael Davidson puts it in relation to recent American poetry, 'Perhaps the greatest challenge to poetry raised by this crisis condition is the question of literariness itself, of whether the category that has historically contested the ordinariness of ordinary discourse can claim some distinctness in an information society.'[12] It can, and does. Its distinctiveness consists in being non-propositional, in constructing its thought in a different way from information discourses, a process to which the lyric mode is central.[13]

Nonetheless, lyric poetry has continued to worry necessarily at the boundary between public and private. It has been customary to think of it as the expression of private emotion such as love, desire, loss, pain, suffering, joy, pleasure, hope, praise, shame, sorrow, jealousy, or fear, in words given memorable intensity through the transformative power of metaphor, metaphor's grace being to increase the value of a state by comparing it to, or transforming it into, something better. The lyric poem's power has often been described as conferring a glimpse of some greater alternative ideality or, as Paul Valéry puts it, communicating 'an idea of some *self* miraculously superior to Myself'.[14] That it has seldom been as simple as this – that self-deception, or deception of some sort, may be a permanent risk – has latterly come to be recognised as a condition of lyric itself. And of course, language not being private, lyric is caught in a fiction between public and private, between social or political and individual or intimate. And lyric here refers not only to poems, but equally to moments or elements in poems (which Sam Ladkin aptly describes as 'apostrophic turns toward personal incident and private knowledge, and scenes recuperable by the poet's memory or the reader's sentiment for nostalgic discourse').[15] So it is hardly surprising that recent critical thinking about the lyric has stressed both its historical specificity and its cultural mediation: 'Poetic language is itself a medium of history. Not only is each word a palimpsest but words and poetic forms carry communal histories of constantly changing usages and functions.'[16] Nor is it surprising that changes in the ways in which the self has been conceived over the last half-century should also have crucial consequences for the writing and theorisation of lyric poetry. The whole idea of personal utterance, the voice of a persona, a subject, or the poet, is refigured in post-Adornian or post-Freudian mode, where consciousness is always already alienated from the object world. The conventional view, still widely held, allows the subject an ontological reality prior to its construction in the language of the poem, such that (to use a reductive formulation) 'we are asked to trust the poet, not the poem'.[17] Oren Izenberg similarly points out that 'for a certain type of modern poet … "poetry" names an onto-logical project: a civilizational wish to reground the concept and the value of *the person*'; given the crises of civilisation of the late twentieth century (he cites decolonisation, national formation, consumer culture, genocide, and 'the specter of total annihilation') there is a cultural 'need to reground personhood'.[18]

The nature and pitfalls of the complicated quest for 'personhood', and its implications for the search for 'one's own voice' in lyric poetry, have been eloquently and perceptively examined by Denise Riley.[19] Reminding us that the materiality of language is 'packed through and through with its own historicity', she locates it in 'the reiteration, the echoes, the reflexivity, the cadences, the automatic self-parodies and the self-monumentalising which, constituting both being called and calling oneself, constitute the formation of categories of person' (p. 111). This raises the question of what it means for a poet to be present in her poem: in what ways do the charac-teristic syntactic gestures of a poet's work respond to the deepest rhythms and drives of the unconscious? The paradox of individuality in language relies on the deep past of both protagonists, individual and language, and on the struggle by the poet to shape the poem she wants out of the mater-ial that arises.

W. S. Graham's repeated question in his poem of the same name, 'What is the language using us for?', adds another dimension to this, conveni-ently reminding us that language is external to us as well as internal, and remains so however virtuosic the poet:

> What is the language using us for?
> It uses us all and in its dark
> Of dark actions selections differ.[20]

An understanding of the performativity of language itself, and the way in which we use it, and it uses us, to perform our social and intellectual func-tions, has necessarily altered the location of lyric authority, and as a conse-quence has also raised more extensive questions about the politics of lyric identity, when the language we find ourselves or lose ourselves in is also the language of a western consumer society whose existence is predicated on exploitation, aggression, and cruelty elsewhere in the world, as well as the inequities and indignities of our own society. Lyric here again becomes the ground of a sometimes painful intersection of private and public.[21]

The production of affect in lyric verse is not directly dependent on per-sonal utterance, or at least not on personal expression. Where the lyric voice of the poem comes from is a creation of the page, brought into being through the process of intellectual and emotional overload that comes with reading the poem, and it stays on the page. No appeal to the accidental authority of the individual writer can be more than a diversion. So much of our language is other people's voices, past and present, that it is not easy to personalise language in the first place. In addition, a number of poets have deliberately sought out other voices than their own to work with, either through translation of various sorts or through the incorporation of words from other mouths and other texts: invisible translations, like John James' *Letters from Sarah* (1973), cast a particular light on the lyric.

Letters from Sarah is a text in which the slowly developing presence of a lyric persona has nothing but the serial form of the poem to give it body. The title signals a relation to the poems of Tristan Tzara, but whatever the process by which Tzara's poems have been assimilated into this new work, no sense of an alien subjectivity is to be found in it. A brief comparison of one passage with the French 'original' is illuminating here:

> le football dans le poumon
> casse les vitres (insomnie)
> dans le puits on fait bouillir les nains
> pour le vin et la folie
> picabia arp ribemont-dessaignes
> bonjour[22]

This, the final, twenty-first section of 'Cinéma calendrier du coeur abstrait maisons' reappears at the end of section 7 of *Letters from Sarah* as follows:

> there are shafts under the mountains
> & my lungs are as wakeful as a trainload of Tottenham supporters
> midgets for beer and madness[23]

It's clear to see what has been used and what ignored, harder to pin down the imaginative process of transformation at work; but the cadence is unmistakably no longer Tzara's, even though the gesture of the last two lines of the French might well make an appearance in another John James poem. This is the case even where the phrasing comes close to absurdity, as in the first line of the second poem: 'at the frontier we gave 'em a lot of madam' (the French is 'madame prit le galop / coup de sifflet à la frontière').[24] In the sequence generally, the montage effects of James' lines create a cadence as recognisable to the ear as a face to the eye, but one that displays none of the exposed interiority of the confessional. There is no particular sense that the instances and utterances of the poem stem from its writer's own life – indeed, plenty of suggestions that they may not, that they are fiction. A sense of ontological steadiness that might in other work derive from self-contemplation comes from a painterly sense of what can be left out, what provides the necessary touch of counter-balance.

A recent poem, 'Pimlico', appears to be making explicit comment on cadence and rhythm, and the relation of intrinsic to accidental language in the following lines:

> & I took flatness as my starting point
> the line made quicker in its shorter pulse
> & slower in its flooded length
>
> the line a slinger to the surface from the depths of things
> where a breath touches the slightest branch
> & bends the stuff of accident to your will

but the ambiguity in 'the line' could just as well be applicable to drawing or walking.[25] Where the terms or phrases come from is not the point: it is the cadence that emerges as 'the stuff of accident' that is shaped by the poem's will-to-form. Lines in James' poems, as in Tom Raworth's or Prynne's or Denise Riley's, are often picked up from elsewhere, sometimes credited, often not. Sometimes they are altered in the process, like the Tzara translations; sometimes they are reproduced like words in the air –

> … but then
> the air is always calling someone's name
> the voice of Springsteen
> drifting from a 1000 radios

– but they all take their place in the poem with equal weight.[26] Words don't originate in the self. This is a matter not just of lyric cadence, but of tonality and an acute sense of the relation between tone and timing, carried out with a curious absence of self-positioning. Writing about James' poetry from the 1970s, John Wilkinson observed that he 'lacks interest even in identity play; he is in thrall to what seduces him rather than to his own propensity for being seduced, which is somewhat unusual for a lyric poet'.[27] What is performed in 'Pimlico' is strung on metonymically connected occasions and the recollections and thoughts they prompt, but the poem's intellectual and emotional coherence, its lyric grace, stems from the level gaze with which the poem encounters matters of very differing resonance. It interweaves different degrees of irony and different kinds of attention in a spectrum from the most personal to the most painful news items to the most contingent encounters ('a black V8 Pilot / on Bruton Place') in a poem that successfully confronts the difficulty of the lyric sublime, so that the 'craving beauty' of line 5, which invites ironic reading, is re-established by the completed poem and is able to be reread at its full value.

In its overall structure, *Letters from Sarah* is more than a collection of lyrics: elements recur across its pages, like the valedictory gesture of 'we're leaving little one', which finally returns in the last poem as 'we will go … leaving the oaktrees to their doom', pointing to another characteristic feature of this sort of work – composition by book. An early and important influence on this conception of the lyric sequence was the San Francisco poet Jack Spicer, whose work Peter Gizzi describes as 'compellingly against the grain of his time [in] its resistance to issues of personality and identity and its placement of the poet in the frankly clerical position of a fatigued copyist or at most, a translator'.[28] Three aspects of his poetics are significant here: his view of writing as 'dictation', his sense of the materiality of language, and his emphasis on the serial poem and on the book as unit of composition. The emphasis on the book as a formal unity goes some way towards answering the question Pound was concerned with when he was wondering about the possibility of the long imagist poem: namely how the lyrical intensity of the 'intellectual and emotional complex in an instant of time' could be sustained or at least used in a longer poem, how the lyric could escape a generic association with brevity and compression and inhabit a more ambitious role for poetry. 'I must speak from within the blinkers of the first person pronoun', as Denise Riley has put it.[29] Spicer's 'dictation', or the poet as radio (more than Heidegger's sense of language speaking through the poem), points us explicitly to what he calls 'the Outside', but there's no need to share his mystical view to recognise that writing poems is not an easy or unproblematic task, and that an important element is 'to try to keep as much of yourself as possible out of the poem'.[30]

Much of the most interesting poetry in this period has been composed as books rather just collections of individual poems: Andrew Crozier's *Veil Poem*, Douglas Oliver's *The Infant and the Pearl*, Tom Raworth's *Eternal Sections*, Peter Riley's *Alstonefield*, Barry MacSweeney's *Pearl*, Andrea Brady's *Liberties*, John Wilkinson's *Iphigenia*, to take a few examples. Most of these are not exclusively lyric, but a lyric mode is crucial to them all and to the ways they work as sequences. All are serious interventions in a complex poetic field. Narrative and argument are not conventionally part of the lyric, but in these sequences lyric becomes essential to both. Metonymic rhetorics suit seriality, and encourage connection between disparate or discrete elements in the series. Parataxis and montage, those

modernist standbys, play an important part in this, as do the variable performances of the personal pronoun and the performativity of language
itself, and structures that use memory, echo, allusion, journeys as ironic
devices that both alienate the subject from itself and structure a will to
make the poems cohere. 'A rage to be some wholeness gropes / Past damage that it half recalls – / Where it was I will found my name.'[31]

The echo of Freud in Riley's lines, the implicit play between 'found' and
'find', and the almost-rhyme of 'rage' and 'damage' point to the kind of
subliminal connection that lyric makes all the time. The early poems of J.
H. Prynne do not exploit this as much as his later work does, but the first
obviously lyric sequence, *Day Light Songs* (1968) uses line endings, *mise-en-
page*, and a breath-mimicking cadence not only to create lyric desire but
also to bend words and reveal their hidden elements, as in the concluding
lines of the fifth poem: 'the entire air a nod / to for / tune, who else', where
the dual sense of 'air' as atmosphere and melody opens the way to the split-
ting of 'fortune'.[32] As the poetry becomes less hortatory, more exploratory,
sound and the music in and of language take on a new prominence, as can
be seen in this short lyric from *Wound Response* (1974):

> As grazing the earth
>   the sun raises
> its mouth to the night
>   rick, ox-eye'd
> and burning, strewn over
>   the phase path
> At the turning-places
>   of the sun the
> head glistens, dew falls
>   from the apse line:
> O lye still, thou
>   Little Musgrave, the
> grass is wet
>   and streak'd with light[33]

Visually, the arc created by the displacement of alternative hemistichs mimics the elliptical movement of the earth, and aurally the poem is full of the
music of repeated sounds. The repetition of 'raise' from 'grazing' to 'raises'
finds its rhyme in 'phase', and further echoes in 'places' and 'Musgrave', with
the 'gra' transforming to 'grass'; a similar connection can be found between
'night', 'eye'd', 'line', 'lye' and 'light', 'strewn', 'dew', and 'streak'd'; there's a
rhyme on 'burning' and 'turning', and 'apse' is a paragram of 'phase' and

'place'. The egregious pun on nitric oxide in 'night / rick, ox-eye'd', which suggests the nitric oxide in acid rain and motor emissions, both products of combustion, eases the transition to 'burning'. The unmarked quotation from the ballad of 'Little Musgrave and Lady Barnard', 'O lye still, lye still, thou little Musgrave', brings death and stillness into a poem primarily concerned with movement.[34] The coincidence of 'grave' in Musgrave adds to the effect created by the sudden opening up of a glimpse into poetry's own history to set beside the technically informed phrases, 'phase path' and 'apse line', but is somewhat offset by the final return to 'light' instead of darkness.

This intense patterning is one of the primary carriers of lyric affect in Prynne's poetry. Rod Mengham has argued that Prynne's work takes a radically new turn in the 1994 text *Her Weasels Wild Returning*. In the earlier poems, Mengham claims:

> the organizing strategies of individual consciousness, lodged in the routines of a speaking voice, were all there, overlapping with, or competing with, or being sidelined by, or being controlled by, the interests of various discursive projects. One crucial point was that … it was a challenged individualism that remained somewhere near the centre of attention. The range of tones and rhythms encountered in reading were ultimately oriented towards the speaking voice, towards the resonance of lyric, towards a proverbial roundness of phrase, towards a gleefully impacted slang. This is just not so with *Weasels*.[35]

But it may rather be that the 'challenged individualism' of the earlier work was more dispersed into a creative struggle with the exteriority of language than this allows: fragmented though the cadence of a speaking voice certainly is in the poems of the last twenty years, it is still textually present, even in as unpromising-looking a sequence as *Streak~Willing~Entourage~Artesian* (2009). But voice may not be the same thing as even a challenged individualism, and may mark a more evenly distributed encounter between the subject and the discursive and political world.

I believe, then, that *Weasels* marks less of a change than Mengham suggests, at least in terms of the lyric component of Prynne's verse. Although it's true that the books since then have seemed more abstract, less controlled by variations on a speaking voice, they still have the power to arouse a powerful sense of lyric exuberance in the reader, a sense that is reinforced in *Weasels* by the titles of each constituent part and by the undefined or unlocated pronoun 'she'. 'She' and 'her' are ubiquitous in the poem, from the title to the last poem, but 'she' never attains narrative personhood. Sometimes evoked through a John Dowland song, as 'she, she, she, and only she'; sometimes, as in 'What She Saw There', the object of unanswered questions: 'what did she really see', 'can't she see the self difference'; 'she' operates as a grammatical ghost inviting the reader to imagine gendered structures, positions, actions, and challenging implicit assumptions about power and knowledge. The absence of conventionally clear discursive utterance foregrounds the presence in each stanza of a variety of lyric moments, as we can see from the poem's final pair of stanzas.

That Now She Knows

> Who with he'll say climbing, to let blood slit imposed
> at a turret elevation to buffer high return. I saw
> her wings in speedy strip like a shadow in the sand
> or in growth like natural reason, her heart so vast
> as justly to make cause with the fiery fountain sealed
> on track right across *terra nullius* overhead. I knew
> that, she made me see the light level cracking along
> her trebled skyline: I held my view. Blizzard loyal
> transgenic pulsation she'll take both up to a dish
> off the bone dropping away to a strut canopy, eyes
> blue on blue aptitude so sweet. I knew that. Evenly
> spaced night fares restore format, leaked to mounting
>
> offshore redemptions; alive droning above tumbled cloud
> for my soft convergence, mine only, only mine. Only
> too small to hold its blood within her option wrappers
> that stake out, spilled through leaves. Light of unclosed
> life comes back, true beyond p/e overturning upfront
> foliar feeds here, its sherbet nectary. This is now
> a near equator or its departure lounge, she closely runs
> as animals will breathe out, he grasping at critical
> backflow fade. Please delete, don't sleep yet, not
> too sure you get shot through upstream. I know that what
> you set under a minded shade tree is hit by first debate
> and the air locks in, at a dab rack roaming the field.[36]

These lyric moments, plastic and volatile as they are, remain potential, shifting their nature both prospectively and retrospectively; shadowing the semantic possibilities and connections of the developing stanza as they come and go; testing the way the poem can be read as encoding and evoking different kinds of utterance, different kinds of value. The phrase that crosses lines 4 and 5, 'her heart so vast / as justly to make cause', besides being a regular pentameter, invokes a lyric tradition and the momentary mental state appropriate to it, while 'I saw / her wings in speedy strip like a shadow in the sand' not only gives 'her' wings (in semantic association with 'climbing', 'turret', elevation' and 'high', and later 'overhead') but divides into two four-stress lines reminiscent of Blake. These rhythmic hauntings and curtailed upwellings of affect counterpoint the grammatical ambiguity of 'speedy strip' or 'the light level cracking' so that we are already prepared to encounter the thought of bombs and rocket explosions when we reach 'the fiery fountain'; and the line break between 'eyes' and 'blue on blue' makes space for the 'sweet' suggestion of blue eyes to be superseded by the horror of friendly-fire attack – in NATO parlance 'blue on blue'. ('Wild Weasels' are, or were, US Air Force planes whose task was to find and destroy hostile anti-aircraft and radar sites: shifting the adjective to a more ambiguous position in the title phrase allows for more deconstructive reference, suggesting a fuller contrast between actual weasels and the prosthetic-human-machines, and underlining the tension between violence and care in the poem.) The interplay of the phonemic echoes of 'She' and 'I' further underscores the relational dialectic that has developed through the poem. Unusually, this stanza is held together by four uses of 'I' – 'I saw / her wings'; 'I knew that'; 'I held my view'; 'I knew that' – the apparent authority of these phrases, with those in the second and tenth lines of the second and final stanza, punctuating both stanzas with a rhythm separate from the prosodic one but contributing to its effect, and making another level of congruence with the 'i'/'ee' sound pattern.

The lyric subject is substantially reshaped here, present less as subjectivity itself than as its interplay with the disparate forces acting upon, limiting, deforming, and forming it. It gives the poem what might be called a written voice, but one that resists actual vocalisation because of the energetic volatility of its grammar and the multiple intellectual and emotional rhythms that make the surface of the poem heave and shift. Instead, the textual voice draws attention to patterns of affinity and opposition that echo those at work in the world. The 'minded shade tree' of the last lines is perhaps the best illustration of the evasive presence of lyric, and the way the reader's fondness for, and complicity with, lyric assumptions are unsettled: 'minded' can mean 'recalled', 'attended', 'intended', 'imagined', 'found annoying or troublesome', 'looked after', 'aforementioned', and other things; and a minded shade tree covers a spectrum from Marvell's green shade to the most meagre landscape.[37] A reader's heart is drawn to the restorative power of the tree's shade, even if it is just a mental shadow of a tree, only to be outraged by the 'hit' as 'the air locks in', and the echo of Iraq in 'a dab rack roaming the field', where the final word, despite or because of containing a homonym of 'feel', overlays any field we might be wishing for with a recognition of fields of fire, fields of force, fields of operations, as well as the field of the poem's engagement with language itself. Lyric still provides the appeal to emotional values, but mocks the idea of such an appeal being an innocent or nostalgic one.

All this helps to cast light on how poetry thinks. This is not the mechanistic insistence on the abolition of personal voice that characterised 'Language poetry' in the United States. In its most extreme form it saw some proponents of that movement arguing (to put it reductively) that political freedom could be promoted through text-generating procedures that allowed the poem's language to escape from conventional syntactic conventions. This approach to writing was attacked by J. H. Prynne, who compared such writing with the supermarket,

> where the consumer is generically trained to value a freedom of choice precisely fetishised by the brand alternatives of late capitalism, the wonderfully smart play of vacuity by which the reader of the labels can rustle up preference, advice, loyalty, thrift, all the bound emotional habits of an old humanism now afloat in the play of signs within which the consumer's arbitration is a highly efficient instrument to maintain market saturation and to ration the efficiencies of decision control.[38]

The comparison was an apt one, and pointed again towards the vexed question of humanism, of the lyric self and the poetic subject, and how to find a vantage-point in the poem that allows a broader take on the relation between interiority and exteriority than simple expression allows, without losing the power of lyric affect. The move from Prynne's early discursive and propositional verse, through the more dislocated sequences of the nineties, to the recent work of *Kazoo Dreamboats*, demonstrates a shift in the function and location of lyric practice in Prynne's work, but not a rejection of it.

By contrast with Prynne, Michael Haslam has maintained a simpler coherence to his writing over the last forty years in a process of charting his life in books of verse in a project he has referred to as one of 'Continuale Song' (*Continual Song* is also the title of a 1986 collection). His poetry, though intensely lyrical, escapes confinement to the condition of the lyric because of its scale. It is explicitly and continuingly a life's work. Haslam is also unusual in that he rewrites his work, with the result that its presence in print can seem, and can be, provisional or fortuitous or regretted. For although the poems spring from Haslam's meditations on his daily life and loves, and his reading and listening and remembering and imagining, their truth is subject to the test of their poetic form and their success as poems. Their occasion, that is, is just that: the work of the poem, not its source, creates its lyric power. This is immediately noticeable in *The Quiet Works*, a recent sequence that starts with a sewage works:

> The quiet works a treat. The water treatment works
>   through falling steps in placid air
> on quiet walks by high top reservoir.
>   Aqueous eases
> as a stallion stales in puddled mud.
>
> A mare for me for equine equanimity
>   on flat slack hope, by small worth mere,
> down rake head stair
>   into a vale of deep deep air
>   love brooks despair.
> I be prepared to de-aspire, no more in sheets
> perspiring pair, no flood of hair,
> no mind to mate nor hope to share
> the quiet works in disrepair,
>   Love brooks the falls endure.
>
> Wet heat, the acid moor, peat sweat
>   is sourly sweet, before down-pour
> whose gushes thrust to groove the grove
> in rushes. Puddles sate the graven delph.
>
> Evacuate what must. Why can't I
>   disabuse myself, of lust?[39]

This is the first page. Two aspects of the verse strike the reader at once: the patterning of sound and the repurposing and transformation of words. Haslam's work is alive with the poetry of the past, histories of rhyme and syntax, word-use and word-change: and a sequence like deep, deep air/despair/de-aspire/disrepair and the tumbling internal rhymes create complex temporalities within the unfolding discourse of the poem. Not in a conjuror's performance, though: 'handkerchiefs on strings, more flutter / funny habits fetched up from beneath the hat. / I saw no art in that.'[40] His poems explore the musical relation of subjectivity and objectivity with an involved but dispassionate compositional commitment. As he has put it, 'I believe there are what I'd call natural plots, and that we live them, and that the truth I want to tell is the truth of a natural plot, which might be realised in art as a musical truth, in language.'[41]

In the title of another of Michael Haslam's books, *The Music Laid Her Songs in Language*, two recurrent lyric tropes are merged: birdsong and the many ways in which birds and their flight have figured poetic imagination and aspiration; and music, the figure of perfect ineffable speech. Haslam and his verse both know these histories intimately and are not intimidated by the weight of the past. Indeed, it becomes the matter of affectionate mockery, self-mockery, and impatience as well as delight.

> The Figure One is watching
> something ancient in the shape of heavy traffic
> through the clearing of the nymphs …
>   … His breathing
> quickly thickens. Breeding, bleeding, nymphs and months
> don't rhyme. And Music still refuses to Personify.
>
>   The Figure I
> can not identify
> the brush-head with his stick.[42]

How the figure of the poet exists in these poems is a function of their engagement with lyric process: sometimes comic, sometimes serious, but always part of a simultaneously prospective and retrospective search for the music in language. The first part of an earlier short sequence of poems is called 'Three of My Chasms', the title phrase a recasting of 'Mike Haslam' indicative of the way in which this autobiographical self is almost as impossible to separate from the landscape it inhabits as it is from the moral consequences of the things it has done.

In John Wilkinson's words:

> writing must never be cathartic or an achieved circle of reassurance or rec-
> ognition: but neither should it just open the sluices to what dwindles to
> the mimetic of a current social awfulness, a storm of part-objects as con-
> sumer durables … The danger … is the separation enjoined by an inher-
> ited literary body … where cadence becomes the frozen gesture of the
> misunderstood.[43]

Haslam's work, poised between lyric pain and lyric grace, embraces all the clumsiness of music and humour as well, in a continually unfolding poetic drama of a situated, and sometimes clownish, self. Wilkinson's own writing provides a very different but equally sustained interrogation of the potential of lyric. In 'Iphigenia', the primary device is tonal-grammatical, the varying of sentences and their tone from peremptory commands to genial interlocutions, further modulated too by the poems' line-endings and layout.[44] Another sequence, 'The Still-Piercing Air' (the title from

All's Well that Ends Well), semantically and lexically overloaded though it appears, makes lucid beauty from its concatenated lines and stanzas. It requires thought and rewards it:

> Answer peels, unbinds the fool, fond
> frittering throughput Mint-pole for an
> answering current shorted in too-swift
> rejoinder.[45]

It's hard to give a sense of the more extended echoes, repetitions, and transformations that give lyric depth to these poems. The final line of this poem, 'Love self-tests & fêtes the empty bed', does something similar in compressed form: the difficulty of getting your tongue round 'self-tests', the repeated short 'e' sounds, the plain short sentence, all work to create a temporary musical ending before the next poem picks up and makes explicit the musical trope. Later poems use rhythm and stanza form to develop the ideas of the sequence. The whole sequence is conducted through poem titles that are variations on each other, another kind of structural repetition to organise time and reference across the array of lyric gestures, from concrete object to abstract calculation, in an increasingly complex pattern. Or in the concluding words of one of the poems, 'The Line of Betrayal',

> the gulls shriek as devising
> ever-new intricacies they reunite
> about the clot of air conjectured.[46]

Through all this work runs a powerful desire to use the resources of lyric against power, to create *détournements* of lyric that take on, ironically embrace, or otherwise critique the violence of late capitalism. The central demand for the lyric now is to unmask and explore the ubiquity of violence, invisible or blatant, and defuse or engage its erotics: reading lyrics has become a sceptical process as well as a constructive one. Andrea Brady, to take another instance, has articulated a dissatisfaction with lyric as hampering her attempts to go beyond subjective experience in her poetry, finding that her use of something like collage, or the poem's hospitality to a variety of discourses, worked counter-intuitively to '[bring] the external world into the space of the personal in order to justify attention to the personal'. She adds that 'if the poems have morals, then the moral always comes afterwards, from the materiality of the language and of the images'.[47] Her most recently published work sets out to avoid the personal by adopting the form of a 'verse essay' on the history of fire – since Petrarch that most lyric of elements – from ancient times to the contemporary use of white phosphorus. In a concluding 'note on the text' she writes: 'A first step towards liberation from the brands and the boils of the most horrific dying is a recognition of the ancient complexity of the desire to burn.'[48]

How far the recognition of a poet's implication in war and the suffering of others becomes, ironically, a claim for the ethical force of a poem is a question that has preoccupied lyric poetry over the last decades, and different responses reflect different ways of conceptualising, and realising, the materiality of language. On one hand, 'to dismiss the materiality of language is to dismiss the emotionally charged history that made us who we are – subjects in language, which is the subject of the lyric'.[49] If the lyric 'I' is a shifter, a positional relation (in both senses of 'relate'), it is not the same as the autobiographical self that, as we've seen, is the implied guarantor of much conventional lyric writing.[50] But even where lyric is fragmented into verse pulses or affective splinters, it entails the struggle of a person to make the poem work, a struggle encoded in the gestures, cadences, and syntax of the verse as the stylistic signature of its author, a lyric identity that is always being re-forged in the language on the page.

Notes

1 Mutlu Konuk Blasing, *Lyric Poetry: The Pleasure and Pain of Words* (Princeton University Press, 2007), p. 28.

2 Jonathan Culler, 'Changes in the Study of the Lyric', in *Lyric Poetry: Beyond New Criticism*, ed. Chaviva Hosek and Patricia Parker (Ithaca, NY: Cornell University Press, 1985), pp. 38–54 (p. 54).

3 See for example Blasing, *Lyric Poetry*. Simon Jarvis points out that the 'oscillation in her important discussion between "poetry" and "lyric poetry"… perhaps constitutes a kind of practical admission that many of the phenomena which she discusses … might belong to verse as such rather than only to "lyric" in particular'; Simon Jarvis, 'The Melodics of Long Poems', *Textual Practice* 24.4 (2010), 607–21 (pp. 620–1).

4 Jonathan Culler, 'Why Lyric?', in *PMLA* 123.1 (January 2008), 201–6 (p. 206).

5 'Lyric did not conquer poetry: poetry was reduced to lyric. Lyric became the dominant form of poetry only as poetry's authority was reduced to the cramped margins of culture.' Mark Jeffreys, 'Ideologies of Lyric: A Problem of Genre in Contemporary Anglophone Poetics', *PMLA* 110.2 (March 1995), 196–205 (p. 200).

6 For the sake of convenience, though, I shall continue to use the terms 'lyric' and 'lyric poem' for the poems of short or moderate length that I shall be discussing in this chapter.

7 This argument is brilliantly pursued in Sam Ladkin, 'Problems for Lyric Poetry', in *Complicities: British Poetry 1945–2007*, ed. Robin Purves and Sam Ladkin (Prague: Litteraria Pragensis, 2007), pp. 271–322:

The conflation of the discourse of Being with love is something O'Hara frequently upsets with his accidentalism … His designation of 'my life' performs the lie that we separate our *true* or *lyric* life, the life which I feel to be integral to myself, out from the ruinous effects this identification causes elsewhere. It makes a farce out of the ethical interleaving we stage-manage between, for instance, wars carried out 'in our name' and the moral sanctity we reinscribe for ourselves by guiltily acknowledging such contingency. (p. 273)

8 Andrea Brady, '"Meagrely Provided": A Response to Don Paterson', *Chicago Review* 49.3/4 and 50.1 (Summer 2004), 396–402 (p. 399).

9 For further details, see Neil Pattison's introduction to Neil Pattison, Reitha Pattison, and Luke Roberts, eds., *Certain Prose of 'The English Intelligencer'* (Cambridge: Mountain Press, 2012).

10 Anselm Hollo, 'Two New Poetries', *Outburst* 2 (1963), n.p.

11 See J. H. Prynne, 'The Elegiac World in Victorian Poetry', *The Listener* (14 February 1963), 290–1.

12 Michael Davidson, 'Introduction: American Poetry, 2000–2009', *Contemporary Literature* 52.4 (Winter 2011), 597–629 (p. 602).

13 'Poetry foregrounds a linguistic nonrational that is not a byproduct of reason; rather it is the ground on which rational language and disciplinary discourses carve their territories, draw their borders, and designate their "irrational" others.' Blasing, *Lyric Poetry*, p. 3.

14 Paul Valéry, 'Poetry and Abstract Thought' (1939), trans. Denis Folliot, in *Paul Valéry: An Anthology*, selected with an introduction by James R. Lawler (Routledge & Kegan Paul, 1977), pp. 136–65 (p. 165).

15 Ladkin, 'Problems for Lyric Poetry', p. 274

16 Blasing, *Lyric Poetry*, p. 21n14. See also J. H. Prynne, 'Poetic Thought', *Textual Practice* 24.4 (2010), 595–606: 'The language of poetry is [the] modality and material base [of poetic thought], but whatever its relation with common human speech, the word-arguments in use are characteristically disputed territory, where prosody and verse-form press against unresolved structure and repeatedly transgress expectation' (p. 599).

17 Andrew Crozier, 'Thrills and Frills: Poetry as Figures of Empirical Lyricism', in *Society and Literature 1945–1970*, ed. Alan Sinfield (London: Methuen, 1983), pp. 199–233 (p. 220).

18 Oren Izenberg, *Being Numerous: Poetry and the Ground of Social Life* (Princeton University Press, 2011), pp. 1–2.

19 See especially Denise Riley, *Words of Selves: Identification, Solidarity, Irony* (Stanford University Press, 2000); and *Impersonal Passion: Language as Affect* (Durham, NC and London: Duke University Press, 2005).

20 W. S. Graham, 'What Is the Language Using Us For?', in *New Collected Poems*, ed. Matthew Francis (London: Faber, 2004), pp. 199–204 (p. 200).

21 Language acquisition and the persistence of the related early psychic structures in or beneath language have led theorists like Denise Riley, Jean-Jacques Lecercle, and Mutlu Konuk Blasing to reaffirm the place of the 'forcible affect of language' (as Riley puts it in *Impersonal Passion*, p. 1) in lyric poetry, and the necessary interplay or dialectic between exterior and interior, between speaking and being spoken. For an illuminating reading of one of Riley's

poems in these terms, see Jean-Jacques Lecercle, 'Unpoetic Poetry: Affect and Performativity in Denise Riley's "Laibach Lyrik, Slovenia, 1991"', *Textual Practice* 25.2 (2011), 345–9.

22 Tristan Tzara, *Poésies complètes*, ed. Henri Béhar (Paris: Flammarion, 2011), p. 159.

23 John James, *Collected Poems* (Cambridge: Salt, 2002), p. 95.

24 Tzara, *Poésies complètes*, p. 172.

25 John James, 'Pimlico', in *In Romsey Town* (Cambridge: Equipage, 2011), pp. 38–40 (pp. 39–40).

26 James, 'On Romsey Rec', in *ibid.*, p. 308.

27 John Wilkinson, 'Unexpected Excellent Sausage: On Simplicity in O'Hara, Lowell, Berrigan and James', in *The Salt Companion to John James*, ed. Simon Perrill (Cambridge: Salt, 2010), p. 188.

28 Jack Spicer, *The House that Jack Built: The Collected Lectures of Jack Spicer*, ed. with afterword by Peter Gizzi (Middletown, CT: Wesleyan University Press, 1998), p. 50.

29 Riley, *Impersonal Passion*, p. 46.

30 Spicer, 'Vancouver Lecture 1: Dictation and "A Textbook of Poetry"', in *The House that Jack Built*, p. 8.

31 Denise Riley, 'Laibach Lyrik: Slovenia 1991', in *Mop Mop Georgette: New and Selected Poems 1986–1993* (Cambridge and London: Reality Street, 1993), pp. 7–10 (p. 9).

32 J. H. Prynne, *Poems* (Fremantle Arts Centre Press; and Highgreen: Bloodaxe, 2005), pp. 26–31 (p. 28).

33 Prynne, *Poems*, p. 229.

34 'Little Musgrave and Lady Barnard', in *English and Scottish Ballads*, ed. Francis James Child, 8 vols., Vol. ii (London: Samson Low, 1841), pp. 15–21 (p. 19).

35 Rod Mengham, 'After Avant-gardism: *Her Weasels Wild Returning*', in *Assembling Alternatives: Reading Postmodern Poetries Transnationally*, ed. Romana Huk (Middletown, CT: Wesleyan University Press, 2003), pp. 384–8 (p. 384).

36 Prynne, *Poems*, p. 416.

37 It is worth noting, too, that '"mind" connects intimately both with memory and with love, the latter as affection rather than desire'; J. H. Prynne, 'Mental Ears and Poetic Work', *Chicago Review* 55.1 (2010), 126–57 (p. 138).

38 J. H. Prynne, 'Letter to Steve McCaffery', *The Gig* 7 (November 2000), 40–6 (pp. 41–2). For a thoughtful and persuasive critique of the adoption of Spicer by Ron Silliman and other Language poets, see Christopher Nealon, *The Matter of Capital: Poetry and Crisis in the American Century* (Cambridge, MA and London: Harvard University Press, 2011), pp. 107–39.

39 Michael Haslam, *The Quiet Works* (Old Hunstanton: Oystercatcher Press, 2009), n.p. [p. 5].

40 *Ibid.*, [p. 14].

41 Michael Haslam, 'Loose Talk by Way of *Introduction* to A Second Verse of Music', in *A Sinner Saved by Grace: The Second Verse of Music (Laid Her Songs in Language)* (Todmorden: Arc Publications, 2005), p. 9.

42 Michael Haslam, *The Music Laid Her Songs in Language* (Todmorden, Arc Publications, 2001), p. 12.

43 John Wilkinson, 'Cadence', in *The Lyric Touch*, pp. 143–7 (p. 146).

44 John Wilkinson, 'Iphigenia', in *Lake Shore Drive* (Cambridge: Salt, 2006), pp. 61–82.

45 John Wilkinson, 'The Still-Piercing Air', in *Contrivances* (Cambridge: Salt, 2003), pp. 107–24 (p. 111).

46 Wilkinson, 'The Still-Piercing Air', p. 114.

47 Scott Thurston, interview with Andrea Brady, in *Talking Poetics: Dialogues in Innovative Poetry* (Bristol: Shearsman, 2011), pp. 103–43 (pp. 105, 107).

48 Andrea Brady, *Wildfire: A Verse Essay on Obscurity and Illumination* (San Francisco: Krupskaya, 2010), p. 73.

49 Blasing, *Lyric Poetry*, p. 6.

50 'The activity of thought resides at the level of language practice, and indeed is in the language and is the language; in this sense, language is how thinking gets done and how thinking coheres into thought, shedding its links with an originating sponsor or a process of individual consciousness'; Prynne, 'Poetic Thought', p. 596.

Afterword

Jonathan Culler

In *The Political Unconscious* Fredric Jameson maintains that genre criticism has been 'thoroughly discredited by modern literary theory and practice'.[1] While one might contest the idea that a compelling theoretical case has been made against the notion of genre, it is certainly true that genre criticism has not fared well of late. Increasingly, what scholars and critics value in literature is the singularity of a literary work, and to expect a work to conform to the conventions of a genre or to approach the work through the lens of genre is to aim at something other than its distinctive literariness. Still, what has been discredited or at least set aside by modern criticism is not the concept of genre per se but the idea of genre as a set of norms to which a work should conform. As readers of Foucault, we know that norms are productive as well as constraining, necessary to the functioning of social and cultural meaning; and there is now a long and varied tradition, running from Ernst Gombrich's *Art and Illusion* through such works as Erving Goffman's *Frame Analysis* to recent cognitive science, demonstrating how essential various sorts of schemata or frames are to both perception and creation. If singularity is what we value in literature, it is most perceptible against the background of conventions of genres. Norms, we might argue, are essential to the identification of singularity; and generic norms themselves emerge most clearly at points or moments of their violation or disruption by the distinctive strategies or novel features of a work. There is no good reason for the valuing of singularity to entail the neglect of genre.

Lyric is an ancient form but one of uncertain generic status. 'Lyric is the most continuously practiced of all poetic kinds in the history of Western representation', writes Allen Grossman.[2] Yet it is marginalised by the traditional theory of genres. Aristotle was thoroughly familiar with ancient Greek lyric and cites many examples in his *Rhetoric*, but in his *Poetics*, which has been foundational for western accounts of genre, he does not discuss lyric because he was writing a treatise on mimetic poetry, poetry

237

as an imitation of action, and he recognised – if only he had bothered to say this explicitly! – that lyric is fundamentally epideictic rather than mimetic (hence more suitable for treatment in a treatise on rhetoric). It is really a matter of unhappy chance – the fact that the greatest systematic philosopher of the West wrote a treatise on mimetic poetry and not on the other poetic forms that were central to Greek culture – that western literary theory has neglected the lyric and, until the Romantic era, treated it as a miscellaneous collection of minor forms, despite the flourishing of lyric in Greece, ancient Rome, the Middle Ages, and the Renaissance. The discussions in this volume amply demonstrate that *lyric* was not a stable or a central concept for poets of most of this period, and that in the nineteenth and twentieth centuries, when it had become an important concept for both poets and critics, it remained a contested concept – the more central the more subject to resistance from various angles. Recent historicist criticism has challenged the notion of a lyric genre, representing it as a modern construction imposed retrospectively on earlier ages, where various types of poetry were produced under conditions quite different from those of the last two centuries.[3] But even if poets of the sixteenth through eighteenth centuries do not use the category 'lyric' as the name of a major genre, they write various sorts of short, non-narrative poems, which they may call sonnets, songs, epigrams, elegies, odes, epistles – none of which are themselves particularly stable generic categories. The complaint about the term *lyric* – that it means different things in different times and places – can be lodged against *elegy*, *ballad*, and even *ode*, which is rather different in the hands of Pindar, Horace, Ronsard, Collins, and Keats. The historical disparities that appear to motivate the desire to abandon the category *lyric* reappear in the case of more narrowly defined genres, and do so more insidiously, one might imagine, since while it is blatantly obvious that the lyric changes, it is less obvious that *ode* might be a slippery, even dubious category. Moreover – this is the second disadvantage of any attempt to focus on narrower categories and avoid *lyric* – there has never been a comprehensive set of sub-categories. If we scrap *lyric* we would always need a further category, such as *short poem*, to accommodate all those lyrics that do not fall under one of the other generic headings – even if we try to include them by multiplying genres defined by content, adding to *aubade* or dawn poem, and *ekphrasis* or poem about a work of art, praise poem, nocturne, lover's complaint, valediction, hymn, epithalamion, and so on.

In practice these chapters demonstrate the need for the concept of lyric or something very much like it in order to launch discussion and make possible a history. The variations that these scholars chart, that is to say, emerge not just from general thinking about poetry but from the assignment to discuss the lyric in their periods, which they do not find difficult, much less impossible, to do. If there is circularity here – a discussion of the lyric illustrates the usefulness of the category of lyric, even if it was not made central in the period in question – it is a condition of fruitful historical comparison: to expose the differences between literary productions of one period and another, we need general categories that will produce groupings where distinctiveness can shine forth. And of course a category such as lyric can connect the poetry of early modern and modern Britain with the melic verse of antiquity, which poets frequently aimed to emulate, and which exercised influence even when poets sought to evade its models. Without a category such as 'lyric', discussion of the history of poetry becomes much more difficult.

The story the contributions in this book tell is not that of the formation of a genre, in which early attempts, with perhaps some false starts, eventually lead by gradual increments to the consolidation of a genre, fully formed, able to realise its rich potential. It is a virtue of these discussions that they do not try to inscribe their reflections in any such teleological narrative. If such a story *were* to be told, it would doubtless have to involve progress towards a certain modern idea of the lyric, as intense expression of a dramatic or reflective moment of individual consciousness. In fact, this idea of the modern lyric, though it is not a *telos* for these contributors, is something of an enabling fiction for their stories of earlier periods: in each case a scholar shows us why it would be wrong to imagine that the lyric in his or her period fits this model. But this particular, restricted modern conception of the lyric, if it serves as something of a straw man for the discussion on lyrics of earlier periods, turns out not to fit very well the lyrics of the Romantic and post-Romantic age either, as the relevant chapters demonstrate, and is certainly not a model whose gradual formation over the centuries the volume records.

In fact, the lyric is already well-formed – splendidly alive – many centuries before our volume takes it up, in Sappho's only complete poem, the intricately self-reflexive invocation of Aphrodite, a lyric whose formal elegance and double perspective on love are not improved on by later lyric efforts. What these chapters sketch for us, then, is not the gradual historical formation of a genre that comes into its own in the last two centuries, but, on the contrary, lyric formations, different historical configurations of the genre, which do not amount to a linear history. One of the distinctive features of the history of the lyric is that, unlike social and political history – which may be irreversible, if not exactly linear – lyric history consists of variations, possibilities of lyric, most of which remain at least in principle available to later ages: what falls out of favour and comes to be neglected is not banished but remains available for reactivation in later times and places. Just as Petrarch is taken up by the sixteenth-century English poets considered here, so Horace is reawakened in the seventeenth century, Pindar in the late seventeenth and early eighteenth centuries, Hebrew Psalms in the eighteenth, early English ballads in the nineteenth century, and so on. The lyric has a history, a particularly fascinating one: linked with social, political, and philosophical developments, certainly, but also involving the repeated reactivation of elements from its own past that have fallen into neglect.

Several themes are pervasive in these analyses and offer suggestive links for thinking about the history of the lyric. The first is the relation of lyric to music, which had long been central to its definition, if usually in a somewhat nostalgic and retrospective fashion. In the first century BCE, Horace presents himself as a singer accompanied by the lyre, but this is already conventional: there is no evidence that he knew how to play or that any of his odes (*Carmina*) were ever sung. David Lindley describes a less radical situation in the sixteenth century, as lyric again separates itself from music and achieves a certain autonomy, despite the frequent references in lyrics and in comments on them to song, lyres, and so on. Renaissance lyricists may not in fact have had much musical knowledge, and Lindley astutely notes 'the abiding paradox that lyrics having the most demonstrably close connection to music are yet frequently those whose metrical shape, or verbal "music", is most incoherent when simply read'. In the seventeenth century, though, Nigel Smith maintains, the identification of lyric with song is simply a given, part of the Classical heritage. He singles out Henry Lawes for his success in setting many lyrics of the age to music, but otherwise music is part of the concept of lyric rather than a reality of lyric composition. David Fairer describes poets later in the century, as they revive the ode and seek to link to its Classical genealogy, once again bedecking themselves with imagery of songs and lyres: 'acknowledging the ancient roots of lyric in the lyre, [poets] were aware of a defining expressiveness in lyric verse'. What seems a new development here is a linking in a figurative register of the strings of imaginary lyres and the strings of the human heart or mechanisms of the mind. The proliferation in poems of adjectives concerning strings shows, writes Fairer, 'how lyric poets thought of themselves as playing skilfully on an instrument and also playing on the responses of a hearer'. Poets claimed not, as in earlier times, to produce words that should in principle be accompanied by music, but to explore a new musicality.

In the mid eighteenth century the further exfoliation of the Classical ode and the quest for sublime effects in the wake of the rediscovery of Longinus sets the stage for a different link with music. Lyrics, increasingly self-reflexive – as Marcus Walsh notes – and appealing to Hebrew songs as well as Pindaric models, deploy a stylised rhetoric and a Miltonic prophetic mode, and rely less heavily on visual imagery. Seeking an adequate form for a modern poetry of imagination, Collins and Smart, for instance, transform in their different ways the models of ancient song into a poetry that is epideictic rather than mimetic, and in its 'articulation of voicelessness' may signify musicality, through its evocation of Greek or Hebrew models, rather than attempt to embody it.

David Duff describes two changing relations to music in the Romantic period. First, the revaluation of music as the highest of the arts, which starts in Germany but finds English exponents such as Walter Pater, gives lyric an abstract, ideal model: music is not an accompaniment but a form to which lyric can vainly aspire. Secondly, while Shelley produces a powerful modernisation of the Pindaric ode, a language that would itself be music, in his 'Ode to the West Wind', there is also a revival of the ballad, imbued with the prestige of origins: in Wordsworth's adaptations but also especially in Burns, whose verses not only allude to an ancient native tradition of song but are themselves frequently set to music as well. These two quite different relations to music – the nostalgic model of ancient native balladry and the abstract ideal of the purest art – are at play in the Romantic expansion of the idea of the lyric.

Peter Nicholls' splendid 'Modernism and the Limits of Lyric' offers an original reading of the impulses or tendencies of post-Victorian poetry. Citing Pound, who argues that 'poetry begins to atrophy when it gets too far from music', he highlights the role of Pound's 'melopoeia' – poetry where 'music, sheer melody, seems as if it were just bursting into speech'. He sees this aspiration to an aesthetics of sound, to poetry aspiring to the condition of music – splendidly exercised by Swinburne, for instance, or Yeats, as well as by Pound himself – as one force that, along with the more frequently cited tendency of the modernist promotion of the image, works to put in doubt or at least severely qualify the notion of lyric as the intimate speech act of a unified speaking voice. He reminds us that Mallarmé's celebration of the music of poetry has no mimetic relation to music or voice as such: it is not a matter of poetry sung to a musical accompaniment, for instance, but of a lyricism that can operate 'with eyes closed', music as writing that is resistant to meaning, as music is. It is this melopoeic lyric that is resisted by the later poets he discusses, such as George Oppen and Susan Howe, where in broken rhythms may be detected 'a deep desire for lyric vision', as Pound's sheer melody is denied.

A second topic that appears at various moments in this book is the question of poetic presence: how does the lyric, this verbal form that often has a nostalgic or aspirational link with music, relate to a moment of performance or consumption? What, if anything, does the lyric make present, and how is the identity of the lyric affected? David Lindley stresses that there is a constitutive gap: the 'I' of the lyric is not just the author but also the reader or singer, and pleasure in recitation implies a distance and not just identification. Heather Dubrow further explores the functioning of deictics in Renaissance sonnets, where the 'here' or 'now' unsettle the simple binaries that may be cited in discussions of lyric and, rather than defining space and time, destabilise them through multiple referents. The spatial *here* can refer to the material manifestation of the poem on the page; as it is presented to someone as it circulates; or, given Renaissance cosmology, it can refer to the sublunary sphere, *here* on earth, as well as to a place of articulation. In the Renaissance there is no presumption of an isolated lyric speaker, as in the dominant modern model of the lyric.

The circulation of lyric in manuscripts, which some Renaissance poets preferred to print, not only marks a break with song, Thomas Healy argues, but enables a certain fluidity that print does not afford. The performance of reading or of recopying supplants in some respects musical performance. From the Romantics on to our own day, manuscripts embody authenticity and personal uniqueness, tying a poem not just to a historical moment of composition but to an authorial intention of that moment seen as originary and determining, but in the English Renaissance manuscript practices illustrate the collective functioning of lyrics, as they pass from hand to hand, separating themselves from a poet and a real or imagined addressee, offering themselves to variable performances and uses in commonplace books. A poem of Wyatt's nicely 'illustrates a literary environment that preferred the mutability of manuscript transmission to the constancy of print. The poets' crafting of their lyrics adopts strategies that collude with a transmission process that expects textual and interpretive instability.'

In the mid seventeenth century, it is taken as given, Nigel Smith argues, that lyric is a genre descended from the Greeks – short poems of charm and sweetness, of varying, often complex metre – but if it keeps the insights of antiquity alive, it is also frequently, in a time of political turbulence, entangled with political positioning. These poems are not simply and easily either timeless artefacts or utterances tied to a particular moment. For David Fairer, the lyric, as manifested in the ode, is striving to be itself an event rather than a representation of an event; and for Marcus Walsh, whose objects of study are designed to manifest the 'poetical character', with oratorical or ritualistic elements and lexical rarities, there is depiction but not expression of feeling. The poem makes present something that never was. In the Romantic poems studied by David Duff, on the contrary, we encounter divergent possibilities: imitation of consciousness and mimesis of speech on the one hand – which looks forward to the dramatic monologue and the poem as discourse of a fictional character – and, on the other, the poem as spell or charm.

In Marion Thain's complex account of the problems of the lyric in the Victorian period, poets such as Browning seek a more objective and dramatic lyric, based on the mimesis of speech, while decadent poets embrace the idea of a solipsistic lyric but give it a new phenomenological cast, through attention to the body and somatic sensations. The lyric seeks to evoke a haptic, bodily presence. But Swinburne and Hopkins, far more central to the poetry of this period than such Decadents as Arthur Symons, practise a sensuous engagement with the properties of words that can scarcely be described as phenomenological. The case of Swinburne in particular poses the question of whether it is somatic references or the ritualistic character of this poetry, its foregrounding of sonorous rhythm, that saves it from the charge of solipsism, giving it a public, collective character that is frequently ignored in accounts of the lyric.

In the twentieth century we encounter a range of strategies that complicate notions of what a lyric might make present, from the intensification of opacity analysed by Peter Nicholls in his account of the blindness of lyric, to the modes of resistance to any integrity of the lyric 'I' deployed by Ted Hughes and Philip Larkin (though from their complex textual influences, mythologies, and vulgarity, as Neil Roberts shows, nonetheless, an 'intending "I"' does emerge). In the more refractory poems Ian Patterson studies, 'No man is an "I".' As he shrewdly observes, it is not easy to personalise language in the first place, and the poems he studies display the fact that words do not originate in the self or present a self. We encounter not a subjectivity but an interplay of forces that would form, act upon, and limit a subject. What the lyric presents is a textual surface in which such forces are imbricated.

This last chapter raises the final question of the boundaries of lyric. This is not a matter of special concern in the sixteenth and seventeenth centuries: when lyric is not a central concept in discussions of poetry no-one need argue whether something is or is not a lyric. In the Restoration and eighteenth century, with revival of Classical models, lyric becomes instantiated in the ode especially, and set against epic, didactic, narrative poetry. Anna Laetitia Barbauld's eloquent preface to Collins' poems, cited by Marcus Walsh, speaks of 'pure Poetry, or Poetry in the abstract. It is concerned with an imaginary world, peopled with beings of its own creation. It deals in splendid imagery, bold fiction, and allegorical personages … while the conceptions of the Poet (often highly metaphysical) are rendered still more remote from common apprehension by the figurative phrase in which they are clothed. All that is properly *Lyric Poetry* is of this kind.'[4] At this point lyric seems to be acquiring a distinct identity, differentiated especially from the narrative and the didactic, but also from popular forms that lack the sublime ambitions of lyric. In the nineteenth century, however, as David Duff and Marion Thain show, when the category of lyric comes to the fore in discussions about poetry, a range of poetic forms, such as the indigenous ballad tradition, are 'colonised' as forms of lyric. The recent historicist critique of the idea of lyric as a modern imposition sees the 'lyricisation' of poetry as a function of modern criticism but, as Marion Thain explains, if the lyric comes to be the central poetic form in the nineteenth century it is because narrative and didactic functions are increasingly taken over by prose, and lyric comes to be set against the novel as the two major forms of literature. But of course, as lyric becomes the major form of poetry grounds for resistance to it arise, from Browning's desire for a more 'objective' form to modernist questioning of a unified lyric voice. Browning's dramatic monologue, though, conceived as a resistance to the lyric, becomes in the twentieth century the very model of lyric, as mimesis of speech. What is especially striking in this history, then, is the way in which, from the nineteenth century to the present, various forms of resistance to the lyric become incorporated into the broad conception of the lyric.

A unifying theme of the three chapters on lyric in the twentieth century is this resistance to lyric as central to the practice of lyric. The rich accounts of particular movements by Nicholls, Roberts, and Patterson describe ways in which lyric is questioned by its practitioners, but they do not pose the questions of the limits of lyric. Are the forms of difficult poetry treated by Patterson still lyric? In so far as they resist association of lyric with voice, resist vocalisation, one could argue that we are approaching a limit of lyric. When we have poems where the visual dominates the oral, where the page rather than the articulable or vocalisable line is the fundamental unit, we have perhaps moved into different territory where the model of lyric is no longer pertinent. In the twentieth century many poets have rejected the notion of lyric tied to the notion of the poetic voice. 'What do we make of poems like Lyn Hejinian's or Charles Bernstein's', asks Marjorie Perloff, 'whose appropriation of found objects – snippets of advertising slogans, newspaper headlines, media cliché, textbook writing, or citation from other poets – works precisely to deconstruct the possibility of the formation of a coherent or consistent lyric voice?'³ They have produced texts that require reading by other models. A wide range of poems have resisted a model that presumes the centrality of sound, in the guise either of a figure of voice or of ritual inscription to be recited. These range from shaped poems and concrete poems that can scarcely be read, only seen or described, to poems that refuse in other ways a relation to voice and an enunciating subject: much L=A=N=G=U=A=G=E poetry for instance. The question, then, is not so much whether particular poems count as lyric as to what extent reference to the parameters of that tradition is pre-supposed, as something to be cited, parodied, deployed, denounced, or worked against – though whether or not we want to call it 'presupposed' may beg the question, since the issue really is whether approaching a given poem or poetic corpus in relation to the lyric tradition enriches the experi-ence of and reflection on the poems in question.

In some cases discussed by Patterson the poem seems to ask to be read in relation to a lyric model, which it is actively resisting and where its functioning primarily takes the form of that resistance. But if lyric is to remain a valuable concept we need to recognise that it has limits and that there are poems that can scarcely be read but must be contemplated, where even though they are made of language the visual overwhelms the aural. A positing of boundaries is important for keeping alive the connec-tions with the vital lyric tradition that the contributions in this volume describe. This tradition is not a linear history but a series of variations that provide much scope for new poems, but do not include everything that we might count as poetry.

Notes

1 Fredric Jameson, *The Political Unconscious* (Ithaca, NY: Cornell University Press, 1981), p. 105.
2 Allen Grossman, *The Sighted Singer: Two Works on Poetry for Readers and Writers* (Baltimore, MD: Johns Hopkins University Press, 1991), p. 211.
3 See the papers in 'The New Lyric Studies', *PMLA* 123.1 (January 2008), 181–234; Virginia Jackson, *Dickinson's Misery: A Theory of Lyric Reading* (Princeton

University Press, 2005); and, most economically, Jackson's entry for 'Lyric', in *Princeton Encyclopedia of Poetry and Poetics* (Princeton University Press, 2012), pp. 826–34.

4 Anna Laetitia Barbauld, 'Preface' *The Poetical Works of Mr. William Collins* (London, 1797), pp. iv–v.

5 Marjorie Perloff, *Poetic License* (Evanston, IL: Northwestern University Press, 1990), p. 12.

Index